Carol J Echtig

Learning to be Litera

B

This book is dedicated to our parents for contributing so much to our own literacy and to our son for contributing to our understanding of learning to be literate.

ALISON GARTON and CHRIS PRATT

# Learning to be Literate

## THE DEVELOPMENT OF SPOKEN AND WRITTEN LANGUAGE

### Second Edition

BLACKWELL
*Publishers*

Copyright © second edition Alison Garton and Chris Pratt 1998.

The right of Alison Garton and Chris Pratt to be identified as author of this work has been asserted in accordance with the Copyright, Designs and Patents Act 1988.

First edition published 1989
Reprinted 1990, 1992, 1993, 1994, 1995 (twice), 1998
Second edition 1998

2 4 6 8 10 9 7 5 3 1

Blackwell Publishers Ltd
108 Cowley Road
Oxford OX4 1JF
UK

Blackwell Publishers Inc.
350 Main Street
Malden, Massachusetts 02148
USA

*British Library Cataloguing in Publication Data*

A CIP catalogue record for this book is available from the British Library.

*Library of Congress Cataloging-in-Publication Data*

Garton, Alison, 1952–
    Learning to be literate: the development of spoken and written
language / Alison Garton and Chris Pratt. — 2nd ed.
      p.    cm.
    Includes bibliographical references and index.
    ISBN 0-631-19317-0
    1. Language acquisition.   2. Literacy.   3. Written communication—
Study and teaching.   4. Children—Language.    I. Pratt, C.
(Christopher), 1950–  .  II. Title.
    P118.G27   1998
    401'.93—dc21                              97-42243
                                              CIP

Typeset in 10 on 12 pt Plantin
by Ace Filmsetting Ltd, Frome, Somerset
Printed in Great Britain by T.J. International, Padstow, Cornwall

This book is printed on acid-free paper

# Contents

# *Preface*

Since the publication of the first edition, our expressed hope about language use as far as commonly acceptable uses of masculine and feminine pronouns are concerned, has not been fulfilled! So, in line with what is now commonly accepted practice, we have removed references to gender (unless a specific individual is named or cited) and where possible have gone with the plural 'children'. Similarly, references to 'mothers' have been replaced with 'parents' except when there is a reference to a specific parent, or when the research was conducted only with mothers.

This volume has been updated since the first edition. The same arguments are presented but some of these have been strengthened in the past nine years by a substantial body of research. The actual literature reviewed and cited covers spoken and written language development, in normally developing children. Again, we have chosen not to include coverage of children with language difficulties in recognition that we could not adequately cover such an important area in the same volume.

As well as those whom we have acknowledged in the first edition, there are many people who have contributed in various ways to our work on this second edition. The Universidade Federal de Pernambuco, Recife, Brazil, provided a haven for early work on updating the text as well as a congenial and stimulating atmosphere in which to work. Special thanks are due to Alina Spinillo, Lucia Rego, Luciano Meira and their colleagues and Masters students.

The University of Western Australia, the University of Tasmania and La Trobe University have been supportive of both authors, but particularly Chris Pratt, while the Australian Psychological Society has provided interesting diversions for Alison Garton. Thanks are due to the lecturers who provided useful feedback on the first edition while we were contemplating this second edition, and also to the reviewers of the drafts of earlier versions of the book. Alison Mudditt, Nathalie Manners and Sarah Howlett at Blackwells have demonstrated patience and encouragement, making good use of electronic mail to ensure we did not forget to work on the book. Many others, some of whom we thanked in the first edition, have continued to offer encouragement over the past few years. We are not able to mention all of these as they include the many lecturers and students who have made positive reference to the first edition over the years. However we would like to make special mention of those who have offered ongoing support, encouragement and the interest to keep working in this area. They are Peter Bryant, Margaret Donaldson, Kevin Durkin, Jessie Reid and Elizabeth Robinson. We would also like to thank Edith Bavin, Jane Oakhill, Nicole Yuill, Michael Johnston and the many students whom we have supervised and who have challenged our ideas, with a special mention to Mary Rohl and Amanda Blackmore.

Finally we again thank our son Stephen for his ongoing perceptive and cutting comments. He may have grown up but he has not lost the capacity to tell us what he thinks.

Alison Garton
Chris Pratt
Melbourne

# *Preface to the First Edition*

In a book about learning to be literate, it seems appropriate that we begin by recognizing a problem with the language that faced us when we began to write this book. This problem required careful reflection before we reached a decision. It concerns the use of masculine and feminine pronouns. We decided finally to use the masculine pronoun for the child and the feminine one for the adult who is interacting with the child. There are exceptions, of course, which occur when we refer to a particular female child or male adult. We made this decision because, like many others, we feel that using non-sexist terms such as 's/he', 'he/she', or even 'he or she' interrupts the flow of the text and interferes with one's comprehension. We hope that that practice will continue whereby authors choose which set of pronouns to use, and that, as a result, we will continue to see some books with male children and some books with female children.

The book in intended to be read by those interested in children's spoken and written language development. It is aimed to be of relevance to undergraduate students taking courses in developmental psychology, educational psychology and early childhood and primary education, as well as specific courses on language development, or reading, or writing. Postgraduate students wishing for specialist information on aspects of literacy development will also find this book valuable. We have tried to avoid using too many technical terms, especially from the field of linguistics, and have not taken to extremes, arguments over issues and methods. The book is concerned with a description and explanation of normal developmental processes in spoken and written language. The omission of topics concerned with children who have language difficulties is made because we recognize the importance of this area and we realize we could not do it justice in this book.

We wish to thank the following people who all willingly gave up their time to read sections of the manuscript and discuss issues with us: Clare Ball, Ellen Bialystok, Amanda Blackmore, Judy Bowey, Lynette Bradley,

Peter Bryant, Lila Braine, Martin Braine, Philip Carpenter, Marie Clay, Ann Dowker, Kevin Durkin, Drew Nesdale and Lucia Rego.

We would also like to thank Jerry Bruner, Alison Dewsbury, Margaret Donaldson, Kay Kovalevs, David Olson, Jessie Reid and Bill Tunmer for helping us shape up our ideas when planning and writing this book. The support and assistance provided by the Department of Psychology at The University of Western Australia, the Department of Experimental Psychology at Oxford University and Wolfson College while writing this book are gratefully acknowledged.

Special thanks go to Herb Jurkiewicz for taking the photographs included in this book. He is a master at capturing on film exactly what is required. Thanks also to Philip Carpenter for his assistance and encouragement throughout.

Finally we thank our son Stephen for talking to us (at times endlessly) over the years, for his patience shown during our many discussions about the book and for the occasional cutting but apt interjections he made during our discussions.

Alison Garton<br>
Chris Pratt<br>
Perth

# *Note on Phonemes*

From time to time in this book, we have made references to *phonemes*. These are representations of the distinctive sounds of language which lead to differences in meaning. Whenever a phoneme has been used in the text, it is enclosed in the conventional manner, between two slashes (for example /s/, /b/). The realization of particular phonemes will be evident from the context in which they are presented. However, we have listed below all those used, with examples of words containing the sounds they represent, for readers who are not familiar with the conventional representations.

| | | | |
|---|---|---|---|
| b | **big, b**at | i | **b**eat, me |
| d | **doll, d**og | I | bit, lip |
| k | **k**ill, **c**at | ∂ | sofa, about |
| t | **t**op, **t**all | ε | bet |
| s | **s**it, **s**ock | u | r**oo**f, sp**oo**n |
| f | **f**it, **f**an | č | **ch**ip, **ch**air |
| š | **sh**op, **sh**y | r | **r**ed, **r**at |
| n | **n**ail, **n**ice | z | car**s**, **z**oo |
| ð | **th**e, **th**at | | |

*Alphabets*

From time to time we take out pen in hand
And scribble symbols on a blank white sheet.
Their meaning is at everyone's command;
It is a game whose rules are nice and neat.

Hermann Hesse, *The Glass Bead Game*

# CHAPTER ONE

# Literacy: The Spoken and Written Language

This book is concerned with the learning of literacy in children up to around the age of 8 years. By the learning of literacy, we mean the development of spoken language and written language from their origins in early infancy to their mastery as systems of representation for communication with others. We are going to consider continuities in the development of spoken language, reading and writing. These systems of representation, spoken and written language, are inter-related in very important ways especially when we examine how they develop in young children. While the major distinctions between these systems will be retained, we will also explore the relationships between them and reveal the extent to which the processes involved in acquiring both are similar (see Pratt and Garton, 1993).

## What is Literacy?

Our definition of literacy must include both spoken and written language, the latter involving both reading and writing. Literacy therefore is to be defined in this book, as 'the mastery of spoken language *and* reading and writing'. This is a much broader definition of literacy than is usually accepted. A more common definition would include *only* the written language – reading and writing. We wish to emphasize the more general nature of literacy and underline the continuities between spoken language and written forms of language. Literacy is directly involved with written language: common knowledge would have us believe so. However, we also expect literate people to speak fluently, to show mastery of the spoken language. Consequently, a definition of literacy should recognize this, particularly when studying the development of language skills. It is thus in this broad sense that we use the term **literacy**.

## The Study of Spoken and Written Language

There are two reasons why spoken and written language ought to be examined together. The first follows from our definition of literacy as there
are clear links between the two systems. While there is always the view
that spoken language precedes written language developmentally, socio-
historically and culturally, there is reason to believe that there is a close
inter-relationship between them. In each case, the structure of language
must be learned and applied successfully so that mutual communication
(including understanding) can be achieved amongst people who, at
least, speak the same language. To illustrate this by focusing solely on the
spoken word misses the important roles of the written word. It also misses
the different ways in which children learn to read and write. The
interconnectedness of spoken and written language has been explored
historically, and so too should this relationship be examined
developmentally. The development of written language is linked to the
development of spoken language – the former is parasitic on the latter;
it is a second- order acquisition. Equally, the development of written
language skills influences spoken language ability, as new language structures and functions are learned for writing which in turn are adopted for
speaking.

A literate person has the ability to talk, read and write, and the achievement of early literacy involves learning how to talk, read and write in a
competent manner. Clearly this definition excludes the more highbrow
definition of literacy which has to do with knowledge of literature (usually a more scholarly activity). However, that is not to say this early
accomplishment is not related to later activities.

The second reason is that many of the processes involved in the learning of spoken and written language are similar. It is generally claimed that
the way in which we learn spoken language is more 'natural' than the
learning of reading and writing. According to this view, written language
is taught – usually formally at school. Nonetheless, the learning of reading and writing depends very much on prior learning of the spoken
language.

So it is usually believed that while spoken language develops naturally,
written language development requires formal instruction. However this
distinction may be simplistic and misleading. For both spoken and
written language the child requires **assistance** – usually adult assistance.
Although the mechanisms for development may be different, we contend
that one vital ingredient for facilitating literacy development is an interested adult, prepared to help the child's spoken and written language

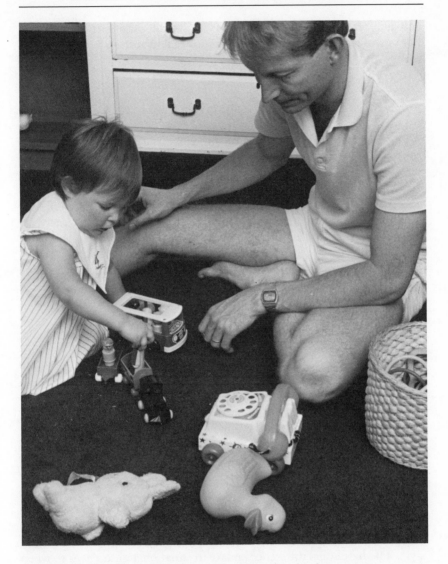

A child requires adult assistance for spoken language development

development by interacting with the child. Further, this adult can provide support and guidance to the child by allowing the child to be actively involved in the language learning process. Thus, in a general sense, the development of both spoken language and written language is facilitated by the child's active interaction with an adult prepared to assist, guide and support the child (see Garton, 1992). Adult assistance is necessary, but as we shall see, not sufficient, for spoken and written language development.

## Differences between Spoken and Written Language

While we have been emphasizing the close relationship between the spoken and the written word, it is important to realize there are also some fundamental differences between the two modes (see Perera, 1984). Any explanation of the development of literacy must take into account differences as well as similarities. There are differences of form, differences of function and differences in the manner of presentation. Firstly there are physical differences between the **forms** of spoken and written language. Spoken language is ephemeral, it occurs in real time and requires the ears for listening. In other words, it is temporary, temporal and uses the aural mode. In contrast, written language is more durable, it is presented in space (rather than time) and requires eyes to read the language. It is thus permanent, spatial and visual.

Further, spoken language tends to be more fragmentary and sociable. You talk **to** (or **with**) someone, and thus tend to involve them. For example, people say such things as 'You know what I mean?', and 'You'll come with me, won't you?', the latter use of a tag question inviting a reply. Talking also takes place much more quickly than writing, although this may be in dispute nowadays as word processors allow greater speeds of producing the written word compared to the laborious task of writing by hand. Written language is durable, the process of achieving it is slow and deliberate, allowing editing both during and after the product, and is frequently a solitary activity: you write alone although usually with a readership in mind.

These differences in the form of spoken and written language produce differences in **function**. As we have indicated, spoken language is used in face to face conversation and is generally more colloquial in form and style. The functional differences relate to situational differences in when and where it is appropriate to use either spoken or written language. Some of these differences are rather difficult to specify and may depend on social conventions. For example, is it more appropriate to write or to telephone your gratitude after accepting the offer of assistance from a friend? In some circumstances it is regarded as more **polite** to write, but it may be equally acceptable to convey your thanks orally, either by telephone, or in direct face to face conversation. What is appropriate depends on various social or situational factors. In terms of the distinction between spoken and written language, the forms of 'thank you' will vary. The written note would likely be expressed rather formally, using correct grammar, the telephone call rather less formal in terms of language and grammar used, and finally, the face to face 'thank you' would be the least formal. This last form would tend to be used when you knew the friend well, and such familiarity does not demand formal language. In the case of saying 'thank you', both the form of the 'thank you' itself and the form of the language used depend very much on social conventions and situational expectations.

There are also circumstances where written transactions fulfil functions that spoken language cannot. Such uses of the written word include the completion of a cash withdrawal form in a bank, the writing of a prescription by a doctor and the writing of a note to the milkman. In these cases, the audience is absent or personally unknown. Similarly, there are occasions when the spoken word fulfils functions that the written word cannot. If you are in danger, you would shout 'Help!', and if you are being interviewed for radio or television, you would talk into a microphone. In these cases, writing cannot serve as a substitute, as immediate communication is demanded.

There are obvious differences between spoken and written language when we look at the ways in which grammatical structures are used. Chafe (1985) listed several of the devices that are used in written language to expand on ideas. These devices include the use of single adjectival modifiers derived from the present or past tense of verbs, for example, 'the *ensuing* discussion focused on the role of *emergent* style on children's language development'. Single words such as *ensuing* and *emergent*, which encapsulate entire notions are often felt to be more part of the written language. Elaboration of an idea in spoken language usually involves expansion and modification. And so, someone might say 'We went on to discuss how style might develop in young children and how this is related to their language development'. In talking, we may use grammatical structures that are seen as 'sloppy' or wrong when the written language is considered, for example 'That guy was really putting it on' (meaning 'The fellow about whom we were talking was showing off').

This view, in fact, does a huge injustice to the importance of spoken language as the means of language change. Of course, spoken language *can* be formal, especially if used by a literate person and the situation demands it. Speakers are very good at gauging the formality of their language and speaking at an appropriate level. Spoken language is far more diverse and volatile than written language, and new words and new grammatical constructions usually have their origins in spoken language. Spoken language too is used by various groups in society, such as teenagers, to alienate themselves deliberately from other groups (adults and especially teachers). There is nothing more frustrating to an adult than being unable to understand a teenager's language to friends.

Another major difference between spoken and written language is in the way ideas are linked. Such **discourse cohesion**, or the organization of linguistic structure in discourse (Karmiloff-Smith, Johnson, Grant, Jones, Karmiloff, Bartrip and Cuckle, 1993), is achieved differently in speech to the way it happens in written texts. In written language, all sentences have equivalent value and force, they are all 'flat', and have no intonation patterns nor associated nonlinguistic features. When speaking, we are quite animated. We use many nonlinguistic and paralinguistic features to accompany our speech. We use gestures, we move our hands and our faces, we use devices such as rising intonation and pauses to add meaning to our speech. None of these is available for the writer, who has to use the ubiquitous exclamation mark to serve a number of functions. It expresses surprise, happiness, contrast and so on. Other devices available include underlining, the use of capital letters and italics. While each of these can be used in writing, none quite captures any of the methods available when speaking.

Olson (1985), in describing two main functions of written language, pointed to further differences between writing and speaking. These functions are **social** and **intellectual** (Olson preferred the phrase 'intellectual consequences' of literacy). The social functions of literacy are to do with the influence the written language has had on the development of society from a historical stance. Spoken language is subject to more variability than written language as it includes such aspects as dialects, accents and slang terms. While people from Glasgow, Edinburgh and Aberdeen speak differently, they all use the same written language. By its very nature then, written language demands that certain conventions be obeyed, since written language becomes permanent and accessible to a larger public. With written conventions, the standard forms (of any language) apply to a wider group than spoken language. Written language conventions become widespread and achieve prestige and authority. These conventions are then taught to children and are thus perpetuated. By allowing all individuals access to the same written conventions, they can gain entry to the world of books and writing which increases their knowledge and consequently, the social world. Written language has the potential of reaching a much greater audience than spoken language.

Compared with the social functions, the intellectual functions of literacy have been considered more pertinent by developmental psychologists and educationalists. Many leading and influential academics believe that it is only through the study of spoken and written language that we can begin to understand relations between how children talk and how they think. Because the basic ingredients of reading and writing are language, and because both reading and writing involve the manipulation of the written word, the strategies children employ to learn and use the skills of reading and writing must tell us something about how they deal with the world. Even more interesting is the fact that such manipulations and strategies are often mental and require that children **represent** their spoken language.

This list of differences between spoken and written language is by no means complete, but is sufficient for us to understand that the relationship between the two modes is quite complex. There are also implications for the teaching of reading and writing, particularly in the classroom, when one appreciates the extent and the magnitude of the differences. Despite the differences, there is ample theoretical and empirical evidence that many of the strategies used in the accomplishment of literacy are sufficiently similar for us to begin to explore the inter-relationship between spoken and written language.

## The Continuity of Literacy

One of the main aims of this book is to explore the continuity of development of language, reading and writing from the earliest period of language development until the child is aged around 8 years of age. The earliest phase of the development of reading and writing is sometimes termed the 'preliteracy stage'. The use of 'stage' suggests this is a distinct period in the child's development and fails to capture the continuity of development for each individual child. Recent researchers have preferred to omit any reference to stages and instead use 'emergent literacy' (Hall, 1987; Bus, 1994; Dickinson, 1995a) or just 'pre-literacy' (Wolf and Dickinson, 1986), terms suggestive of development towards a period of literacy. During the early period of development, the focus has typically been on the types of reading and writing experiences children have before they attend formal schooling. However, this focus has usually been on **only** the child's experiences with the written mode. So studies have looked at the influence of having been read stories on children's later reading development, or the relationship between scribbling at a young age and the development of writing skills at school. The study of spoken language development tends to dwell on the emergence of different language forms, again often charting development in stages.

More recent studies have looked at how these forms of language are acquired and how they are used. Some of the lines of research seem outwardly similar to those used in studies of early reading and writing. Many studies of both spoken and written language involve children looking at picture books, being read to or indeed reading themselves. We agree with those researchers who contend that the study of children's early experience with books is a good starting point for exploring in depth some of the continuities in the development or acquisition of literacy.

One link between early and later literacy has been proposed through awareness of language, or **metalinguistic awareness**, suggesting that knowledge of language, developing in the preschool years, facilitates later reading. The precise nature of the awareness that is necessary is still being debated although some argue it is via phonological processing, beginning with an awareness of **rhyming** (Bryant and Bradley, 1985; Goswami, 1994). Children's knowledge of nursery rhymes and their awareness of rhyme at age 3 years has been positively linked to later reading ability (MacLean, Bryant and Bradley, 1987; Kirtley, Bryant, Maclean and Bradley, 1989). The notion of awareness providing the crucial link between early and later literacy, and between language development and the skills of reading and writing, has been the subject of intensive (and extensive) study over recent years, particularly the relationship between phonological awareness and early reading (for example, Goswami and Bryant, 1990; Rohl and Pratt, 1995), and grammatical or syntactical awareness and early reading (for example, Rego and Bryant, 1993; Bowey, 1994). This issue will be discussed in chapter 7. In addition, many researchers have focused on the nature of the phonological deficit(s) found in children identified as having specific reading disabilities (for example, Rack, Snowling and Olson, 1992; Stanovich, 1993)

## Consequences of Not Being Literate

There are two ways (at least) of addressing the issue of not being literate. It can be examined from the perspective of children who, for whatever reason, fail to develop skills in talking, reading or writing, or it can be examined by study of non-literate cultures. Both approaches have considerable bodies of research and literature, and while it is beyond the scope of the current volume to explore these in any depth, each is worthy of brief mention.

### Children Who Fail to Achieve Literacy

Children who, during development, are unable to speak, read or write (usually a spelling or orthographic difficulty rather than a motor disability) can be classified according to the type of disability (such as specific language disability, specific reading disability/dyslexia or dysgraphia), or according to the purported cause(s) such as sensory impairments (hearing, vision), intellectual disabilities or delays, or other developmental disabilities including autism and other genetic, hereditary or birth defects. Messer (1994) provides a convenient and up-to-date review of some of the issues in this area with respect to the development of spoken language, while much of the work on reading disabilities can be found in useful reviews by Prior (1989) and Snowling (1991). Work on specific populations is rather more diverse, with research examining the range of difficulties and delays, including language, associated with particular impairments (for example, Frith, 1989, on autism; Chapman, 1995, on Down's syndrome). Finally, research on difficulties with physically writing language is less commonplace, although research on phonological processing frequently examines orthographic processing, and the relationship between the two (for example, Cunningham and Stanovich, 1990).

In general, however, there is little consideration given to the consequences for literacy (as defined in this volume) from failure to achieve competence in any or all of the relevant domains. Lists of educational, social, psychiatric and possibly occupational consequences of such impairments can be drawn up, but the causal links, if indeed any exist, between the particular difficulties and the particular consequences are not specified. There may be good reason for such a lack of specification, which if made explicit could have implications, both positive and negative, for teaching and remediation strategies. It is apparent however that there are educational implications if any delay, deficit or deficiency in speech, reading or writing is manifested, and remediation programmes can be offered to assist the child. By inference then, it is recognized that such abilities *must be* important for achievement and accomplishment in the educational system and in society more broadly. Greater questioning of this assumption may be necessary to advance further our theoretical and practical knowledge of the consequences for children of not achieving literacy, either at developmentally the 'correct' period, during schooling, or even, at all.

Other work has focused on the consequences of not learning to read, usually as a result of not attending school or as a result of not being exposed to print (Cunningham, Stanovich and West, 1994). This work has tended to examine the abilities of such children that are associated with reading, such as phonological processing or awareness, or more general cognitive outcomes. Stanovich (1986) discussed some of the consequences of individual differences in literacy acquisition, in terms of the 'rich-getricher' and the 'poor-get-poorer' phenomena. Referred to as 'Matthew effects' after the biblical analogy, Stanovich presented alternative views regarding the relationship between cognitive processing and reading. After an extensive review, he proposed an overarching framework, characterized by marked improvements in reading by children who demonstrate good comprehension skills which contrasts with the lack of improvement and lack of reading in children who do not demonstrate such skills, to account for individual differences. His approach was based on trying to reduce the number of causal explanations for reading problems and he advocated a 'bootstrapping' whereby a truly reciprocal relationship exists between vocabulary and reading. The Matthew effect in reading arose because 'the better readers . . . have the more developed vocabularies' (p. 381) and those with more developed vocabularies demonstrate superior reading skills. Conversely, Stanovich discussed the poor-get-poorer effects noted in less skilled readers and the negative consequences of reading failure, suggesting ways in which this interacting cycle might be broken. Increased phonological awareness training and computer-aided reading systems were proposed as programmes that can remediate or prevent reading problems.

## Non-literate Cultures

There has also been considerable research examining non-literate, and very often, non-schooled, children whose place in the society or culture is not dependent on achieving literacy. Most of this work focuses specifically on the non-achievement of reading and/or writing rather than a failure to learn to talk, the consequences of which are largely similar across all cultures. For many so-called non-literate societies, spoken language skills are highly developed and the oral tradition for communication, for example through story telling and narrative, is far superior to that found in societies and cultures that rely more on the written mode for communication.

Some studies have examined different cultural experiences in relation to child-rearing practices and expectations regarding children's spoken language development (for example, Ochs and Schieffelin, 1995). There are cross-cultural differences in the kind of assistance that mothers provide to their children's learning of language, and, if theoretically such support is essential to the acquisition process, then there must be implications for the child's subsequent language development, and possibly beyond. Differences in the ways infants are treated as communicative beings influence what is learned and when. However, the communication patterns that are learned reflect the socio-cultural context in which the child is developing and in which he or she will later take a place. So, language acquisition not only reflects the child's developing needs but also the culture in which this development is occurring. This is consistent with the Vygotskian framework described in chapter 3.

## Methodological Issues in the Study of Literacy Development

One of the most difficult problems facing researchers studying spoken and written language development is that we, as adults, are already competent users of language. This competence means that we judge children's developing capacities in our own terms. The analysis of children's developing language is tempered by our own knowledge of language. This has meant that children's language use is usually seen as imperfect in comparison with that of adults. Their language skills are not as good as ours, though one day they will be.

We typically regard the child as striving to learn the language we use and we examine children's language for evidence that they are acquiring this language. We look for the child's production of linguistically correct and socially appropriate words and sentences. By viewing children's language as developing towards an adult model (whatever that may be), we tend to regard as errors language structures and functions used by young children that do not conform to those expected or commonly used. It is important to look carefully at errors however, rather than to dismiss them as deviations from an adult model. Errors can be extremely illuminating as mistakes can highlight the model of language children are trying to develop. For example, one area where errors have been taken into account is in the over-regularization of past tense verb endings – she goed, he bringed – and so on. This phenomenon is very widespread and recognizable. Such mistakes are taken as evidence of children mastering the -ed rule for the past tense of verbs (Clark and Clark, 1977).

As well as making errors of interpretation based on our own knowledge of the language and its implicit rules, the data base used can vary. For studies of spoken language, video and audio tape recordings are made of children's **production** of language in various settings. These may be the home, the child care centre, the preschool, or the psychological laboratory equipped with toys and furniture to be 'home-like'. The child may play alone, with the experimenter, with a parent, with siblings, or with peers. Recordings are made two-weekly, three-weekly or monthly over a specified period, ranging from a few weeks to years, depending on the requirements of the investigator. Analysis takes the form of transcriptions of **everything** recorded, both verbal and non-verbal. This is an extremely expensive and time-consuming way to conduct research, but it is the conventional way of studying spoken language development. One benefit in the long run is that the transcripts (and the audio and/or video tapes) can be re-analysed or used for examining different hypotheses at a later date. The same tapes can also be used to explore other developments such as the development of number (for example, the work by K. Durkin, Shire, Riem, Crowther and Rutter, 1986). In such a way it is possible to relate language development to development in other conceptual domains. The danger with this tactic is, however, that errors of fact or interpretation remain and may affect later usage, quantification and interpretation.

Once the child begins to use language, the methodologies change. Experiments involving children's **understanding** of language become commonplace. Children's ability to understand complex grammatical structures is tested by an experimenter, usually manipulating some pertinent materials or showing relevant pictures and requiring the child to respond verbally or to demonstrate some level of understanding through further manipulation of the materials. On the basis of children's understanding or lack of understanding, conclusions are drawn about their developing language capabilities. There is a great danger of underestimating children's language by this method. Typically, children of different ages are tested in only one experimental situation. It is then concluded that the younger children do not have the language structure under scrutiny while the older ones do; that is, the older ones can apparently understand the language used by the experimenter. Children must be studied in a greater range of situations, and both their production and their comprehension of the particular language structure examined. Otherwise all that really can be concluded is that in a particular context (that is, an experimental task), children of a particular age understand that language structure or grammatical construction. Again, most of the research on language development in children older than age about 3 years has been conducted in this fashion. There are, however, notable exceptions and the work conducted by Wells and colleagues at Bristol is a good example. They undertook naturalistic, observational studies of children's language development from the very early period when speech appears through to primary school, in both the home and school contexts. Similarly, studies of children's peer interaction have been undertaken as they occur naturally in classroom settings (French and Boynton, 1984, cited in French, Boynton and Hodges, 1991).

Studies of reading and writing have similarly relied on both methods of data collection. Early reading and writing have been studied through young children's production. So naturalistic data on early attempts at reading (in the home) and early scribbling can be gathered. Later studies, while again relying on the production of reading and writing skills, tend to be more experimental rather than studying the spontaneous productions. Children are asked to read a standard passage, lists of words or non-words, to write a particular story or to spell particular words or non-words. These are then assessed, usually in terms of the correct pronunciations or orthographies, or the errors made.

This consistent change in the methodology used to study the development of literacy must influence the way in which we view literacy. Coupled with the fact that our interpretations of what is going on must inevitably be adult, and experience based, then can we be sure that we have any idea which aspects of the child's language are developing and changing? When we are looking for continuities, some of these problems seem to disappear because the focus is on similarities across contexts and in trying to find the ways in which developments in one domain affect and influence developments in another. Commonalities are being sought. So although the problems still exist, by adopting an integrative perspective, different studies can be drawn together under the same umbrella. In this book, we will try not to place too 'adult' an interpretation on what children are striving to achieve as they learn to talk, read and write.

## Structure and Scope of This Book

In emphasizing the continuity of the acquisition of spoken and written language abilities, not only will the developmental aspects be examined, but the continuities across contexts will also be explored. It is common to examine the development of language in terms of the child's chronological age, focusing on the preschool period in particular. Thus the context is usually the home, and frequently involves looking at the mother interacting linguistically with her child. Once a certain competence with spoken language has been achieved, then it is assumed language development is more or less complete. Reading and writing are skills typically acquired at school, where the context is different from the home. Research, as well as theorizing, is now beginning to cross these traditional boundaries, and there are studies of language development comparing language in the home and language at school, and studies of reading and writing in the home (though these are usually regarded as *pre*literacy skills) as well as in the school. We will draw more explicit parallels between children's language experiences (both spoken and written) in various contexts, in particular, the home, the preschool and school. Reading and writing accomplishments will be linked to the developing spoken language skills of the child and to the context of their development and use. Within this integrative framework, a range of developments can be discussed, including structural developments in language, experiences of reading and writing, the development of awareness and the development of communication skills.

The book has been organized to capture the types of continuities we wish to emphasize. It has not been strictly organized by chronological age. Instead, the chapters are arranged by *topic*. Chapters 2 and 3 consider theories of spoken language development and how these have been translated into psychological studies of the process of language development. In particular, chapter 3 examines theories and processes that are applicable to both spoken and written language. While these chapters probably contain some of the most difficult sections in the book, the reader is encouraged to persevere. Knowledge of the theories and processes are important for an understanding of the content of spoken and written language development presented in later chapters. Chapters 4 and 5 trace the development of spoken language and chapters 8 and 9 describe written language development, both writing and reading. Topics that are central to both spoken and written language and serve to link the two areas are discussed in chapters 6 and 7. Chapter 6 examines issues in communication such as the use of language in different social contexts and how to deal with issues in successful communication. Chapter 7 considers metalinguistic awareness and its role in the development of literacy. A final synthesizing chapter completes the book.

The content of the chapters focuses almost completely on the acquisition of spoken and written English. Nonetheless much of what is said about the development of spoken language applies to *all* spoken languages. Similarly, much of what is said about written language applies to other languages, particularly those with an alphabetic script like English.

We have also confined our considerations to those children who do develop at least some degree of mastery over both spoken and written language. Some seem to do so almost effortlessly, while others appear to struggle more. Nevertheless, given the complexity of language, children do develop a remarkable command of spoken and written language within a relatively short period of time, generally by the time they are 8 years of age. Although some of the more cynical claim that many children learn to read and write despite the educational system, they all require some input to achieve literacy. In confining ourselves to those children who master spoken and written language, we do not wish to overlook the importance of those children, who, as a result of possibly some perceptual handicap or learning disability do not achieve such mastery. We acknowledge that by addressing probably only a small percentage of the world's population and around 85 per cent of the western literate population, we are limiting our study of literacy. We think, nonetheless, that the focus we have adopted will be useful for all those interested in the development of spoken and written language and that our framework will have explanatory value for all those concerned with language.

# CHAPTER TWO

# *Explanations of Spoken Language Development*

In this chapter two opposing theories of language development are described. These two theoretical positions, the **nativist** and the **empiricist,** have received the most prominence over the past few decades, and have been the most influential. These theories have been influential because not only have they attempted to explain how language may be acquired, but also because they have implications for the role of the child in the acquisition process.

Firstly, we will consider what these language theories have to offer, and what their explanatory shortcomings are. The very act of proposing a theoretical explanation for the development of language draws attention to the possible inherent problems with that theory. It is essential therefore to review these two theoretical positions first in order that subsequent changes of direction can be described and evaluated in the light of what has gone before, particularly the theories discussed in chapter 3. Extensions of these two broad perspectives will be described, both theoretically and in terms of the type of research studies that have been conducted in the two traditions. After the theories have been discussed, the ways in which they have been translated into psychological explanations of **how** spoken language develops will be considered, illustrated with relevant research studies. Finally, shortcomings of the two positions will be presented.

The rest of the chapter is devoted to an extended examination of the role of maternal speech, and more generally, maternal behaviour, in children's language development, derived largely from the prevailing orthodoxy of the 1970s, namely the nativist view. Furthermore, focus is predominantly on the role of the mother as opposed to any parent or care-giver in language development, reflecting the typical research design. Research examining the motherese hypothesis is followed by work that considers the mother–child dyad as a system for the development of language. Implications of this shift to a broader social-interactionist perspective lay the foundation for further theoretical considerations of language learning.

## Learning Theory of Language Development

The first major influence on the study of behaviour including language was the prevailing Behaviourist tradition in the USA in the 1930s. Behaviourists believed all behaviour was learned. Language was classified as a behaviour – verbal behaviour. The Behaviourist learning theory account represented the first attempt to provide a theoretical underpinning to the development of language by accounting for the processes of language learning in children. Skinner (1957) was the principal exponent of the view that behaviour, once reinforced, would continue, particularly after further reinforcement. Desirable behaviour could be systematically reinforced, while undesirable behaviour could be extinguished through the removal of reinforcement. Such changes in behaviour constituted learning. Skinner was concerned only with observable behaviours and believed that the processes of learning were the same for all species (including rats, pigeons and humans) and for all actions (running through mazes, pecking discs, learning language).

In the early stages, before children produce recognizable words, it was claimed that they produce all sounds of all languages. According to Behaviourist learning theory, parents selectively reinforced by attention or approval, only those sounds that occurred in the child's native language. Reinforcement could take a variety of forms and could be verbal, such as saying 'Good boy', or physical, for example, hugging or kissing the child. This selective reinforcement resulted in the child producing words. Now being able to talk, the young child could produce an utterance (the 'operant' in Skinner's terminology) to achieve some end which in turn reinforced the utterance. For example, the child may utter 'juice' and be reinforced by being given some juice to drink. This desirable outcome increased the likelihood of the utterance being repeated by the child.

One major problem with this account of how children's language develops lies with the fact that no one has specified precisely what ends or outcomes are reinforcing to each and every child learning language. While Skinner provided the definition of a reinforcer being something that increased the likelihood of the behaviour occurring again, it is very difficult to specify what constitutes a reinforcer. At best we could predict that hugging and kissing the child are reinforcing, as are drinks, food and sweets, but are these equally reinforcing to *all* children *all* of the time? Or are the reinforcers individual? The desirability of a reinforcer can only be ascertained *after* the utterance has been made and hence can only be defined after the utterance. We can make no prior predictions regarding the desirability of reinforcers.

Even if we could be certain about our choice of reinforcers, it is still difficult to understand how a child could possibly learn to speak and to utter sentences solely as a result of reinforcement. For example, there are problems in identifying the stimulus in language. Once an operant is established, then its occurrence is contingent on the presence of a stimulus. Again, taking the utterance 'juice', while its use depends on being reinforced, what prompts the child to make the utterance both in the first place and every time it is uttered from then on? Is it an internal drive – is the child thirsty? Or does the child see a cup, or see the tap, or see a bottle of lemonade, and *then* utter 'juice'?

It might be feasible to chart the environmental stimulus events that precede the child uttering 'juice'. But children do not restrict their uses of words to specific identifiable contexts, and utterances are usually produced in response to different stimuli. Indeed one of the major characteristics of language is its decontextualized nature. Language is not produced simply by 'seeing' a particular stimulus in the environment. It may result from other stimuli, including internal ones. For example, the child may utter 'juice' in response to feelings of thirst. Yet, as only observable behaviour is taken into account, we know nothing about what **motivates** the child to produce a certain utterance in the first place.

In addition to attributing the development of language to the successive shaping of sounds by reinforcement, some Behaviourists have acknowledged that the **imitation** of parental speech is an important component of learning language. Children can imitate their parents' correct utterances and receive reinforcement for so doing. However, it seems as though this process is unlikely to be of such paramount importance, since children produce novel linguistic constructions, never heard or used by adults, and still receive approval or reinforcement for their speech from their parents.

Brown and Hanlon (1970), in a classic study, found that parents paid greater attention to the meanings of their 2- to 3½-year-old children's utterances than to the grammar. Thus, instead of giving approval to utterances that were well-formed structurally, parents were concentrating on the veracity (the truthfulness) or the semantic value (the meaning) of the child's statements. There was no evidence of approval or disapproval based on the syntactic correctness of the children's utterances. Even when the syntactic form produced by children was very deviant from anything they could have imitated, for example, 'You goed church', parents did not disapprove, unless the statement were factually untrue. This study therefore cast doubt on the role of reinforcement in the child's acquisition of the **structure** of the language. Parents talk to their children a great deal, and may not reinforce selectively. Perhaps any (verbal) response to children's utterance signals attention being paid which in turn may reinforce their speech. Hirsh-Pasek, Treiman and Schneiderman (1984) replicated Brown and Hanlon's study but extended the argument to suggest that parents are not indifferent to grammatical form as evidenced by parents' tendency to repeat the ungrammatical sentences of 2–year-old children. Hirsh-Pasek et al. remained unsure of how these young children were actually able to make use of subtle environmental feedback regarding correct language use.

Thus in the Behaviourist account, language behaviour is considered only in terms of external events such as reinforcement and imitation, and no intervening variables are considered. What was true of all other behaviours was also true of language learning. It seems reasonable to accept that parents may indeed reinforce early attempts at language, and we are all well aware of parents who enthusiastically respond when their small infant 'talks'. Parents apparently become more selective in what they give approval to, and demand utterances increasingly closer to the acceptable (adult) ones as the child gets older. This too, seems distinctly possible. But is it unlikely that reinforcement is the sole means available for language development.

Nonetheless, it seems amazing that despite the fact the learning theory account of language development depends on parental reinforcement of children's language, parents are frequently not aware that they are reinforcing their children's language. Also, in spite of the varied assortment of reinforcers parents supply, and the consistency or inconsistency with which they do supply reinforcement, most children learn language. It would seem clear then that there is something lacking, or not fully specified, in the learning theory account of language development. However, there are still some advocates of this approach who regard language learning within a Behaviourist paradigm (for example, Stemmer, 1987).

One of the major shortcomings of learning theory is that it views the child as a passive recipient of environmental stimulation and reinforcement. There is no consideration given to the view that the children might be actively constructing their language. The only activity acceptable is imitation, a passive response to the language of the environment. It would appear that learning theory cannot account for the complexities and the creativity of language development, as it offers too simplified an account of the language learning process. Further, the relationship between the learning of language and other cognitive phenomena was never fully explored by learning theorists (with the possible exception of the work by the Kendlers on verbal mediation in problem solving, for example, Kendler, 1969). The principles of Behaviourism and learning theory have been invoked to account for memory, spatial and even social skills, but the inter-relationship between these different aspects of the developing child has not been examined in any depth.

Although there are clear drawbacks in the explanatory adequacy of learning theory as applied to language development, it is important to acknowledge the role of the environment in language development. We must be wary of rejecting all the concepts in a learning theory explanation too hastily. Some of the processes, such as imitation, may play a part in language development, but they are by no means the whole story. Language learning is far more complex and complicated and requires that the child play an active role in the process.

Reinforcement may assist in language learning, and certainly learning theory is most usefully applied in the treatment and remediation of language disorders in children. In order to facilitate language growth or language change in children with disabilities, behavioural techniques, concentrating only on external conditions and involving reinforcement for correct language production, have been found excellent for teaching purposes (see, for example, Crystal, Fletcher and Garman, 1976) especially in facilitating language in preschool children.

## Nativist Theory of Language Acquisition

The leading exponent of the nativist view of language acquisition is Noam Chomsky. In contrast to the Behaviourists, who were concerned with explaining behaviour and who regarded language as simply another observable behaviour, Chomsky was first and foremost a linguist concerned with explicating universal structural properties of language. This subsequently led him to an examination of the processes of the acquisition of language. However, instead of talking about the learning of verbal behaviour, as the Behaviourists had done, Chomsky (1965) concerned himself with the **acquisition** of language.

Chomsky's formal theory of language postulated universal rules which could distinguish grammatical from ungrammatical sentences in any language. These rules were applicable to every language in the world. The rules therefore had to be of sufficient generality to cover all the world's languages (including 'primitive' languages, manual languages of the hearing-impaired and possibly computer languages too).

Chomsky proposed two levels of grammatical rules, one level containing very generally applicable rules, and the other level containing specific manifestations of the more general rules. The two levels of grammar corresponded to what Chomsky called the **deep** structure of language and the **surface** structure of language. From the surface structure, that is, language which is spoken, the deep structure or grammatical constituents of sentences could be derived. These deep structure constituents were the universals of language. Specification of these universal rules would enable the generation of grammatical surface structures in any language, even if the actual forms of the language were different. The deep structure rules could only specify grammatical sentence forms. This process of specification was called **generation** by Chomsky. Chomsky's overall contribution, and the one that provided the impetus for subsequent language studies, was to describe a universally applicable generative grammar, capable of accounting for every grammatical sentence uttered the whole world over. Clearly the project was an ambitious one and not without difficulties, but Chomsky (N. Chomsky, 1986) continued to contend that there are universal general rules of language, with different spoken and written forms, depending on particular languages.

## Language Acquisition Device (LAD)

Since the rules of generative grammar were considered universal, it was a logical extension to assume that because everyone learned language, it must be an innate ability, that is, something everyone is born with. McNeill (1966) and Chomsky (1968) thus likened the child to a Language Acquisition Device (LAD) (see figure 1). LAD, a hypothetical entity, receives primary linguistic input in the form of sentences of the language heard by the child, and produces, as output, grammatical sentences of the language.

*Figure 1*   Language Acquisition Device (after McNeill, 1966)

What goes on in the mysterious LAD? It might be regarded as a black box, wired to receive language input data and to output or generate sentences. In all cases, LAD is wired to produce a grammar of the language, capable of generating comprehensible sentences. This grammar was the universal grammar, so was achieved by all children, regardless of the particular language community in which they were growing up. LAD was also proposed to account for the assumed poor levels of language input children received. LAD could deal with incorrect grammar and other irregularities of spoken language as the primary linguistic input. Chomsky proposed that individuals were genetically endowed with a specific facility for language, and this facility required only input data from the particular language community for the child to generate appropriate and grammatical sentences. In this way, he was able to account for the fact that features of language are universal.

Children are not predisposed to learn any particular language; all are born with the same facility and will develop as 'native speakers' of the language of the community into which they are born. The child has innate knowledge of the universal principles that govern the structure of language. These principles are resident in the mind of the child and are triggered by linguistic input.

## Competence and Performance

Here it is necessary to consider the distinction Chomsky made between linguistic **competence** and **performance**. Competence was equated with knowledge of the rules of grammar, while performance was the output actually produced. Again, this represents the distinction between the universal, general knowledge of language and grammar, and the specific knowledge for producing spoken language comprehensible to others. Technically, the output from LAD should be competence but traditionally, it is derived from performance. That is, knowledge of the rules of language is inferred from what the child (or the native speaker) actually speaks with all the imperfections of spoken language. However, for Chomsky, the acquisition of competence, of knowledge about the grammatical rules of the language, was more important.

The child learning language can be likened to a linguist trying to decode the principles of a language just discovered. For both the child and the linguist, the task is to process the input – the primary linguistic data – and from this, output grammatical sentences. From the language performance of native speakers (the input), the child must adduce the universal rules of language in order to output acceptable sentences. For the linguist, this is a comparatively easy task as the work is usually undertaken from written records of the language, or tape-recorded utterances of adults in a particular speech community. After extensive examination and re-examination of the language forms (the performance data) the linguist creates the grammar of the language (the competence model). The linguist, like the child, must create rules of grammar from the primary linguistic data. The linguist, however, brings to bear on the task existing competence with his or her native language. The linguist is already an accomplished language user and in establishing grammatical rules for another language can use existing linguistic knowledge, both implicit and explicit.

In contrast, the input the child typically deals with is the output from another person. Such speech is not only transient but may include ungrammatical sentences, unfinished sentences or errors of various kinds. It may also be restricted in scope, both spatially and temporally, as speech to very young children is frequently to do with the 'here and now', although this may be regarded as an advantage. The input is further subject to the child's hearing, the child's attention span, or what is being done at the time, what the adult is doing at the time, the level of noise the language is competing with, and so on.

Chomsky's thesis thus depends on the belief that the child is innately predisposed to acquire linguistic competence. How the child does so remains largely a mystery, although not without considerable debate and speculation. Chomsky's critics have been quick to point out his lack of concern for environmental influences on language acquisition. Chomsky, of course, represents the extreme opposite theoretical position to that adopted by the learning theorists where innate mechanisms were not even considered. But Chomsky (and other early workers in the area of child language acquisition, such as McNeill, 1966) did fail to take into account things that might affect the acquisition process. It is precisely this possible shortcoming that has provoked the bulk of research on issues connected with the processes of language development.

## Constraints on Language Development

A recent theoretical advance has been to consider what might be the **constraints** on language development. In other words what assumptions have been made regarding the innate unfolding of language capabilities, and the level of specification of these innate components or modules and what triggers their manifestation during language development. According to this view, there are limits to the child's capacity for language and exposure to the linguistic community allows these assumptions to be confirmed or disconfirmed. This view draws heavily on the tradition begun by Chomsky, since he made some strong assumptions about the learning of language. Constraints on language (both syntactic and semantic development), as evidenced by the inability to produce or understand certain grammatical structures or meanings or by the errors made or not made, allow a theoretical view of the development of language that involves the interface between language and cognition. Much recent research has been concerned with exploring this issue, in terms of the extent of the specification of the innate knowledge and its domain specificity (cf. the volume edited by Gelman and Byrnes, 1991).

Answers to questions such as the origin of the constraints and their operation are currently being sought. In addition, there is a body of research that assumes modularity of components in the linguistic and cognitive domains (for example, Fodor, 1983; Karmiloff-Smith, 1992). Work is being conducted to determine the theoretical importance of assuming that there are highly specific modules available for use by children as they develop, how these modules operate separately yet are inter-related and how they are manifested and articulated during development. Chomsky claimed that a nativist approach required modularity and conversely, that a non-nativist approach could not admit modularity for mental systems. The advantage of these recent extensions of Chomsky's nativist approach is that they consider both language and cognition as part of a more complex system that develops during childhood.

## Theoretical Advances

Recently there have been some theoretical shifts in linguistics which have implications for the study of language development. Linguists have continued to propose that children acquire structural rules but now allow for greater flexibility on the part of the child learner. There are two major theoretical positions – **learnability theory** and **parameter setting**. Both owe their origins to Chomsky (1981, 1986).

### *Learnability Theory*

Learnability theory as described by Wexler and Culicover (1980) and Atkinson (1986, 1987, 1992) has been proposed to account for the innate constraints that are imposed on the child to learn only adult grammar. Admitting that children learn grammar, then one has to describe how and why only one grammar is learned. There are two principles to learnability theory (Wexler, 1982). The first principle is that language is learned (by the child) and is hence grounded in experience, while the second principle states that the adult representation of the grammar (the final state of the learning process) is the representation given by linguistic theory. In order to reconcile these two positions, Wexler proposed that children derive the meaning of adult language from contextual cues and experience and then derive the grammatical structures from these meanings. In order for this mapping process to be successful, there must be constraints imposed on the grammatical rules and how they operate. These constraints are innate. While learnability theory is plausible in so far as children undoubtedly do learn language, it accounts only for the learning of grammatical structures.

It has also been claimed that learnability assumes that negative information is not available for children and therefore how can children know when they are producing incorrect, ungrammatical utterances. It has been proposed that child learners have certain constraints that bias production. For example, Wexler and Manzini's (1987) 'sub-set' principle assumes that if more than one grammatical description of an utterance is possible, the child will select the simplest one. It is not clear however how children can make such value judgements in the absence of a sophisticated knowledge of the language and a capacity to distinguish simpler from more complex representations of grammatical structure.

## Parameter Setting

With the modifications made to the original Chomskian theory, the mechanisms required to account for the acquisition of grammatical rules have likewise been altered. While still admitting a set of fixed linguistic principles as innate, some linguists now concede that there are some more flexible principles. This then leads to the belief not simply that children have to learn the rules of grammar (as learnability theory would have us think), but that they have to use their innate knowledge to complete and fix the more flexible principles. This work has been called 'parameter setting' (Chomsky, 1981; Gleitman and Wanner, 1982; Roeper and Williams, 1987; Meisel, 1995). According to this theoretical position, children are innately equipped with some important principles, but what develops, in what order and how these are specified linguistically, are determined by the linguistic community in which the child is growing up. Thus, these parameters can shift and change in the light of linguistic input. There is now an acknowledgment that children actively work on their linguistic input, and that language development does not occur in isolation.

Psychological research has focused on how children set limits to linguistic principles by working on the linguistic input (for example, Gleitman and Wanner, 1982). For example, linguistically relevant precursors in infants for later parameter setting have been identified. These include infants' reported preference for pauses in spoken language on clause or word boundaries rather than within words (Hirsh-Pasek, Kemler Nelson, Jusczyk, Wright Cassidy, Druss and Kennedy, 1987; Myers, Jusczyk,

Kemler Nelson, Charles-Luce, Woodward and Hirsh-Pasek, 1996) and a reported preference for certain acoustic properties of mothers' speech (Fernald and Kuhl, 1987). Such early abilities are leading researchers to conclude that infants are equipped with innate mechanisms to perceive units of spoken language. These mechanisms then constrain the hypotheses entertained and tested during the language acquisition period. Innate constraints on the perception of input language act as 'perceptual scaffolding on which language-learning strategies can build' (Hirsh-Pasek et al., 1987, p. 282)

The possibility that some parameters have default settings has guided the psycholinguistic research on the topic. According to this view, if children do not detect examples that would enable the setting of a parameter, then the default controls speech output. Such a view would account for why children learning different languages often use the same form at the beginning of language development. Further research on parameter setting includes the work by Hyams (1986, 1987, 1992) on the acquisition of what is termed the 'pro-drop' parameter, in other words, the null subject principle whereby languages like English require a subject at the beginning of the main clause while others like Italian, do not (see summaries in Garton, 1992 and Messer, 1994) and on the development of appropriate use of pronouns (Solan, 1983; Stevenson, 1992). However, this research has only served to increase uncertainty about the usefulness of a view that requires the single setting of a parameter per linguistic form (see Weissenborn, Goodluck and Roeper's 1992 book for chapters that discuss this issue in depth; also Meisel, 1995). In particular, Valian (1993) argues that instead of one setting which can be reset, a more useful analogy is of 'balance scales' whereby if the parameter is incorrectly set, then the child will not recognize incompatible linguistic structures. So, for example, if the pro-drop parameter is set, a child will not recognize sentences containing a subject. Therefore, it is hypothesized, that a level balance is set at birth, and the parameter then set according to the linguistic input. Further confirmation of this setting will raise the side of the balance while disconfirmation will lower it. In this way, the original setting (for example, prodrop) can be altered to reflect the input language (assumed to be correct) which will affect children's language production. Other areas of concern with the notion of parameter setting include the precise specification of the parameter (which explains why much of the research is crosslinguistic) and what happens if a parameter is incorrectly set at the start. Furthermore, it has been claimed that many of the apparent omissions from children's early language are due to processing or performance limitations and have nothing at all to do with parameters.

## Shortcomings of the Learning and Nativist Theories

Overall, both the nativist and the empiricist theories as described earlier fall short of providing totally adequate accounts of language development and of the process of achieving language. They are both polarized theories of spoken language development, and rely too heavily on *either* the environment *or* innate capabilities to describe and explain development. There is little, if any, consideration given to the acquisition of written language (including reading), not even as an adjunct to, nor as a consequence of, learning to speak the language.

The child's language development is generally regarded as occurring in a social vacuum, the child merely being a passive recipient of conversation and other language input. Environmental **stimulation** is acknowledged only in the learning theory account, while the nativist account considers the environment as **input** data for the child to develop abstract notions about language. The child is not accorded an active role in the language acquisition process – it all occurs as a pre-programmed sequence with modules becoming operational. Further, there is generally little or no consideration given to the parallel development in the child of other abilities such as cognitive (the development of intellectual abilities), perceptual (the development and refinement of the senses of seeing, hearing, and touch), and motor (learning to crawl and walk, hop and jump) abilities, although there is greater acknowledgment now being given to the relationship between language and cognitive development. One of the major functions of language, both spoken and written, is to communicate with other people, and it would seem necessary to study the importance and influence of social interaction on children's language development.

The emphasis has moved from studies of innateness and/or environmental reinforcement as mechanisms for language development to studies examining in depth the role of input language provided by an adult to a child's language development. It must be recognized that there is probably still an innate component to language acquisition, although a consideration of research on the relationship between input and output language has led many psychologists to shift away from the polarized theories discussed here. Chomsky's theory would predict that any input would suffice for LAD to generate a grammatical output, and hence initial studies categorized characteristics of language used to children. Myths about the possible detrimental effects on the child's language acquisition of a less than adequate (that is, impoverished, ungrammatical) input have largely been dispelled, even within the more recent theoretical frameworks which recognize constraints that operate to set limits on what input data will suffice.

A substantial body of research studies since the 1970s has been focusing on the direct influence adult speech has on the rate and course of grammatical development of children aged between 1 and 3 years. We will therefore trace the research that has examined the direct impact adult speech may have on the development of language forms in young children. Most of these studies assume that children have an innate capacity to work on the input data and use the input language directly. Children then output grammatical language, evidence of their knowledge of the grammar of the language. This impact can thus be measured by looking at the emergence of the forms found in the input language in the child's own language. Researchers have mainly concentrated on clearly observable language forms such as parts of speech, aspects of language that affect the way language is produced by the child (the output), such as the rising intonation pattern used with questions, and broad functions of speech forms, such as the use (frequency of occurrence and appropriateness) of question forms.

This research provided the impetus for subsequent studies into the role of adult, especially maternal, speech on children's linguistic development. Further, the studies have moved to look not only at the child's developing linguistic structures but also at the functions of children's developing language in relation to maternal speech input. Before discussing the role(s) of maternal speech input, we examine in more general terms some of the proposed broad processes by which mothers may assist their children with the development of language.

## Are There Specifiable Acquisition Processes?

Researchers studying language development have always acknowledged (perhaps not overtly in all cases) that there must be specifiable processes by which children learn language. For some, these processes are **intra**personal, within the child, and might be neurological and physiological, or modular in some way; for others these processes are **inter**personal, environmentally or socio-culturally determined, requiring the social support of other persons. Some individuals admit both biological and environmental processes as being necessary for language. The study of the biological prerequisites for speech and the research into the growth of neural networks for language development will not be considered in depth here. Many of the researchers in this area take the view that there are centres in the brain without which there would be no language.

Typically, the evidence comes from individuals who lose the capacity to talk (or write and read) after removal (either surgically or because of a stroke) of parts of the brain. However, there is a number of adherents to the biological **predeterminism** view in which it is admitted that there is an innate propensity for language in human beings. Partly because of the rapidity with which language development takes place, most psychologists acknowledge that the infant must be pre-wired to receive language input, if only admitting that infants are equipped with mechanisms such as vision and hearing which facilitate language development (Garton, 1992). Without going into details, we too subscribe to the view that there is some in-built or innate propensity in the infant for language. At what level this should be specified is largely irrelevant to our argument.

We also adopt some of the processes for language development set out by learning theory. The imitation of parental utterances by the child, coupled with reinforcement, have often been cited as important processes in language development. Much of the research influenced by learning theory aimed to investigate precisely the direct relationship between a child's changing linguistic output, and the input and language support offered by the parents. As we discussed in an earlier section, this was achieved by invoking processes such as reinforcement to account for the child's developing language.

However, in 1965, the American psychologist Courtney Cazden undertook a study comparing two different types of adult response to children's utterances. Instead of simply suggesting that reinforcement was sufficient for language to develop, she explicitly compared two possible processes whereby children's language structures might be enhanced. This study differed from previous research in the area because instead of looking at the child's language and how it related to preceding adult talk, the issue became one of how adult speech was causally related to the child's subsequent language development. Although the children Cazden studied were already talking competently, the study was sufficiently novel to influence much of the later research looking at the relationship between adult speech as input data to the child and the child's subsequent language development (and hence, knowledge of or competence with language structures). The principle that adult speech could determine child's language acquisition became widely held.

In Cazden's study, 12 children attending nursery school and aged between 28 and 38 months were divided into three groups. The children in the first group received, for 40 minutes of the 'school day', intensive and deliberate **expansions** of their utterances by a tutor allocated to them. That is, each utterance made by the child was expanded fully taking into account the context. It was hypothesized that the children in this group would manifest the most rapid growth of syntax (or grammar) since the expansions were the full realization of the child's intended meaning. The adult's utterance would therefore be directly related to the child's preceding utterance. For example, if the child were to say 'Want those', the adult would then say 'Oh, so you want the scissors. Here are the scissors.' The adult expanded the child's language appropriately, drawing on the context for interpreting the child's demand. In usual conversation, the response might be 'Here y'are', as the child is handed the scissors. The children in the second group received **modelling** whereby they were talked to by the tutors but no attempt was made to expand the child's own utterances. Thus the tutors provided grammatically correct and socially appropriate linguistic forms in speech and when reading to the children. These were to be the examples from which the children could learn. The third group was composed of four children who received no additional linguistic input from the adults. They were talked to in the usual manner.

At the conclusion of the study, six measures of the children's grammatical development were taken (for example, number of grammatical sentences, and the use of complex grammar such as the agreement of plural endings). It was found that the children in the modelling group made the most progress in terms of grammatical development, followed by the group who had received expansions. Although the original hypothesized benefits of expansion were outdone by the 'success' of modelling, Cazden interpreted her findings as showing the importance of adults talking to children. Adults need not necessarily deliberately expand each and every utterance. The richness and variety of the linguistic input to the children provided in the modelling group may be precisely the type of language that determines acquisition.

Despite being highly innovative and immensely influential, this original study has been criticized mainly on methodological grounds (see, for example, K. E. Nelson, 1977; Snow, 1986). In the group of children whose utterances were expanded, all language was subject to expansion, regardless of its content. So children were receiving expansions to ambiguous and nonsensical utterances, something that would not occur in real life. It has been pointed out that expansions did not, apparently, help the language acquisition of these children as much as modelling did because continual expansion may have caused the loss of confirmation that the occasional expansion of selected utterances provides (Nelson, 1977). Secondly, the children in the study were all lower class black children and the tutors, white, leading to social class differences which could have affected the results. Also, the numbers of children in each group were very small.

Subsequent replication experiments (for example, K. E. Nelson,

Carskaddon and Bonvillian, 1973) aimed to evaluate the effect on children's syntactic development of expanding only incomplete utterances. The shift in terminology from grammatical to syntactic development reflects a shift from focus on abstract and general principles of sentence construction to specific elements of word and sentence construction. Instead of indiscriminately expanding children's utterances, Nelson et al. **recast** only the incomplete utterances into a different sentential frame while maintaining the meaning intended by the child. So, for example, adults created a question out of a child's statement such as 'Is that a duck over there?' when the child said 'That's duck.' These recastings invited participation by the child in conversations. This technique, they found, improved subsequent syntactic development. Thus, the later studies, looking at the possible facilitative effects of adult expansion of children's utterances as a potential device aiding acquisition, not only found specific effects but have also confirmed the linguistic benefits.

Research has also examined the **direct** effect of maternal speech variables on children's later language development. Studies such as those discussed in the next section have sampled the speech of an adult while interacting with a child learning language. Through the use of statistical, usually correlational, procedures, they have examined relationships between forms in the adult's language and emerging forms in the child's language. By focusing on small developments in language form, conclusions can be drawn regarding the role of adult speech on children's language development. All this research assumes an innate predisposition on the part of the child to act on the input language. The child must be regarded as actively trying to make sense of the language and deriving rules from it. Variations of this research have compared different types of adult input speech such as mothers versus fathers or high socio-economic groups versus lower socio-economic groups, or compared different groups of children, such as 'normal' children versus hearing impaired children. Across all these studies, the basic contention remains the same. Adult input speech to children is causally related to children's language development, though the processes by which this happens and the extent to which it is sustained are possibly subject to variability (see also Garton, 1992, for a discussion).

## The Correlation of Parental Speech with Children's Language Development

The study of the correlational role of the speech of adults on children's language development has been concerned almost exclusively with

**maternal** language input to the young preschool child, often aged between 1 and 3 years. The imbalance has been redressed to a certain extent by research examining the influence of paternal speech on children's language development and also by research comparing language at home and at school, some of which will be reviewed later in this book. The original studies (for example, Snow, 1972; Cross, 1975) were prompted by a realization that perhaps the nature of the mother's speech would actually be at best **facilitating** (or at worst, hindering) the language development of the young child. Thus the initial research in this area aimed to describe the characteristics of maternal speech input and to correlate these with the eventual growth of language forms in children. The studies have been conducted with children of various ages, but always beginning once language has appeared, usually around 12 to 18 months. The studies then examined the input and output language during the period of rapid growth of the child's language, tending to stop somewhere between the child's third and fourth birthdays. Both age and linguistic ability are customarily reported by researchers.

It is now fairly evident and widely accepted that mothers (and all adults, including older children) do indeed talk differently to children in the early period of language development. In a broad sense, the nature of the interactions between mothers and their young children is different to adult–adult interactions, because not only does the content of the interaction vary, but the type of speech varies, as does the form of the language used. Early researchers dubbed these systematic variations of speech either **motherese** or **baby talk**.

Both motherese and baby talk refer to language specifically directed to the young child and should be distinguished from any other form of language to which the child is exposed, such as the television, radio, or conversations between adults carried on within earshot of the child. Although the child is exposed to quite a considerable amount of indirect environmental language, we are concerned here only with that language directed to the child. However, there is an important distinction that must be made between motherese and baby talk. Baby talk is best characterized by the use of a 'baby' vocabulary such as the use of words with syllable reduplication, for example, 'doggie', 'gee-gee' and 'nana'. There is also a tendency not to use personal pronouns, but to use nouns and pronouns in a deviant fashion. For example, a mother might say 'Now Mummy is going to get baby his breakfast' instead of the more normal 'Now I'm going to get you your breakfast.'

These deviations of adult speech characteristic of baby talk are also noted in motherese, but motherese includes further modifications of normal adult speech. Mothers' speech to children includes sentences that

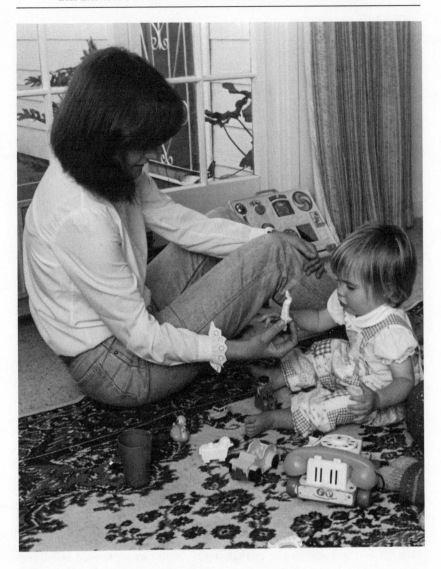

Parental speech facilitates language development

are characteristically very short, and, although elliptical, are usually gram-matical. They are spoken and enunciated very clearly. Further, motherese refers to the speech expressly addressed to young children. The major characteristics reported in different studies such as Snow (1972) and Cross (1975, 1977, 1978) are summarized in table 1.

*Table 1*   Major characteristics of motherese

| Category | Characteristic |
| --- | --- |
| Paralinguistic | High pitch |
| | Exaggerated intonation |
| Syntactic | Shorter utterance length |
| | Fewer verbs and modifiers |
| | Fewer subordinate clauses |
| | Fewer embeddings |
| | More content words |
| | Fewer function words |
| Discourse | More imperatives |
| | More interrogatives |
| | Speech more fluent and intelligible |
| | More repetitions |

There is broad consensus amongst investigators regarding the nature of the input to the child. Maternal speech certainly does deviate from adult speech along definite describable parameters, though there is no suggestion that this input is actually degenerate in any way. Maternal speech to children is structurally simpler in form than adult speech and there is a tendency to talk about the 'here and now' both in terms of space and time when addressing children. It is also reasonable to conclude that maternal speech constitutes the primary linguistic input to young children. Therefore it seems justifiable to predict that maternal speech as input data must have some influence on the acquisition or learning processes. Descriptions of maternal speech input are reasonably robust from study to study and there are some important implications of this research.

Firstly, the linguistic input to young children is ongoing and continuous which would suggest that the acquisition process is not something that happens instantaneously. Language acquisition occurs gradually. This then raises the issue of the changeability of the input speech to young children. Are the speech modifications the same to children of all ages? Or are there differences in the nature and extent of the modifications depending on the age of the child? That is, do parents, or other caregivers, make changes to their speech modifications in the light of the developing child's increasing linguistic capabilities?

Cross (1979) argued that we must regard the child's acquisition of language as an interactional process, incorporating the changing nature of the child's learning strategies, the possible changing nature of the parent–child interaction pattern and of the linguistic input provided. Cross attempted to examine this issue by studying mothers' speech adjustments in relation to the linguistic ability of their young children learning language. Not only is it important to confirm whether mothers' speech is finely tuned to the linguistic capacities of their children, as suggested by Snow (1972) and Cross (1975), but methodologically, if parental speech does change over time, then research into the role of input speech in child language acquisition becomes more problematic.

By correlating maternal speech variables with measures of children's language development, Cross (1979) found relationships between many of the aspects of maternal speech and the linguistic capabilities of the children. She was thus able to confirm the hypothesis that mothers do adjust their speech in tune with relatively small differences in age and linguistic maturity of their children. Cross concluded that mothers were sensitive to even very minor increments in the language of their children. She suggested that study of the processes of language acquisition must take account of the two-way, interactional, dyadic nature of mother–child interaction. That is, not only is maternal speech important for the child's subsequent language development directly, but it is also related to the child's present language level.

However, still further questions start to be raised by an examination of maternal speech input. For example, do the modifications of the language make the child's task as learner any easier? The answer to this question, in the light of the research just discussed, would seem to be 'Yes', since the mother is clearly modifying her speech to meet the child's linguistic needs. In so far as adjustments are being made in direct relation to changes in the child's own output, it would appear that mothers are sensitive in gauging the appropriate level for their speech. Presumably, the current level reflects the mother's expectations of her child's present linguistic capabilities. Research has pursued this topic, guided by the **motherese hypothesis**.

## The Motherese Hypothesis

The **motherese hypothesis** states that it is precisely the 'SPECIAL properties of caretaker speech [that] play a causal role in acquisition' (Gleitman, Newport and Gleitman, 1984, p. 43, their emphasis). Instead of hypothesizing differences between the structure of maternal speech to children and speech between adults, the motherese hypothesis makes claims about the **role** of the input language on the child's learning of language. In its strongest form, the hypothesis states that the restricted linguistic structures and functions selected by mothers to use to their children are necessary for language learning. A weaker version of the hypothesis exists, stating that the restrictions merely hasten language learning and reduce the error rate (cf. Newport, Gleitman and Gleitman's, 1977, claim that general language development was relatively unaffected by the specific properties of the speech heard).

Gleitman et al. (1984) provided an examination of 'the current state of the motherese hypothesis', comparing and contrasting many of the correlational studies of maternal input speech and child language development conducted in recent years. They were critical of the different methodologies adopted by researchers, and they also criticized the definitions used and the types of language selected for investigation. In particular, they were critical of the study by Furrow, Nelson and Benedict (1979) which demonstrated that simplified maternal speech was indeed related to faster linguistic development in children. To substantiate their confirmation of the strong version of the motherese hypothesis, Gleitman et al. analysed maternal speech and correlated certain aspects with young children's developing language. They concluded that the influence of the structure and function of maternal speech was modulated to a large extent by the predisposition of the (child) learner to learn language. This predisposition concerns how input language is organized and used by the child. This notion of a predisposition to act on the input language reiterates our point, made previously, that we should assume an innate component in language development. It is also consistent with the view that there are certain constraints or limits on the way the input language is accessed and used by the child language learner.

In support of the strong version of the motherese hypothesis, Gleitman et al. (1984) cited the selective use of input language by young children, both in *what* (language)they use, *when* it is used and the *purposes* for which it is used. The young child does not use all input language indiscriminately. They are selective in those aspects chosen to use, or needed to be used, both in terms of the actual language forms produced and the (limited) uses to which it is put. The child is regarded as being an active participant in the language learning process, working on the input language provided by the adult. Further, Gleitman et al. argued that simplification of the language by mothers when they talk to children may not necessarily be conducive to rapid and trouble-free language development. Children ought to be exposed to a range of linguistic structures and functions from which they can make hypotheses regarding the language being acquired.

More recently, Messer (1994) has reviewed all the above evidence, including the methodological debates as well as the substantive concerns, and concluded that 'the majority of the studies have failed to find strong support for the effect of A-C [adult-child] speech' (Messer, 1994, p. 227, our elaboration). He supports a view that some simpler and less potentially confounding methodology is necessary to demonstrate any correlational relationships between maternal speech and child language development, a view shared by Harris (1992), and hence infer any causality.

Snow (1986) continued the theme of the child as an active processor of input language in a useful review of the issues regarding the relationship between what she called **child directed speech** (CDS) and language acquisition. Although CDS and motherese are equivalent, Snow believed the term 'motherese' to be misleading as it implied only mothers talked in the special way. Instead of placing emphasis on the adult speech input to children, she regarded the child as the important component in the language learning process. Snow concluded that the main contribution of the study of CDS and its facilitating features has been to 'constrain hypotheses concerning the nature and variety of language learning mechanisms' (Snow, 1986, p. 88). That is, she believed that the study of the role of the features of maternal speech influential for children's language acquisition was far too limited, impeded by a narrow theoretical stance and consequent focused research enterprise. She argued for expanding the study of child directed speech and for uniting the study of social aspects of language development with studies looking at cognitive, information-processing, aspects (such as the studies by the Gleitmans and colleagues), rather than studying each in isolation.

Snow (1989; see also 1995) subsequently expanded the notion of social influences that facilitate language development to include the mechanisms of fine-tuning, recasts, negative feedback and joint attention. Of these four aspects of social interaction, it is joint attention that has received the most research work in recent years. Of the other three, only recasts seem to have any facilitative effect on language development *per se* (see Keith Nelson's work reviewed earlier in this chapter), while fine-tuning and negative feedback may, in a more limited way, assist. Joint attention, that is the mutual establishment of a shared activity usually between a mother and a child, provides a context within which the mother and her child can develop a mutual focus for conversation (Bruner, 1983; Snow, 1989; Garton, 1992) and shows most promise as a facilitatory a mechanism for language development.

Joint attention includes such behaviours as prelinguistic infants' following of adults' pointing, adults' gazes and the head turning of adults (for example, Scaife and Bruner, 1975; Murphy and Messer, 1977; Butterworth and Grover, 1988; Butterworth and Jarrett, 1991; see also review in Messer, 1994). Other studies have examined the relationship between joint attention (defined as maternal responsiveness) and language development (defined as vocabulary development) in children using longitudinal designs (for example, Tomasello and Todd, 1983; Tomasello and Farrar, 1986). These studies generally obtain findings that support the view that vocabulary size is related to maternal sensitivity and responsiveness in directing her child's attention to objects. Similar findings are also reported in experimental studies for joint attention and the child's acquisition of object words (Baldwin, 1991) and action words (Tomasello and Kruger, 1992).

The research on adult speech to children was instigated as a response to the Chomskian claim that the linguistic input to children acquiring language was in some way 'degenerate'. It then shifted to an examination of the way adult language influenced children's language learning. It overtly acknowledged that the child's innate capacity required input data on which to work. The research therefore implicitly acknowledged that environmental, or social, input was necessary. However, in pursuing the particulars of this process, the overall perspective was lost. The social domain, in a broad sense, must be reintroduced into studies of how language is acquired. Further, and more importantly, the child's part in this process must be examined. The child is an active processor of environmental information and any contribution to language learning should not be neglected. The research on adult speech to children all too quickly became an end unto itself, forgetting other aspects of the child's development. In this sense, Snow's urging of taking into account the complementarity of parallel developments in the social and the cognitive spheres is timely. It must not be forgotten, therefore, that there is the need both for an infant predisposed to process information and to interact with others *and* for appropriate environmental input and support. Only in this way can development proceed, both in terms of the child's language development and of our theoretical understanding of the relationship between complex human behaviours.

## Social Considerations in Language Learning

Theoretical advances such as learnability theory and parameter setting make an important contribution to our understanding of language development by extending the nativist perspective and acknowledging the importance of environmental input in the language acquisition process. However, there has been an even greater influence on the study of language development, particularly when we wish to consider spoken language and written language as literacy. In order to consider spoken language, reading and writing together and how developments in one domain influence developments in the other, and how continuities between developments can be studied, it is necessary to examine in depth the influence of social interactionist approaches to the study of spoken language development and written language development.

For spoken language, up to now the focus has been on the input language to the child and how it may influence the course and rate of language development. A theory to explain how learning occurs has still not been formulated, although Snow (1989), Garton (1992) and Messer (1994) have made attempts. It is becoming more and more obvious that social considerations must have a role to play in language development. It is therefore proposed here that competence with language is part of a wider developmental competence. The role of the child's **social** environment in shaping, encouraging and moulding these competencies must not be ignored. Language does not develop in isolation. The child is not only acquiring other cognitive competencies and developing intellectually, but is developing in interaction with other social beings. The social interactional domain must have some impact on the child's language development, if not on all aspects of cognitive development.

CHAPTER THREE

# Social Interaction and the Development of Language

## Vygotsky's Theory

Guided by the theoretical notions put forward by Vygotsky (1978) and Bruner (1983, 1984), there has been increased research into the role of social interaction in spoken language development (for reviews, see Garton, 1992; Messer, 1994). Further, this research has been extended to look at the social interactional roots of written language development (Assink, 1994) and development more generally (Bornstein and Bruner, 1989; Rogoff, 1990). Consequently, we believe that the social interactionist theories have the most to offer for the empirical study of literacy development in young children. Although other researchers clearly adopt similar views to Vygotsky and Bruner regarding the child's development, few articulate any notable theoretical advances. Those crucial links between data description and theory building are still missing. We intend, at least, to provide some guidelines for the construction of such a theory.

Vygotsky (1896–1934) was a Soviet psychologist and educationalist with a wide range of expertise. Writing and researching during the period after the Russian Revolution, his influence was suppressed in the subsequent Stalinist years and resurrected only after 1956. Beginning his academic career by studying literature, philosophy and the arts, he gradually moved into psychological studies after attending lectures at university. He initially taught literature at school, and also organized a psychological laboratory at a nearby teachers' college. He continued to read extensively, particularly poetry, fiction and philosophy, including the works of Freud, Marx and Engels. In 1925 he successfully completed his doctoral dissertation on 'The psychology of art'.

As an academic and as a practitioner, Vygotsky got caught up in the wave of enthusiasm for the incorporation of western ideas and thinking into the Soviet ideology that followed the Revolution. The debate over the origins of mind that had raged for centuries in Europe and America took on political overtones as the Soviets sought to adopt a position in keeping with their ideology. Vygotsky was part of the 'paedology' movement which attempted to unify the study of children from a Marxist perspective. This movement was not only a reaction against the prevailing adoption of mentalist theories but was also an attempt to relate theories of psychological development to educational practice.

However, the year 1924 marked the beginning of Vygotsky's profound impact on psychology. As an unknown scientist, he presented a conference talk which was not only magnificently delivered, but the content of which highlighted the magnitude of his intellect. His talk explored the relationship between conditioned reflexes and the development of conscious behaviour in man. The inclusion of 'consciousness' as part of the human mind clearly dissented from the paedologists' empiricist position, but equally, Vygotsky did not advocate a return to mentalist theories. What Vygotsky did was to take Marxism at a philosophical level and apply it at the psychological level. The theory assumed individual mental processes have socio-cultural origins; that is, individual change receives its impetus from historical and social change.

Vygotsky's radical theory brought him into ideological and political opposition with the Soviet mainstream in the late 1920s, and while eventually his views prevailed, he was never accepted as the leader of the psychology movement in the USSR during his lifetime (see Vygotsky, 1986, for an introduction to both his life and to the history of Soviet psychology; also Wertsch, 1985a).

From that point on however, Vygotsky was recognized as a psychologist and accepted an invitation to join the Psychological Institute in Moscow. For the next ten years, his scientific output was prodigious. There are two major ways in which Vygotsky has proved to have been influential. He wished to reformulate psychological theory especially regarding the development of intellectual abilities in humans. He also wished to develop ways to deal with practical problems in Soviet education, such as remediation for the handicapped. It was in this latter connection that he founded a research institute for 'defectology'. He began serious investigations of, among other things, the relationship between literacy and schooling. Thus, our concern here is with Vygotsky's interest in and impact on psychology and education in both theoretical and practical terms.

Vygotsky's theory encompasses the development not only of language but also of other 'higher mental processes' including all forms of intelligence and memory. In fact, he wished to 'describe and specify the development of those forms of *practical intelligence* that are specifically human' (Vygotsky, 1978, p. 23, our italics). He was concerned first and foremost with those aspects of intelligence that fulfil useful human functions.

Such activities include speech, perception, memory and attention.

Vygotsky's influence on Soviet psychology was and is profound; he was contentious, and yet his ideas have achieved recognition. In the west, the first English translation of his work appeared in 1962, but it is really only since the late 1970s that the importance of his work for the study of children's developmental processes has been acknowledged. In particular, his theoretical work has been influential on recent studies of cognitive development in children, especially memory processes, problem solving, and the relationship between language and thought (for example, Wertsch, 1985b; Bornstein and Bruner, 1989).

### Vygotsky's Theory of Mental Development

Vygotsky made substantial contributions to the study of mental development including spoken language and written language. Because he regarded specifically human activities as **tools** (after Engels's concept of human labour and tool use as means of achieving change and of transforming the self), any process that successfully achieved a particular end must also lead to changes in the individual. Humans and animals were alike in their use of external tools to bring about changes, but only humans were able to master such changes by their use of specific tools. Further, Vygotsky extended this argument to cover the use of **signs**. Sign systems include spoken language, written systems and number systems, which are created by societies over the course of history to fulfil uniquely human needs. These systems are also amenable to change as society changes and as history changes. For Vygotsky it was precisely the mastery of such sign systems that marked individual development, for both the child and for society, historically and culturally. The child's development with spoken and written language is paralleled by cultural changes in the use and mastery of such sign systems. Sign systems were used for symbolic activities, according to Vygotsky, which permitted greater intellectual accomplishments than the use of tools for practical activities.

In essence, Vygotsky's theory rests on the fundamental premise that development occurs on the social level, within the cultural context. Specifically, for cognitive development in children, it is postulated that intellectual functioning takes place on the social plane to start with, then proceeds to the individual level. The child internalizes the mental processes initially made evident in social activities, and moves from the social to the individual plane, from **inter**psychological functioning to **intra**psychological functioning. To take the example of arithmetic, Vygotsky believed that this should be taught to children through the use of concrete materials, and careful step-by-step demonstration by a teacher.

As children begin to work out the rules, say for the addition of single numbers requiring a double digit answer, they initially use concrete material such as counters. Increased levels of abstraction are introduced and the child becomes capable of reaching solutions alone. The social transmission of the rules precedes the child grasping them and using them. The same principle can be applied not only to school learning, although this was the area where Vygotsky was most interested, but also to learning in infancy, where children learn to stack nesting cups, or learn to do jigsaws.

In fact, Vygotsky's position is that individual functioning is determined exclusively by social functioning, and the structure of an individual's mental processes mirrors the social milieu from which it is derived. Despite his claim that language and thought have separate roots and develop independently for a time, Vygotsky maintained that 'The child's intellectual growth is contingent on his mastering the social means of thought, that is, language' (Vygotsky, 1962, p. 51). Thought, and intellectual development, thus depend on language. Social interaction, itself derived from the present culture or historical perspective, in some senses **creates** the language. Through language and communication, cultural information can be passed on to children, who then internalize this knowledge and use it as they need. According to this view, children's development best takes place in social settings, from which the culturally appropriate intellectual, cognitive and mental structures and their functions are internalized.

In social interaction, children learn the use of the tools that will enable them to achieve the ends or goals they require. For the pre-verbal child, such tool use is non-verbal, limited to external tools or practical activity, rather like monkeys and apes. Children learn, for example, simple give-and-take routines, where object exchange is achieved without the need for language. Later development allows for the use of increasingly sophisticated tools, namely signs – spoken language and then written language (both reading and writing). What is uniquely human is the independence yet the unity of these two activities, the use of external tools and the use of internal tools or signs. Only humans can use both tools and signs separately and together to reach a specified goal. The use of both tools (for practical activities) and signs (for symbolic activities) enables higher, human, levels of functioning because 'symbolic activity [is] accord[ed] a specific **organizing** function that penetrates the process of tool use and produces fundamentally new forms of behavior' (Vygotsky, 1978, p. 24). In other words, the use of a sign system such as language allows for greater organization, flexibility and creativity in the use of more practical tools.

There is thus an underlying unity between all the various cognitive processes of speech, perception and action. Vygotsky emphasized the importance of speech, especially in accompanying action to attain a goal.

In fact, this clearly demonstrates what was meant by mastery via tool use. For the young child, speech accompanies activities. That is, young children talk as they play, solve problems or whatever. In solitary activities, children can achieve what they have been learning in interaction with other people. They often talk to themselves as they work towards the solution of their tasks. This talk is sometimes termed 'egocentric', in so far as it is non-communicative and is not meant for anyone else. Nevertheless, it is related both to later social, communicative speech and to inner speech, speech used for **planning** activities.

Children faced with a task or a problem they are unable to solve alone may well turn to an adult for help. In order to do this successfully, they have to be able to communicate the nature of the problem and the attempts they have made to solve it. Children use their language to appeal to the adult. That is, their language use is social or interpersonal. As children mature, this use of language becomes in addition intrapersonal, and they are able to appeal to their own knowledge. Their language comes to guide their activities, to precede their actions, to plan. For example, Wertsch and his colleagues have shown how, in problem solving tasks such as jigsaws, young children gradually take over the strategic functions of language and other behaviours initially used by their mothers. Wertsch, McNamee, McLane and Budwig (1980) examined how mothers use language and behaviours such as eye gazes and pointing to guide their children towards the successful solution of a task. Mothers and their young children were requested to make a simple jigsaw puzzle in accordance with a model. The extent to which the children consulted the model while doing the jigsaw constituted evidence that they were monitoring their task behaviour. Regulation of eye gazes to the model could be undertaken by the mother or by the children themselves. Self-regulated gazes were those not immediately preceded by a behaviour such as a point or the mother calling attention to the model verbally. The ontogenesis of monitoring skills was manifested by a shift of responsibility from the adult to the child, as evidenced in a decrease in the proportion of other-regulated gazes.

Wertsch et al. also found that with age children were able to use the mother's utterance and/or gaze or point more effectively. This was evidenced by a decrease in the number of maternal interventions needed for correct placement of each piece of jigsaw. Thus as children learn the strategic significance of being told to look at the model they are supposed to be copying (as this will enable a correct copy to be made), they can then incorporate this into their own actions. They can internalize the sentence 'Look at the model to see where to place the piece of jigsaw I have in my hand.' The functions of social speech become internalized

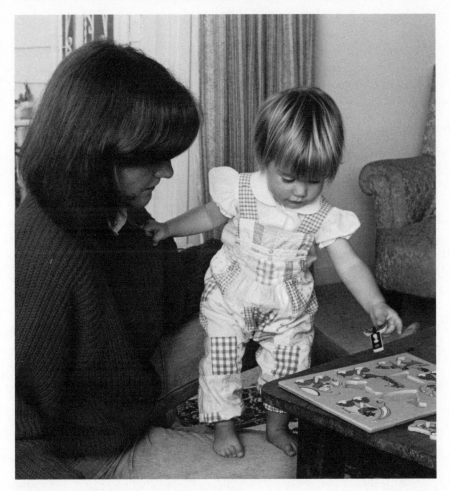

Mother and child completing a jigsaw puzzle

while the speech also retains its communicative functions. Social speech becomes totally integrated into the development of the child's practical intellect, ultimately leading to the development of cognitive processes.

## Development and Learning

An important distinction made by Vygotsky was between **development** and **learning** in children, two processes he believed to be inter-related but not coincidental (see also Bruner, 1971; Pratt, 1985; Garton, 1992).

Learning characterized what went on in the classroom at school. Vygotsky however did not mean to imply that no learning could or should occur prior to school entry. However, distinguishing (school) learning from development enabled Vygotsky to describe a central tenet to his theory, namely the **zone of proximal development**. Much of the thinking on this concept derived from his dissatisfaction with the use of intelligence tests to assess children's intelligence. He believed that such tests were able to measure only the extent of the child's knowledge at that point in time. They told us nothing about the process whereby the child arrived at a solution. To account for this discrepancy between product and process, Vygotsky proposed the zone of proximal development. This theoretical concept was introduced to explain the distinction between the child's **actual** developmental level, as measured by the intelligence test for example, and the child's **potential** developmental level. The latter level is characterized by what the children are capable of achieving, given their socio-cultural development to date.

To assess the potential level of development, it was necessary to present children with a problem, the solution to which was just beyond their mental capacities, and allow them to interact with another person while working out the answer. The processes by which children arrived at the solution would provide a more accurate assessment of the child's intellectual capacity than merely examining what they already knew. More formally, Vygotsky defined the zone of proximal development as 'the distance between the actual developmental level as determined by independent problem solving and the level of potential development as determined through problem solving under adult guidance or in collaboration with more capable peers' (Vygotsky, 1978, p. 84). Delineating the zone makes it possible to ascertain what the child is currently capable of achieving and also what the child will be able to achieve in the near future.

This theoretical construct is totally in keeping with Vygotsky's broader theory, emphasizing the social nature of knowledge acquisition. In collaboration with an adult or a more capable peer, the child is able to solve more complex tasks, since through the use of practical intellectual activities such as speech and action, the adult can guide the child's progress towards a solution. What the child can achieve today with appropriate help and guidance, can be done tomorrow alone. There has been internalization of the processes required for working out that particular task.

Vygotsky thus believed that collaborative functioning was a more useful indicator of a child's ability than individual performance on an intelligence test. In order for a child to learn, tasks slightly in advance of the child's actual developmental level should be set, and instruction geared to the child's potential developmental level. Instruction therefore plays a central role in Vygotsky's theory, especially as by instruction he meant teaching *and* learning combined. Instruction is the mechanism whereby the child can grow intellectually and internalize the processes necessary for such development. The adult or more capable peer in collaborating with the child conveys the tools of that society, which the child can utilize in interaction and subsequently use alone, independently. The notion of the instructional aspect of the zone of proximal development has spawned a great deal of research interest in recent years and psychologists are beginning to identify processes of individual cognitive functioning that have their roots in social interaction (for example, Garton, 1984a; Tudge and Rogoff, 1989; Garton, 1992). The zone of proximal development has also been shown to be of relevance for the study of reading (for example, Berninger, 1994).

According to Vygotsky, learning and development are inter-related from very early in the child's life. Within this framework, Vygotsky was able to consider how the **functions** of spoken language change for young children. Speech turns inward because its function changes as children develop. Egocentric speech is inner speech functionally, in that children are using the language for themselves. In this sense, egocentric speech is a precursor to internalized speech with its planning and monitoring functions, albeit it communicative to a certain extent. Vygotsky's major contribution was to have incorporated the development of language into his theory of cognitive development.

In language development, Vygotsky claimed children learned language from adults by assimilating the names of objects in the environment. Children ask adults questions, and not only acquire linguistic information, but information about a range of phenomena. In general, children are used to being instructed, to learning, even before the period of formal learning takes place in school. Children have dealt with some of the intellectual concepts that will be taught to them at school, as school learning must build on the learning and experience that has gone before. However, there are some important differences between preschool learning and the learning that the child encounters in school, and Vygotsky used the example of the development of writing to illustrate his point.

## *Writing*

Vygotsky was concerned not only with the way in which children develop speech (spoken language) but he also addressed the antecedents to and development of writing. Language and thought were regarded as originating from separate roots, but coming together later in development. By language, Vygotsky meant both speech ('the linguistic tools of thought',

Vygotsky, 1962, p. 51) *and* the child's social and cultural experience. Language was regarded as the means through which thought was transmitted and created. Fundamental to the use of language however was socio-cultural and historical thought, itself created through language. There was thus an intimate relationship between language and thought, the social and the individual, the spoken and the written word. Part of the child's social experiences must include the written word, since writing is the permanent record of a society's culture and history with which the child is becoming imbued during development. By writing, Vygotsky intended written language rather than the processes of writing. Consequently, in developmental terms, this entailed learning to read as well as learning to write.

The process of writing is typically taught within the narrow constraints of the school curriculum. It is not regarded as a continuous developmental activity. As Vygotsky (1978) pointed out, this is in stark contrast to the prominence and utmost importance placed on writing as a cultural and social activity. Learning to write is also overshadowed by learning to read. According to Vygotsky part of the problem lies in the fact that writing is difficult to teach. Children are encouraged to make marks on paper but do not *need* to write. Teaching writing requires effort on the teacher's part and requires fine motor skill and incentive on the child's part. Vygotsky in fact addressed the crux of the issue (and one that perplexes and confounds researchers today) when he wrote of the 'second order symbolism' of writing. That is, written language comprised signs designating spoken words that themselves **stood for** objects or entities in the environment. The developmental history of writing in part consisted of removal of the middle link, the spoken word, so that the child realized that the signs stood for objects and entities. Such a realization did not simply appear when the child mastered the intricacies of neat handwriting; instead it only occurred when the child's mental development had reached the required level (Vygotsky, 1978).

The physical, motor process of writing, that is, making marks on the writing surface, requires teaching. Vygotsky thought this situation rather artificial in comparison with the ease of learning the spoken language. In the natural course of growing up, children have opportunities to display many of the skills required for writing later. They learn about gestures that communicate, and gestures and other symbolic systems that 'stand for' other things. For example, in pretend play, children learn that a box can be a dolly's bed or a long stick can be a sword. Vygotsky drew parallels between these children's games and the early graphic drawings produced by young children. The level of symbolism in both is often quite crude, but there is rudimentary evidence that children can understand that everyday objects can be represented in different ways. This all happens naturally and spontaneously and is a precursor to later developments.

In the case of writing development, there is then a movement from the drawing of lines and squiggles to realizing that these in fact might mean something, Further, there is a distinction being made between drawing and writing. Marks symbolizing objects such as men or houses, trees or horses, come to be distinguished from lines and marks that are signs. The child becomes aware that speech can be represented in writing too. Vygotsky postulated that the developmental progression was from 'drawing things to drawing speech' (Vygotsky, 1978, p. 115). Attempts to introduce this sequence as a rationale for teaching children writing should be made, as Vygotsky urged that we try to organize and ease the child's transition from drawing things to drawing speech.

Vygotsky argued convincingly for recognizing continuities in the development of writing from the earliest scribbles to the discovery of the symbolic function of writing, and argued firstly for shifting the teaching of writing to the preschool. Writing should be a developmental activity with the adult teacher only providing suitable organizational structures to ensure young children's writing (and reading too) are necessary. There should be a purpose to the child's reading and writing. Secondly, writing should be meaningful to children – 'relevant to life' as Vygotsky so strikingly commented (1978, p. 118). Only in this way, concluded Vygotsky, can we claim to have **taught** the written language and not just 'the writing of letters' (Vygotsky, 1978, p. 119). Vygotsky referred to the teaching of writing as the cultivation rather than the imposition of the skill. Both the child and the teacher must be motivated, and the development natural.

While Vygotsky's work was sadly curtailed by his untimely death, his influence is found in the research of a number of other psychologists and educationalists. Vygotsky was primarily interested in school-aged children (including nursery school children and handicapped children) but much of his research dwelt on the older age ranges. The origins of language were theoretically explored, but Vygotsky's notions were not empirically tested. The social origins of language are conceptually sound and not in dispute. However, we need some evidence that spoken language development (and hence reading and writing development also) has its roots in early social interaction. More recent theorists have been examining precisely the social interactional origins of both spoken and written language. Their work, by and large, supports Vygotsky's views, while providing some interesting refinements and additional evidence. One prominent theorist who has examined the social interactional origins of language is Jerome Bruner.

## Bruner's Theory of Cognitive Growth

Bruner is one of the most notable contemporary exponents of the view that language develops in children through the processes of social interaction. He was clearly influenced by Vygotsky, but his theory differs in scope both across psychological domains and across the life span, from early infancy to adulthood. Like Vygotsky, Bruner has been concerned both with language development and with children's learning. While his views on education (Bruner, 1966, 1971) have been a major influence on modern curricula and educational practice, his views on language development have only more recently permeated theory and research. There is a fundamental continuity in his conceptual thinking so although his particular focus may have shifted over the years (for example, from perceptual to cognitive to linguistic development; from adults to school aged children to infants), the basic tenets remain the same (see Bruner, 1973, for a 'compendium' of his earlier writings).

### The Growth of Knowledge

In Bruner's theory of the development of knowledge, or the growth of **competence**, the human being is regarded as an active creator and learner. Knowledge can be acquired in many different ways and via different modes. For example, motor skill mastery, language acquisition and concept attainment are all aspects of knowledge that are achieved with increasing competence. Each can be viewed as a problem which the child must come to solve, through active construction with the relevant materials, be they concrete or abstract. Such construction usually takes the form of hypothesis-testing, children seeking confirmation or disconfirmation of incoming information in relation to their existing stored knowledge base.

From his earlier work on the higher mental processes of adults (Bruner, Goodnow and Austin, 1956), Bruner turned to study the growth of competence in children and the development of skilled activity from infancy. This he termed 'growth of mind' (Bruner, 1965). Bruner took account of the **social** environment in which the child was developing and the child's interaction with other people. Like Vygotsky, he allowed for instruction to play an important part in the child's learning process. Bruner's model of mental development involved both an internal representation of experience plus the active construction of reality. Mental tools facilitate cognitive growth, but social participation and instruction are equally important components.

The most important tool for cognitive growth the child has is

**language**. Language is a mental tool that facilitates representation of the world. The development of language enables more flexible thinking, allowing for planning, hypothesizing and thinking in abstractions. Bruner, in his studies of language acquisition, focused directly on language as the object of his research, instead of regarding language as a necessary adjunct for thinking and the growth of knowledge.

## Learning to Use Language

Bruner was attracted to the study of language development in the 1970s because of the shift away from the emphasis on structure (as dominated by Chomsky) to the study of the functions of language. Like other aspects of cognitive competence, language was regarded by Bruner as a tool: what the child was acquiring was how to use that tool efficiently and effectively.

In his studies of the development of language, Bruner tried to synthesize three aspects which he believed to be crucial. These were concerned firstly with learning and how the infant comes to learn language at all. Bruner dismissed both imitation and innateness as plausible mechanisms. His theory sought to span both 'an impossible empiricist position and a miraculous nativist one' (Bruner, 1983, p. 39). Instead he believed children learned language for a purpose. Secondly, Bruner was concerned to explicate *how* the infant comes to give utterances 'meaning' and how the infant uses linguistic (and nonlinguistic) resources to refer to things. Thirdly, and most importantly, Bruner was concerned with the functions of language, the communicative intent of the child. Bruner tried to convey the interdependence of these three domains of language, and also the fact that much goes on before children utter their first words.

## Processes of Learning to Use Language

In explaining the processes by which children learn language, Bruner introduced what he called **LASS** – an acronym for **L**anguage **A**cquisition **S**upport **S**ystem. Bruner maintained that through interaction with the mother who guided and supported the child's emerging language, children learned to talk, and learned the language of the socio-cultural-historical group in which they were growing up. For LASS to function as a language support and teaching mechanism, Bruner proposed a predisposition on the part of the child to acquire language (essentially LAD, as explained in chapter 2). For language development, there thus needs to be both a child component, incorporating an innate propensity for active social interaction and language learning, that is to work on the input language, together with a component consisting of adult support and help. LAD, the innate predisposition, requires an interactional framework to function. Indeed, LAD can only function with LASS, as the social interaction format enables children to learn the language. The interactional partner provides a structure appropriate for the child, allowing for entry into the linguistic community (and ultimately, to the culture).

Like Vygotsky, Bruner believed that for learning to take place, appropriate social interactional frameworks must be provided. Bruner (1977) called this **scaffolding**. In the case of the young child learning language, the instructional component consists of, most commonly, the mother providing a framework to allow the child to learn. To do this, the mother should always be one step ahead of her child, and by using contexts that are extremely familiar and routinized, can facilitate the child's learning. The mother's pedagogy consists of staying finely tuned to the capabilities and capacities of her child, allowing for progress at a reasonable pace.

Characteristically, the mother and her young child engage in routine play or work interactional activities, **formats**, as Bruner called them. These highly predictable routines, such as peek-a-boo or reading books together, bath time or meals, offer the mother and child a structure within which the mother can continually raise her expectations of the child's performance. For Bruner, this meant specifically the child's linguistic performance, because, he argued, it is within these formats that children learn how to use language.

In addition, Bruner related the use of formats to the transmission of a culture. Not only do formats provide a useful framework within which we can study language development, they also enable the constitution of culture for the child. Language is a cultural phenomenon, and it is only through language that we can come to adopt and alter cultural mores. Thus, according to Bruner, 'Culture is constituted of symbolic procedures, concepts and distinctions that can only be made in language. It is constituted for the child in the very act of mastering language. Language, in consequence, cannot be understood save in its cultural setting' (Bruner, 1983, p. 134).

## Prelinguistic to Linguistic Communication

Bruner undertook a detailed examination of the child's prelinguistic period and the transition phase into the early linguistic period. He was aiming to chart continuities in the functions of children's communicative resources be they linguistic or otherwise. Continuity between the prelinguistic period and the early stages of language can be best described by the continuity of communicative functions, achieved in no small way by the mother and her use of routinized formats. Language continuity is also marked by the constitutive role of formats. These microcosms of the social world allow for the creation of language functions as well as being created by language. Bruner believed that these become increasingly abstract. The social processes required to sustain language are also part of continuity in development – turn taking, making requests (of another person) and so on, are as much a part of an adult's social interactions as they are the child's.

Bruner (1983) described his study of two male children (and their mothers) and how they came to learn the uses of language. By examining a number of formats longitudinally, he was able to study how certain linguistic processes developed and were then generalized to other contexts. In these studies, the interactional nature of the social world in which the child is learning language predominated. The mother was regarded at all times as helping the child to get things done by using existing linguistic and communicative resources. Bruner argued that regardless of the quality or the quantity of the innate component for language, it still needs to be deployed, to be **used**, appropriately. That can only be done in interaction with another person.

A number of formats is games or regular household tasks or events, within which the mother can use the highly familiar structure to 'teach' the child to attend to different aspects that she deems important. In particular, she can highlight different aspects of the routine through the use of language. Words can be introduced and used at juncture points in the formats, the mother expecting the child to come to recognize the predictable nature of the routines and also to come to use language. Bruner was interested in not simply how children come to learn the structure of language, but also how various functions of language are learned. We will now examine two of these formats – the appearance/disappearance game and book reading – in more detail.

*Appearance/disappearance game*  The appearance/disappearance game described by Ratner and Bruner (1978) and Bruner (1983) typically involves the disappearance of an object closely followed by its reappearance, designed to 'surprise' the young child. Another variation is peek-a-boo (see Bruner and Sherwood, 1976), where the adult performs the disappearance and reappearance herself. There is therefore a relatively invariant and routinized structure to the format. Bruner traced the progression of such a game in one mother–infant pair and firstly described the clear and regular structure of the game. The game occurred several times over a period of some months and while its surface manifestations altered, the basic structural components were retained. The element of

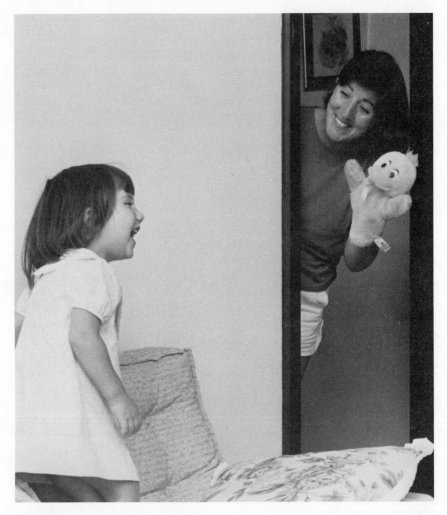

'Boo'

'surprise' was maintained by variations in the surface structure by the mother. For example, the speed at which the mother caused the re-appearance of the object could be altered, the pitch or loudness of the mother's vocal expressions such as 'Boo' could be changed and the actual points of the game at which she chose to vocalize varied.

Within the game then, not only did the mother continually alter the constituent parts, but the child's role altered. At the start, the child (aged about 5 months) was fairly passive, but as the child's attention to the game and to the actual object increased, so did the mother elaborate her use of language. The child then began also to vocalize at particular juncture points in the game. Bruner described in detail the development of this format and the child's increasingly active participation in it, both as a language user and as manipulator of the action.

Bruner concluded that during the course of learning to play this game (and others like it), children are learning a great deal about social inter-action and its management, especially its linguistic management. Children are learning about the language, that is, they are learning when and how to use their developing linguistic structures. Children are also learning conventions about how to indicate whose turn it is and how to acknowledge completion of the action. Language is only one part of such conventionalization.

*Book reading*    Another study by Bruner (Ninio and Bruner, 1978; Bruner, 1983) was concerned with book reading and how the simple joint reading of books by mothers and their children can aid the development of gram-mar, of pragmatics and of possibly later literacy skills. As a format, its reported appearance was relatively late (the child was aged about 12 months at the start), and the child already knew many of the conventions surrounding conversation, such as turn taking and the use of rising intonation for a question.

The most interesting aspect of this study here is the mother's changing participation in tune with the child's developing language capacities. The mother constantly strove to make the child achieve more and more, in terms of what she believed to be either truthfully correct or linguisti-cally correct. For example, the mother would point to a picture and ask 'What's that?'. The child was obviously expected to provide an answer, and initially the mother would accept any vocalization, provided it involved some approximation to a speech sound. After some months, the child began to produce a reasonably acceptable (phonological) label. The mother was constantly providing feedback, often making comment on the veracity of the child's utterance or providing comment on the referent itself.

In subsequent book reading sessions, which occurred over the next six successive months, the mother continually raised the criteria for accept-ability of the child's response. She would expect the child's vocal response to resemble the adult linguistic form more closely. Or perhaps, she would expect the child to respond at the appropriate point in the sequence, that is, after she had fully asked the question. The mother's role became more pedagogic or instructional as the child's linguistic capabilities increased. The child was further expected to make contributions to the interaction,

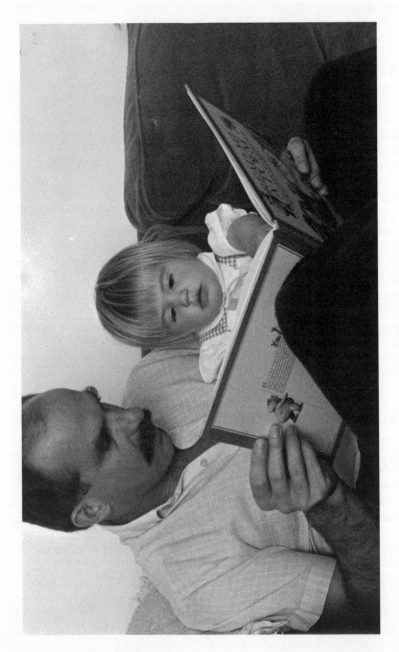

Book reading

initiating the activity, turning the pages of the book and asking the mother questions.

While there are many implications for the study of language development and language learning from the study of book reading (see, for example, Ninio, 1983; Bus, 1994; Dickinson, 1995b), Bruner suggested that it made possible the specification of how the child progressively attained language. At each 'level', the child is mastering routines, both linguistic and nonlinguistic, within the format. As each level becomes more automatic, the child's information-processing capacity alters, so that new information can be dealt with. This capacity is the 'pull' factor in the development of language. Further, Bruner believed that there was also a 'push' factor involved and here he reiterated the importance of the scaffolding provided by LASS – the mother and the format. Thus, the language learning process required both forces 'inside' and 'outside' the child. But spoken language learning encompasses more than just learning about the structure of the language, the child is also learning how to mean and how to communicate, both vital for subsequent social interactions.

Throughout all of these ritualized formats, the mother is providing cues for the child to assist in the learning of language. The mother's role is one of scaffolding. She provides the ritualized dialogue and the constraints within which the child is acquiring many different uses of language. The child is learning from the mother in the 'zone of proximal development', as Vygotsky called it. The mother is allowing the child to achieve his potential as she supports the efforts to learn language (French, Boynton and Hodges, 1991; Garton, 1992). The actual content of the language used in the formats seemed to matter little in Bruner's account. It was the *principle* of acquisition that he was explicating. However, it is still difficult to see how the specifics of language are actually learned by young children, given that there is no one-to-one mapping of language to format nor, according to Bruner, does the mother actually directly instruct the child in particular word forms. Yet Bruner viewed interaction as the major form of assistance provided by adults for language development.

## Philosophical Theories of Language Development

A clue to how language *per se* is acquired through interaction can be found in some of the philosophical theories of how children acquire meaning. That is, interest lies in how children come to understand the language used by others to them, and how, in turn, they can achieve communicative objectives through the use of language themselves. The issue of how children come to acquire meaning when they begin using words has been at the heart of philosophical and linguistic debate for many years and has also taxed developmental psychologists wishing to explain language development (Forrester, 1992).

The fundamental question to be answered in a consideration of the acquisition of meaning is whether it is the words or the child who provides the meaning. Each is partly true as words obtain meaning via their conceptual or representational realization (cf. Wales, 1993), but equally children (and adults) can use words in other than their conventionalized meaning, as is noted in metaphor or sarcasm for example. Understanding the communicative significance of words, both as a speaker and as a listener, is the developmental task faced by the child as well as the philosophical matter to be resolved. Grice (1957) put forward a theory to account for the acquisition of meaning in which he claimed that meaning is derived from a speaker trying to convey intentions and the listener trying to work out those intentions. The notion of intentionality in communication has laid the basis for much psychological research (for example, Bruner, 1975; Siegal, 1991). Furthermore, this view was expanded by Austin (1962) and Searle (1969) in **speech act theory** which assumed that communication can involve behaviour, or actions. A distinction can be made between locutionary acts, that is, actually speaking, illocutionary acts which try to achieve some objective, and perlocutionary acts, which have an effect (intended or unintended) on the listener. The application of these philosophical theories to children's acquisition of language has permitted the inclusion of meaning in the process, as well as consideration of the grammatical forms acquired. It was the influence of theories such as these that initially prompted Bruner to shift our way of thinking about language development, a tradition that has continued in current ways of examining children's language acquisition, in particular those views that consider social interaction to be a necessary, if not sufficient, aspect.

## Adult Assistance to Children Learning Language

Cazden (1983) proposed three models in which the adult provides **assistance** to the child learning language. Rather than there being a direct relationship between the mother's language to the child and the child's language development, the mother's assistance is generally regarded as indirect. The mother actively guides and supports the child's learning of language. The first model is called **scaffolding**. Vertical scaffolding involves the adult (most frequently the mother) extending the child's language by, for example, asking further questions. So in response to the child's utterance 'dog', she might say 'Yes, that's a dog. What does a dog say?, or she might ask for elaboration, 'And what did we see when we went to the library today?'. Scaffolding is also found in the games mothers play with their young children, in routines and in conventionalized activities such as meals and bath time. The predictable nature of such routines in itself provides a supportive framework in which language can be acquired.

The second type of adult assistance described by Cazden was the use of language **models**. This echoes one of the processes she originally proposed as helping children's later language develop. Adults occasionally supply children with models of the language, sometimes in response to the incorrect production of a language form. So a child may say 'We choosded two lovely books to read' and the adult may explicitly correct this, saying 'Yes we did, we *chose* two lovely books', emphasizing the correct form. Language modelling may also involve elaboration and expansion of the child's language. Scaffolding and modelling, as types of adult assistance, are probably not mutually exclusive. Cazden does qualify her account of models by suggesting that adults should not expect children to *copy* the correct language provided, but should *learn* from these correct models.

Finally adult assistance can be provided through, what Cazden termed, **direct instruction**. This is best seen in instances where an adult says 'Say "Thank you"' or 'Say "Goodbye"' to a child, expecting the child to repeat the given word or phrase. Direct instruction is noted especially in the teaching of social conventions, where the context will likely provide useful clues for later use of the phrase. Adults also sometimes expressly teach their young children the words for things, and again, routines can be used to establish a predictable framework for the teaching of spoken language, particularly vocabulary. For example, the mother and her child may sit at a little desk for this activity, or it may evolve during bath time when items are labelled or named.

These possible ways adults assist in the development of spoken language have implications for the study of the development of written language. In particular, scaffolding and direct instruction have proved useful when looking at the development (and teaching) of reading and writing. Further the book reading format is a clear link between spoken language development and written language development, using, as it does, a similar explanatory framework. We will now turn our attention to an examination of some of the processes of written language acquisition.

## Processes of Acquiring Literacy

The processes of acquiring spoken language, according to a social interactional interpretation, demand the active involvement of the child

with another person, usually an adult. Both Vygotsky and Bruner proposed that spoken and written language should develop in a natural way
through children's interaction with the people of the culture in which
they are growing up. To this point, we have said little about the processes
of learning to write and to read. If we adopt a similar perspective, then it
must be argued that learning to read and learning to write can be facilitated by the presence of an adult providing assistance to the child. One
line of research looking at the processes by which reading is learned
has used the book reading context. Book reading (whether looking at
pictures or actually reading stories) is a possible facilitatory process for
the acquisition of both spoken language *and* written language.

The research on book reading described earlier has obvious links with
the study of the processes of reading and provides a clear example of how
one task can assist both spoken language development in the early years
and reading development in the preschool years. An explicit link can be
found in the research study reported by deLoache and deMendoza (1987)
who examined the structural aspects of book reading between mothers
and their infants aged between 12 and 18 months. They used the
scaffolding model of adult assistance proposed by Bruner. Rather than
relating the joint picture book reading only to the child's later language
development, they examined in detail the mother's role as a scaffolder
for the child's learning. DeLoache and deMendoza acknowledged the
potential benefits for spoken language acquisition of maternal labelling
during book reading, and also the benefits for later reading development.

Book reading with a supportive mother facilitates the child's entry into
the world of written language. Learning about books and the printed word,
and being read to by one's mother, provides children with early experience of decontextualized language and the nature and conventions of
print. DeLoache and deMendoza provided evidence at least that book
reading facilitated vocabulary acquisition, and that the mother's supportive teaching role was essential to elicit the highest ability level from the
developing child. Their research also potentially supplied the crucial link
between the child's development of spoken language and the later development of reading, by focusing on the use of the book reading format as
a common element which can be used by the mother to teach the child
about various aspects of literacy.

More recently, Bus (1994) reviewed the evidence for the parental role
in emergent literacy, using the book-reading paradigm. Literacy was used
to refer to reading and writing and encompasses such things as letter
knowledge and printing as well as formal conventions, and the linguistic
procedures associated with the written language. Bus stressed the importance of the active involvement of the child in the process, and she drew

on Bruner's scaffolding analogy to illustrate the type of adult-child relationship that might facilitate literacy acquisition in the child. Bus reviewed
a range of studies conducted by herself and Van IJzendoorn and concluded that book reading as an activity lays the basis for literacy, and
furthermore, that adults are attuned to their children's emergent abilities.

An interesting aspect of the work by Bus and Van IJzendoorn is the
investigation of the relationship between attachment and literacy. Their
research has demonstrated that children's interest in reading books
with their parent(s) is more dependent on the nature of the parent–child
relationship than on characteristics of the child. For example, Bus
(1994) cited evidence demonstrating that securely attached children have
qualitatively different ways of reading story books with their parents, and
conversely, that insecurely attached children often show problems in
maintaining and sustaining attention to joint book reading and such
adult–child pairs are less inclined to engage in this activity. Bus concluded
that securely attached infants benefit from the close physical relationship
afforded by joint book reading. The inclusion of emotional factors in
literacy acquisition is an interesting development and is further noted
by Dickinson (1995a).

Other researchers (for example, Wells, 1985a, 1985b, 1985c; Olson,
1977, 1984; and contributors to the recent edited volume by Dickinson,
1995b) have studied the relationship between spoken language acquisition (via book reading) and later reading and literacy skills, in terms of
the processes required for learning. The basic argument runs like this.
During the acquisition of spoken language, the context provides cues
for interpretation of, for example, the language input the child receives.
In early book reading, as we have described, the context is used as a
vehicle for the child learning such things as social routines and linguistic
labelling techniques, together with rather more sophisticated ways of
representing information. The books involved are frequently those that
have predominantly clear pictures of items believed to be reasonably
familiar to young children, and arranged either alphabetically (all the A
words on one page, then the B words) or in 'meaningful' conglomera-
tions, such as 'All kitchen implements' and 'Clothing'. As well as the
picture, the label is often included (for further comment on the content
of books read to young children, see Bus, 1994).

In homes where books are read to children, there is frequently a shift
when the child reaches about 2 years of age to the reading of stories from
books. Again, the text is often simple and is supported by illustrations. As
children progress through the preschool years, graded (that is, more and
more complex) stories can be read, along with the old familiar tales. Wells
and Olson believe that through listening to the language of stories being

read to them, young children are learning a lot about the organization of *written* language. Compared with spoken language, written language does not have a shared context for interpretation. Spoken language exists within the context of a conversation between at least two persons. In contrast, written text exists often independently of the context in which it is being read. For young children, a context is supplied through the provision of pictures in the book. The adult and child reading the story can use the pictures to contextualize the written words, and can also elaborate on the illustrated characters and scenes.

Such contextualization can vary, depending on the circumstances of the story telling. Many children's stories are now available on audio cassette (usually accompanied by the book). While children will sit and listen to such tapes, they would be unlikely to be able to follow the accompanying text alone. Indeed, there are some children who will not sit and listen to such cassettes (with or without the book) on their own. What is important is the establishment and maintenance of a context shared by parent and child, whereby the parent and child together listen to the tape and follow the text as if the parent were doing the reading. In the case of narratives that parents 'make up' and tell to their children without the support of pictures, there is frequently a shared context for the child to work out the story. These stories are often based on shared experiences between the adult and the child; the child knows what is being talked about. Again however, the important component for the story telling is the joint adult–child participation.

In understanding a story, whatever the context, children must pay attention to the language in order to interpret what is going on. They begin to realize that a context must be created through the language of the story which then provides them with the meaning of language. Even when stories have pictures, these can only present or represent a small part of the action, and children have to come to appreciate that the meaning is inherent in the structure of the language used to tell the story. Accordingly, children gradually realize that language can be used as a system of representation. That is, language can be used independently of the objects, people, events, actions and places it stands for, and can be further used and interpreted in other, different contexts. In other words, while being read stories initially extends children's experiences, it then allows children to begin to reflect on these experiences as the language becomes more detached from the immediate context and children realize how powerful language can be. The use of language to formulate hypotheses, to solve problems and to delve into the realms of the imagination, the hypothetical or impossible, finally emerges. Wells argued that reading stories to children enabled all of these to develop, with the proviso that not just any old story will do. Rather parents have to choose wisely and also are required to talk about the story, either during its recitation or afterwards.

The usefulness of parents reading stories to children can be judged in terms of the positive benefits noticed on starting school (Hewison and Tizard, 1980; Wells, 1985a, 1985c, 1987; Cunningham, Stanovich and West, 1994; Dickinson, 1995b). In fact, Wells claimed that the early experience of stories is the single best preparation for school. He found that listening to stories being read was positively correlated with measures of knowledge of literacy taken on school entry and reading comprehension taken at age 7 years.

The relationship between the early hearing of stories and later success in beginning reading has also been reported by Tough (1977, 1983) and Bus (1994). They both claimed that by being read stories from an early age, children's beginning reading benefited because, among other things, they, the children, had greater familiarity with the language of books; they had developed the concept of a story; they had certain important 'book skills' such as knowledge of print orientation (top-bottom and left-right) and they knew about page turning; and perhaps most importantly, they knew that meaning could be extracted from the printed page.

Because of the reported success of early book reading on later literacy, Dickinson (1995a) emphasized the need for intervention programmes in this area. In particular, home intervention programmes attracted attention because of the strength of their theoretical underpinnings as well as their practicality of implementation. Four characteristics of book reading are appealing: it is a discrete activity that can easily be duplicated; it is a regular feature of home and school life; it is valued in literate cultures; and once established as a routine, fosters emotional closeness. The volume edited by Dickinson (1995b) brings together a range of intervention programmes that have been used successfully in homes and schools to promote higher levels of literacy in the target populations. Dickinson (1995a) reminds us of the intricacies of assessing the effects of programmes, with both short- and long-term evaluations being necessary of behaviours, attitudes and beliefs. There is however a firm commitment to such intervention programmes and their value in enhancing literacy and educational opportunities for young children and their parents.

There is therefore consensus regarding the benefits to be had from introducing children to books (or vice versa) from a very early age. Both language and reading skills can be encouraged through the use of books. It could be argued that books are very much part only of western literate societies and such obvious benefits accrue only to those children fortunate enough to be reared in these cultures. Clearly, books are important, but not essential to language development. The early introduction of books facilitates later reading and writing skills, which are essential for functioning adequately in a literate civilization. The caution researchers urge regarding the type of literary material given to young children and the sensitivity with which it is handled by the adult further limits the generalizability of the findings. But the point must be made that the more we can encourage parents and other adults to read to their children, even if they believe their children are too young to understand, the greater the benefits to everyone, especially the child, in the long run.

## Individual and Social Differences in Influences on Language Development

The large individual differences in language skills that children exhibit in the preschool period are often of concern to parents and educators. Many of these differences can be traced to variations in the social circumstances of children and the nature of the social interactions they have. Most of the research examining acquisition processes has been conducted on the children of middle-class, western parents, although there are several studies that have looked at lower socio-economic groups (for example, Tizard and Hughes, 1984). Higher socio-economic parents tend to value language and literacy more highly than lower socio-economic groups and other cultures, although this has no implications for claims about the richness of different early experiences. However, even within the narrow socio-cultural domain studied, there are differences between children and their language skills. Both Tizard and Hughes (1984) and Wells (1985c, 1986) quite clearly pointed out some of these differences and the implications of these in relation to the school environment.

There are some obvious inherited differences between children which have been shown to influence language development (Wells, 1986). Girls are commonly regarded as 'better talkers' than boys, and there is evidence that young girls learn language more quickly and also show fewer language problems. It has been proposed that the greater talkativeness of girls, rather than being genetic, is directly attributable to differential types of parental communication to girls than to boys. Research by Wells (1985a) showed that there were noticeable sex differences in the contexts in which mothers initiated conversations with their 3-year-old children. For example, mothers were more likely to talk to their daughters in the context of home-based, domestic activities (when they were cooking or doing the washing). Mothers with sons were more likely to talk to them during times of physical play. There may also be subsequent differences in the content of the language spoken by girls and boys once they reach school (Wells, 1983).

Twins, triplets and other multiple births are particularly interesting for the study of language development (for example, Savic, 1980). Most researchers agree that children of multiple births are delayed in their language development, and many show speech problems. The reason for the language delays and deviations is now believed not to be biological but due to the differential treatment of twins and triplets by their parents (Messer, 1994). Not only is there reduced social interaction between parents and each individual child, but there is also the opportunity for the children to communicate with each other possibly using inappropriate words and strategies.

Children do not all develop at the same rate, and even given the same inherited characteristics and the same type and level of parental input, children will show different capabilities. In particular, and as noted in chapter 1, we should be aware of the difficulties faced by children born with an intellectual disability (see Snyder, 1984) or born hearing impaired (see Wood, Wood, Griffiths and Howarth, 1986). These impairments usually affect language development by delaying spoken language. Other handicapping conditions that may affect aspects of the development of spoken language include visual impairment (Mills, 1983; Dunlea, 1989), cleft palate and other oral malformations affecting the production of speech (for example, McWilliams, 1984), and other prenatal or postnatal influences that adversely affect the foetus or neonate and prevent or delay 'normal' development. These forms of disability handicap or impede spoken language development, either because of the nature of the acquired or inherited problem(s) or because parental expectations and interactions change as a consequence of the child's disabling condition and perceived or real limitations. In turn, impaired spoken language development has been linked to later problems with reading (for example, Rutter and Yule, 1975; Silva, McGee and Williams, 1985; Share and Silva, 1987). To assist children with disordered spoken language development, an optimal social environment should be provided (Schiefelbusch, 1984), within which interaction between adult and child can take place. Sensitive contingent social responding can aid children in their language development, and this is true for children who are normal or those with disabilities. Communication skills can be fostered from a very early stage, to be supplemented with specific language teaching later if required.

The size of the family may also affect the rate of language development. As Tizard and Hughes (1984) pointed out, the opportunities for one-to-one conversation between mothers and their children increase as the number of children in a family decreases. Such intensive, one-to-one, conversations facilitate language development. There is evidence that position in the family may affect language development, with certain advantages accruing to the first born and different advantages to later born children (see Rutter, 1985). The spacing between children is also regarded as an influential factor in the growth of language. Much of the work on family structure and linguistic outcomes is both contentious and inconclusive because of the variety of advantages and disadvantages claimed.

The social differences between children that result from socio-economic or class differences are often cited as reasons for differential rates of language development. This topic has received widespread research coverage because of the supposed problems encountered in school by children from lower socio-economic homes. According to Bernstein (1960), children from lower socio-economic backgrounds were being exposed to impoverished language compared with their middle-class counterparts. The debate over this issue has continued for some 30 years (see Wells, 1986 for a succinct review). The home environment provided by parents, itself related to socio-economic status, influences language development. In general, the uses of language at home vary enormously and the opportunities for talking to adults may differ. A child may be growing up in a small, one- or two-roomed house along with five or six siblings and the type of talk most commonly encountered could be squabbles or fights. The television might be on constantly, as well as music being played loudly. Surely this home environment cannot be as conducive to later literacy development as that of children growing up in a smaller family unit with the attention of their parents?

Theories of spoken and written language development have to encompass a range of individual differences to have any explanatory value at all. In principle, it could be argued that any social interaction involving language with a more competent communicator is beneficial for a young child's language development. Thus, a child growing up in a home surrounded by several older brothers and sisters might in fact have an advantage over the single child. Certainly the amount and types of language would be more diverse. There may not be one-to-one interaction, but talk is certainly evident. While it can be argued that such talk is not the sort of talk the child will meet in educational settings, the debate is not closed. Studies comparing children from a range of home language and literacy environments and the subsequent effects on language or reading skills still have to be conducted before we can provide answers to these questions.

## Implications of Early Spoken and Written Language Development

As this chapter has shown, by describing the processes of spoken and written language development in social interactional terms, we have to consider the practical implications of the research. Obvious implications concern the universality of the underlying theories, particularly in relation to different socio-economic and cultural groups. The more general applicability of social interactional theories also relates to the cultural importance placed on early literacy skills. Many of the acquisition processes in language, reading and writing are apparently the same. The extent to which these processes are of relevance for reading and writing will depend on the socio-cultural-historical value placed on them. Different socio-economic groups and different cultures place different values on reading and writing. However, spoken language can still be acquired through interactional processes, regardless of cultural values and expectations.

A thorough examination of the processes involved in language, reading and writing has clear practical implications for parents. Parents should be encouraged to talk to their children, to listen to them and to respond when they ask questions. Even from the earliest period, parents should interact with their children, as there is evidence that even from a few hours or days old, infants can respond to parental speech patterns. Such fine tuning should then encourage parents to continue talking to their infants and responding to their vocalic output. There is also evidence that it is the *quality* rather than the *quantity* of parental attention and language that is of utmost importance, so even brief periods of time should be set aside for parents to talk exclusively to their young children.

In addition, parents must be encouraged to read books to their children, so that they can gain all the benefits of listening to narrative stories and getting meaning from connected prose or discourse. Hearing stories seems to be one of the most important ways children learn about language as a system of representation, which then facilitates their use and understanding of both writing and reading. Little has been said so far regarding the processes of acquiring writing and reading as separate skills, but these will be discussed in chapters 8 and 9. What we have considered in depth are the more general processes that seem necessary for children to learn things about the spoken language and about language as a representational system. Once this latter ability has been achieved, only then can we begin to look at early reading and writing.

## A Theoretical Overview

From the discussions in this and the previous chapters of theories of the development of language, reading and writing, it would appear that the interactionist theories have the most to offer in terms of unifying literacy development. In rejecting traditional and apparently rather simplistic accounts of the acquisition process, it has been suggested that the empiricist and nativist theories can only partially explain language development and cannot adequately account for the development of reading and writing. These latter aspects are definitely not innate, since there are cultures where the written word does not exist. Indeed, the development of reading and writing can be regarded as an indication of a culture 'coming of age'. Nor can the acquisition or development of reading and writing simply be explained by a process of reinforcement. While it cannot be denied that such an approach has been found extremely useful in the teaching of these skills to children who are disadvantaged or disabled, in the main the behavioural theories are unable to explain the processes involved in the development of reading and writing.

It therefore seems most appropriate to view the child as developing language through interaction with other people. Such early interaction can also form a very firm basis for subsequent reading and writing development, particularly in the preschool years. This then lays a strong foundation for more formal approaches at school. There is good evidence that many of the early sensory and motor developments during infancy are geared towards enabling the developing organism to be able to recognize mother from father or parents from strangers, and interact in more and more sophisticated ways with others. The lure of increased social interaction would seem to encourage early development, and there is no reason to believe language does not develop from similar origins.

Certainly, if Vygotsky and Bruner are to be believed, it is only through social interaction that linguistic skills develop and children learn how to use their language. These interactionist theorists, instead of placing the source of development either totally within or totally outside the child, prefer to shift the emphasis. Not only do they relegate the acquisition of language structures to second place, they strongly advocate the study of the functions of language, that is, the study of how children use their language.

The interactionist theories also offer a useful explanatory perspective for the study of early literacy and both Vygotsky and Bruner have provided indicators as to how this might be achieved. One of the underlying themes is the *continuity* of development and the inter-relationship between spoken and written language development. Spoken language fulfils a communicative function. In social interaction, reading and writing can be regarded as useful activities, the purpose of which is also communicative. Children are able to see *why* they are being asked to read or being required to write. Allowing children to read and write in rudimentary ways prior to formal school instruction enables children to develop literacy skills continuously in meaningful ways.

Children must be given the opportunity to develop their spoken language skills in interaction with others, *and* also to learn the contexts for and the uses of reading and writing. These latter activities should be introduced when the child shows an interest in, for example, books or making scribbled marks on paper. Like language development, the ensuing collaborative interaction should facilitate further development. Bruner has demonstrated that mothers make inordinately competent (even demanding!) teachers of their infants while they acquire language. It seems that early interactions in the home may well foster other abilities such as numerical/mathematical abilities (Hughes, 1986) and emotional links (Bus, 1994) as well as reading and writing.

Within a broad social interactionist theoretical framework, we now turn to describe the course of spoken and written language development in the following chapters. Chapters 4, 5 and 6 concentrate on spoken language development, while chapters 8 and 9 examine writing and reading development. The sequence of development of each aspect of literacy will be traced and the implications of the developments discussed.

# CHAPTER FOUR

# Learning Spoken Language: From Precursors to First Word Combinations

Although the major emphasis throughout this book is on the use of language as the medium for both spoken and written communication, it is useful to provide a broad description of the development of the spoken language capabilities of children from the earliest prelinguistic period through to school age. It is popularly assumed spoken language development is complete once children produce recognizable sentences and further developments are merely extensions and refinements of existing language forms. As we shall show, this is a false conception, and in particular, knowledge of the productive capabilities of children (both in terms of what they can and can not do) has far-reaching implications for our understanding of the child's development of reading and writing.

The study of spoken language involves **phonology**, the sounds of the language, **syntax**, the grammar of the language or how words are put together to make phrases or sentences, and **semantics**, the meanings of words or sentences in the language. It is also concerned with **pragmatics**, how language is used. This last topic will be addressed separately in chapter 6.

The development of phonology is charted first, because if there were no sounds, there could be no further spoken language development. Sounds are the first evidence that spoken language is being acquired and lay the basis for further language development. We will then examine the developing language structures of the young child, focusing on one- and two-word utterances. At times, syntax and semantics, or grammar and meaning, will be considered separately as this was the way early research proceeded. At other points in the chapter, they will be considered together, emphasizing the interconnectedness of grammar and meaning in the developing language of the young child. During development, the complexity of the language spoken by the child increases, the length of the sentences uttered increases, the number of words in the child's vocabulary increases and a greater range of meanings can be expressed. With both an increasing vocabulary and greater command of the grammar of the language, the child can communicate in more sophisticated ways and is more understandable to others.

The previous chapter examined some of the processes (the 'how') of language development in young children. This chapter charts the 'what' of language development from the prelinguistic period to first word combinations, focusing mainly on the linguistic and grammatical forms produced. Further linguistic accomplishments are described in chapter 5 where developments in grammar and meaning after age 2 or 3 years are explored.

It is of immense value for those involved in the education of young children to know what spoken language skills children have. To work effectively with young children, it is necessary to be fully aware of their linguistic capabilities and limitations. We should also be aware of the extent to which young children can communicate with others and how they perceive conversations. Before the teaching of reading and writing can begin, children's spoken language development and what they can produce and use must be taken into account. Therefore, we intend tracing the phonological, syntactic or grammatical and semantic developments of language from the babbling period through to the one- and two-word stages, at which point preliminary hypotheses can be made about the nature of the grammatical developments that enable the child to communicate more efficiently and effectively. The relationship between grammar and meaning, and how knowledge of one may assist in the development of knowledge in the other, will also be considered. The language acquisition process is regarded as a progressive sequence. The child is at all times trying to communicate by means of presently available linguistic and nonlinguistic resources. The sequence of language development is embedded within the social context.

Starting with the prelinguistic period, we will examine some of the precursors to and possible prerequisites for later language. The area chosen as a starting point is phonological development, the study of the development of sounds of language.

## Phonological Development

There is a good reason for beginning with the development of phonology because the sound system is fundamental for later language (Wales, 1993). There is a feeling however that the sounds made by children in the first year of life are not 'proper' language. Indeed the word 'infant' is derived from the Latin word *infans*, meaning 'without language'. It is undeniable that children make many sounds and noises during the first year of their life, before they begin to 'talk properly'. These early sounds include crying, cooing, bubble blowing, making 'raspberries' and babbling.

Phonological development refers to the development of the child's understanding that different combinations or patterns of sounds in the language convey differences in meaning. For example, 'dada' and 'mama' refer to different individuals. Subsumed under the topic of phonological development are two other important developments, namely the physical development of the articulatory mechanisms required for the production of speech sounds, and the development of the auditory perception of differences in sound.

When one examines these two developments together, it is of interest to note that differences between the sounds of language are distinguished at a very much earlier age than these distinctions are produced. Further, the auditory perception of speech sounds occurs before the infant appreciates the importance of making such distinctions. Speech perception studies (for example, Morse, 1979; Menyuk, Menn and Silber, 1986) have shown 2- to 4-month-old infants can discriminate between two speech sounds, such as 'ba' and 'ga', which differ in the place in the mouth where they are produced. Such an ability is important because it means very young infants are able to hear slight variations in the language spoken around and to them. In infant auditory discrimination tasks, one sound is repeatedly presented and the other one then introduced. To measure whether the infant has heard the distinction, some behavioural indicator of signalling the change in sound is taken. Very often infants signal 'surprise' when the new sound is introduced by increasing their sucking rate on a dummy or by turning their head. If such a behaviour is found, it is then concluded that the infant must be able to distinguish the sounds. As this ability has been noted in infants of only 4 to 6 weeks of age, then it may be that humans have an in-built tendency to respond to important distinctions among speech sounds (for a review, see Aslin, Pisoni and Jusczyk, 1983).

The major importance of the research on early speech perception can be recognized in terms of the distinction between 'bet' and 'get', words used by adults. For adults, being able to distinguish between these two words is important for understanding the speech of others, as the two words convey different meanings. Infants therefore seem predisposed for the active processing of the different sounds of the language they hear around them. This propensity becomes more specific as the infant grows and listens to more and more adult speech, and eventually learns the significance of these auditory distinctions in conveying different meanings.

This ability to hear distinctions in the language from an early age is in contrast with the physiological development of the articulatory mechanisms. The sequence of phonological development depends on the physiological speech mechanisms and the progressive maturation of the vocal apparatus (Stark, 1986). Much of this maturation occurs over the first 12 months of life. Children also gain increasing control over these mechanisms, including being able to control the place of articulation of the sounds. These vocal productions are usually referred to as 'babbling'.

It seems reasonable to assume that babbling is related to later speech development in rather complex ways. Jespersen (1922) suggested that babbling resembles play with words and sounds, while speech represents controlled planned language use. During the babbling phase, children are practising their speech production, trying out articulatory mechanisms such as their tongues, lips, and teeth, and are gaining increasing control over these apparatuses. With the auditory feedback provided through their own ears, young children come to work out what sounds can be made where, and conversely, the place of articulation of particular sounds that they want. Deaf children babble until around the age of 9 months. They then cease as they have no auditory feedback to enable control to develop (Stark, 1986).

There is relative agreement amongst researchers about the order in which the sounds appear. Although the development begins in infancy, it is not completed until children are at school. Broadly, consonants develop from those articulated at the back of the mouth such as 'g' to those produced at the front of the mouth such as 'b'. Vowels, on the other hand, develop from the front of the mouth for example, 'a', and the place of articulation moves upward and outward in the mouth, so that by the end of the first year, almost all vowel sounds are produced. A sequence of speech sound development in terms of the child making progressive contrasts between sounds was proposed by Clark and Clark (1977). In this sequence, children make a fundamental distinction between consonant and vowel sounds. After that, the first consonant distinction is between 'p' and 'b', illustrated by children's attempts at uttering 'pa' and 'ba'. These sounds are then contrasted with the nasal sound 'm', as in 'mama', which are then contrasted from dental sounds such as 'd' and 't'. This sequence simplifies the order in that it does not dwell on why the sounds of English appear in this order, although linguists and phoneticians have speculated on possible reasons.

Stark (1979, 1986) described a more detailed developmental sequence of the vocal productions of infants up to the age of 18 months. She examined the acoustic qualities of infant sounds and based her analyses on phonetic transcriptions of such sounds. The derived sequence is claimed to provide evidence for continuity between early vocalizations and later language. The sequence described by Stark is adapted and condensed in table 2.

*Table 2*   Stages of vocal development (after Stark, 1986)

| Stage | Age | Vocal behaviour |
|---|---|---|
| 1 | 0 – 8 weeks | Vegetative, reflexive sounds. Crying and fussing. |
| 2 | 8 – 20 weeks | Cooing and laughing. Nasal, consonant sounds. Sounds produced at back of mouth. Frequency of crying decreases. Greater control over sounds produced e.g., 'goo' sounds. |
| 3 | 16 – 30 weeks | Vocal play and exploratory language behaviour. Consonant sounds made towards front of mouth. Increased control over speech mechanisms. Beginning of sequencing and resequencing of sounds, e.g., buh-buh-buh, mum-mum-mum. |
| 4 | 25 – 50 weeks | Reduplicated babbling (production of consonant-vowel syllables in which the consonant is the same in every syllable) e.g., dada, gaga. Ritualized and stereotyped. Vocalization more likely to occur when in interaction with an adult than when playing with a toy. |
| 5 | 9 – 18 months | Non-reduplicated, variegated babbling. More control over stress and intonation. Overlaps with production of first words. |

Stark argued that her sequence provided evidence for a general progression of vocal productions. Stark also claimed that there was a strong relationship between the vocal productions made prelinguistically and the later production of language. However, Stark (1989) has now cautioned against a strong continuity view, at least early on in the sequence, with a recognition that cooing may mark a reorganization of the speech sound system. Stark in fact did claim that the sounds the infant was capable of producing at the end of the prelinguistic period were precisely those sounds which find their way into the adult phonological system. The research implied a relationship between babbling and identifiable phonological universals. She has further found that deviant phonological development may be related to later problems with reading, thus strengthening her view that phonological development is continuous with later achievements with spoken and written language. The common consensus is that babbling and later word production are continuous and that prespeech vocalizations are precursors to later abilities.

Because of the constraints on early productive abilities, children often realize the importance of making a spoken distinction while being unable to produce one. For example, Grieve, Tunmer and Pratt (1983, p. 293) quoted an example from a 4-year-old child, who understood the distinction between /k/ and /d/, but was unable to pronounce /k/ and instead said /d/.[1] So, on being asked what he wanted to be when he grew up, he replied 'a dowboy'. The conversation continued as follows:

Adult: 'So you want to be a dowboy, eh?'
Child (irritated): 'No!, not a dowboy, a *dowboy*'.

Sometimes articulation errors that involve the substitution of phonemes persist into the preschool and early school period. Problems with the development of speech sounds (such as the úse of /d/ instead of /ð/ in 'dat' [= 'that] or lisping with an /s/ sound) are quite commonplace in children in the early years of school. In many cases these errors are corrected spontaneously by the child as the following dialogue indicates. It took place between two children, C1 and C2, and the mother (A) of C2. At the time of this conversation neither C1 nor C2 showed any sign of being able to produce the sound /k/:

C1 *(aged 1 year 7 months)*: Dar, dar *(pointing to a car)*
C2 *(aged 4 years 5 months)*: It's not dar, it's *car*
A *(in surprise to C2 who usually pronounced car as tar)*: I didn't know you could say *car*
C2 *(after a slight pause)*: I was keeping it a secret.

Other errors may be corrected by the child if an adult points out that the pronunciation is incorrect and encourages the child to try to say the word or sound correctly. In other cases, persistent articulation disorders may require the skilled intervention of a speech therapist. While certain problems with the production of speech sounds may persist into the early school years, many of the sounds of the language are produced during the infant's first 12 months. It now widely accepted that these sounds lay the basis for subsequent phonological development. However, there are other important aspects about the structure of spoken language that infants learn during their first year of life.

## Other Pre-speech Structural Developments

As well as developing a comprehensive range of speech sounds during the first 12 months, the infant is learning other things about speaking and the

---

[1] Examples, giving the phonetic transcriptions of the phonemes referred to in the text of this book, are given in the Note on Phonemes on page xii.

spoken word. For example, features such as intonation patterns and stress variations have been recorded in the vocalizations of infants. At around the age of 6 months, most sequences of sounds seem to be produced with a falling intonation pattern. After this, both rising and falling intonation patterns are noted in the spontaneous vocalizations of infants. There is also some imitation of adult intonation patterns (Lieberman, 1967).

Although we can identify different intonation patterns in these early vocalizations, there is a tendency to describe them in terms of adult speech patterns. Thus, the early patterns of falling intonation have been compared to the adult use of declarative sentences. So, in straightforward sentences uttered by adults such as 'I'm going to the shops now', the intonation is quite flat and may drop towards the end. Questions are usually said with rising intonation: 'Are you going to the shops?'. Infants have similarly been 'heard' to produce 'questions' (with rising intonation) and other adult speech forms. Further, adults *infer* an intention on the part of a child to produce a question, and will respond accordingly (Menyuk, 1977). Therefore adults might interpret a sequence like 'da-da-da' as 'Where's daddy?', and reply 'Daddy's at work.'

Finally, it has been claimed that there are syntactic precursors to speech (Bloom, 1973). There is limited evidence that children have mastered aspects of grammar prior to their producing multi-word sentences. For example, when Bloom's daughter was about 16 months old, she produced 'widð' (pronounced 'weeda') for a period of three weeks. This uninterpretable word form always followed another word. She produced 'mama widð', 'dada widð', 'more widð' and 'no widð'. The word form widð seemed to have no specific meaning and did not refer to anything in particular. The interesting thing was the consistent word order adopted in relation to the use of widð, which was interpreted by Bloom to be evidence of emerging grammatical knowledge.

## The Transition to Speech: Functional Prerequisites

There are important functional origins to language, which possibly facilitate the transition to speech. Even when the only sounds an infant can make are cry sounds, mothers infer an intention to communicate. Indeed, as Pratt (1978, 1981) showed, the cries of infants during the first 6 months or so are interpreted as being for **physical** needs, such as hunger, wind and pain. These cries are also distinguishable acoustically. Mothers interpret the cries and will provide the infant with necessary intervention to enable the crying the stop. By 6 months of age, and in some cases much earlier, mothers begin to interpret the infant's crying

**psychologically**. For example, the infant might be frustrated because he or she is unable to reach a dropped object. Crying will cease as a result of psychological intervention, such as distraction, talking to the child or providing the child with an object. The crying patterns of an older infant show **conventionalization**. The patterns become ritualized and are acoustically different to the previous cries. Consequently, by the time the child makes the transition to speech, the mother is already adept at interpreting the child's psychological needs and intentions, based on vocalizations and nonlinguistic cues.

Mothers and infants have also established routines that are essential for efficient and effective linguistic communication. Bruner's (1983) research on the prerequisites for and precursors to language showed clearly how looking and vocalizing are the first forms of communication between mothers and their infants. There is a continual modification of the adult's communicative behaviours in direct relationship with the child's developing communicative (linguistic and nonlinguistic) capacities. The mother's repertoire exhibits many behaviours judged to be finely tuned to the infant's existing abilities. Therefore, by the time the infant is actually talking, a great deal has been learned about how to modulate conversation in accordance with social expectations.

## One-word Stage

There is an identifiable period usually some time after the child's first birthday during which single words are characteristically produced. When early researchers first charted the developmental sequence of language development, they merely recorded in diaries these single words as they appeared. Today the issue is far more complex as researchers focus on both the forms and the functions of single word utterances (Harris, 1992; Messer, 1994; Barrett, 1995).

It a fairly difficult task to try to characterize the forms of children's first words, because the vocabulary of each and every child is different. While many people and parents try to keep lists of the increasing vocabulary of young children, the task very quickly becomes out of all proportion as more and more different words are added. It is feasible to chart the first  50 to 100 words. From such lists we can find some common words in the vocabularies of young children. Amongst the early words of most children (in most cultures) are forms such as 'mama' and 'dada' or 'papa', words referring to mother and father. Phonologically, these forms are reduplicated syllables, with the lips and front of the mouth as the place of articulation. These forms quickly and reliably come to refer to the infant's parents. Many other reduplicated syllabic forms of this type are produced and can be used as 'words'. For example, one infant produced 'deedee' to refer to 'Stevie', while for many children the word 'nana' (= banana) is one of the first words acquired.

For those families with young children, they will be aware that it is often difficult to decode children's early single word forms. There are two reasons why this should occur. The child's meaning may not overlap with the usual adult meaning of the word, or the child's word form may be idiosyncratic, seen for example in one child's coining of the neologism 'zhadow' to refer to a supermarket trolley.

Barrett (1995) summarizes most of the research in this area, examining both the characteristics of early lexical development or first words, as well as the theoretical explanations for these developments. Some of these are discussed in the following section.

## Acquisition of Single Words

First words are typically identifiable by having a recognizable and consistent phonetic form although the actual form may not correspond to the adult word. Many deviations from adult language occur, and some of these idiosyncratic word forms may be rough approximations to adult forms while others seem to be totally different to adult forms. The fact that parents recognize those forms again emphasizes the importance of social interaction and mutual sharing of the context in language development. Parents are often more tuned into their child's language forms than others less familiar with the child, and can thus act as interpreter, for example, translating the child's word form 'buppy' into 'He wants his blanket.'

Because these idiosyncratic forms are used in particular contexts, some will be adopted by the adults, perhaps in a slightly different form. As a result some neologisms remain in families for years (cf. Clark, 1991). This is often found in the case of words for children's comforters. Two cases from our own experience are 'weeda' derived from 'feeder' and 'buppy' from 'blanket'. Neologisms are not restricted to comforters however, and there are many other examples that could be quoted. Three that we have encountered in family life are 'donni-della' referring to a certain variety of flower whose actual botanical name is now totally lost; 'dawdle-awdle-awdle', a rather unusual word for 'button' which was also generalized to 'belly button'; and 'weh-weh' to refer to 'scissors'. These shared meanings for unconventional forms of single words would not continue to exist if they did not occur in social interaction between the child and others.

In discussing these lexical innovations, Clark (1991) highlights the adherence by children to other lexical principles in a systematic way. These principles are: transparency of meaning (to the child); simplicity (of form); and finally, productivity. These principles reflect the child's underlying conceptual organization as applied to the acquisition of syntax and can be used to predict the types of neologisms that children will produce.

Many of the referents for these first words belong in the familiar here-and-now world of the developing child. So we find that not only do familiar people such as parents and siblings receive labels, but so do family pets, such as the dog or cat. Children often acquire words for food, such as for milk, juice and biscuit. They acquire labels for body parts such as words for eye, nose and mouth, and words for clothing, such as shoe, sock and hat. Objects in the child's daily routine also acquire labels, so there are often words for spoon, cup, bath and potty (see Clark, 1983, for a full review of early vocabulary domains).

As well as developing words for concrete objects, young children also develop other words that perhaps enable them to begin to adjust to the social world. For example, Gopnik (1982) provided evidence for the early development of non-referential words such as 'more', 'no' and 'all-gone', the expression of any of which will elicit action on the part of the hearer (and can also result in more food, more play activities or more toys to play with!).

## Vocabulary Spurt

Many researchers have commented on the so-called vocabulary spurt or naming explosion towards the end of the child's second year. This can be regarded as an increase in the variety of word forms that children use, though it is not unrelated to increased capabilities in associating meanings with different forms. The increase in the production of words by young children, in particular, nouns, has been linked to a shift from context-dependent, interpretative use of words, to a cognitively more complex way of organizing the world (for example, Gopnik and Meltzoff, 1986). Other researchers have suggested the naming explosion is related to the constraints under which children operate (Markman, 1991) as it is evidence that some principle has been learned. Bates, Dale and Thal (1995) explored two related problems in the explanations offered for the vocabulary spurt, namely, lack of universality and the lack of a definable inflection point. The former stems from the fact that not all children display this single, large burst, with many children acquiring vocabulary in a slowly accreting fashion and others moving in smaller 'bursts'. Secondly, the notion of a burst implies a discontinuity development. Bates et al. argue that this does not fit with the data, nor, theoretically, is it a sustainable argument. However, it is acknowledged that there is an acceleration in vocabulary development during the child's second year and that this, according to Bates et al., still requires some explanation.

## Nouns in Early Language

Whatever the mechanism for acquisition of words, it is clear it is important that the 'word' should be used consistently in a particular situation or in relation to a specific object or event. That is, the referent of the 'word' should remain constant. The examples illustrated in this chapter certainly all share that characteristic. We have now considered both single word meanings and single word forms, but throughout, we have treated single words as if they are labels. In so doing, it is clear that there are problems of interpreting these single words. We have also assumed that single words are used to refer to or to name objects, although this need not be the case (K. Nelson, Hampson and Shaw, 1993). Single words can also be used to represent propositions and ideas, and other semantic categories, and we will turn now to discuss research that has examined how meanings might be ascribed to single words.

## Meanings of First Words

In looking at what a young child's first single word utterances mean, we are faced with a problem of interpretation. As adults we tend to judge the language of children as being an incomplete deviation from adult speech. We do, however, tend to interpret the meaning intended by a child from a number of cues, not only the verbal production (Bates, Bretherton and Snyder, 1988). But it is likely that children's meanings are also incomplete and only partially overlap with adult meaning, or may not overlap at all. Children, by virtue of their age, have a limited knowledge of the world and have to try to work out word meanings by various means. For example, young children need to hypothesize about the appropriate context for the use of a word and to do so, they have to rely on non-verbal cues plus the uses of that word by others. They can also invoke their possibly incomplete knowledge of the meanings of other words.

## Mismatch

Five mismatch conditions between adult meaning and child meaning have been identified (Clark, 1983). These are **overextension, underextension, mismatch, coincidence** and **overlap**. Here we will con-

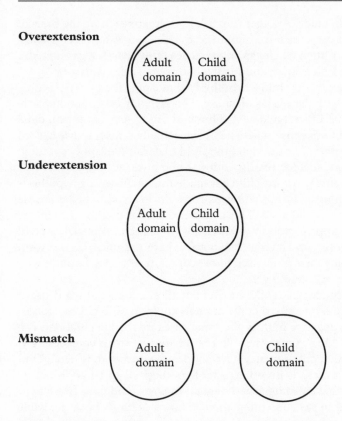

*Figure 2* Three possible mismatches between adult meaning and child meaning

sider the first three as they are sufficient to explain the principles involved in children's early word meaning development (see figure 2).

In *overextension* of word meaning, there is overlap with adult meaning, but there is further extension past the normal range of meaning applied. That is, a word is used in a range of contexts, the hypothesized meaning being based on some characteristic of the original object, but one that is insufficient to distinguish that object from others in different categories. The child may use a word in many contexts judged to be inappropriate by an adult. The research literature abounds with examples of overextension by children (for example, Bowerman, 1976; Clark, 1973a), where there are overextensions based on the similarity (same size, same shape, same 'four-leggedness') of referents. Thus, we can find overextension on the basis of **size**, where the word 'fly' was applied initially to a fly, then to specks of dirt, dust, all small insects, the child's own toes, crumbs of bread and small toads. Another example is overextension on the basis of **shape**. A child used the term 'tick-tock' to refer to a watch, then a clock (so far so good), then all clocks and watches (still okay!), a gas meter, a fire hose wound on a spool and finally, bathroom scales with a dial.

In *underextension*, the child's hypothesized meaning for a word has only partial overlap with the adult's meaning. This is much less common partly because it is very difficult to detect. The child's usage can never be judged inappropriate in this sense unless he or she actually refuses to use a word in a certain context. For example, the child may call the family pet 'dog' and not use that label for any other dog, using instead 'bow-wow'.

*Mismatch* occurs when the child has made the totally wrong hypothesis about the meaning of a word and usually results in an adult being unable to understand the child at all. This assumes the word used by the child is a recognizable approximation to an English form. Occasionally, a child may coin a neologism, such as 'zhadow', where the idiosyncratic form acquires meaning only when used in the company of a specific adult who has 'interpreted' the new word.

It is often argued that children overextend conventional word usage because they do not realize that the animals are from different categories. Thus cats and dogs are both in the same category for the child and can both be called 'dog'. One other alternative that is worth considering is the possibility that children may have an idea that the word is wrong, but it is used when there is no other label hypothesized to be appropriate. The child may have distinguished dogs from cows, and have two labels, but on wanting to say something about a cat, says 'dog', because, while appreciating cats are in a different category to dogs, conceptually the cat is more dog-like than cow-like (because it is a small, furry, domesticated animal perhaps). Such utterances are indistinguishable from those where the child simply has the incorrect word.

It is believed that young children make hypotheses about the meanings of words and seek to have these predictions supported before adopting them as rules for language use. Children therefore are actively exploring the possible meanings of words being learned by seeking environmental evidence to confirm or disconfirm possible predictions. By hypothesizing about the meanings of words, there are, as we have discussed above, several outcomes, most of which involve a mismatch between the child's meaning and the adult's meaning. The adult may then assist in clarifying the meaning of the word for the child.

For example, the child on seeing a cat may utter 'dog'. In such instances, there are possible strategies that the adult can adopt to provide feedback to the child regarding the differences in meaning. Under most circumstances, the feedback should have the effect of indicating to the child that the word meanings do not coincide. So when the child says 'dog' for cat, the hypothesized meaning might incorporate elements of 'cats', possibly their 'four-leggedness', their tails or their furriness. In this case, an adult, 'understanding' the child, might say 'No that's not a dog. That's a cat.' Here the child's attention is drawn to the mismatch between the use of the word (that is, using it with the meaning the child has attached to it) as the adult corrects the meaning by introducing a new or another term.

Occasionally, it may be that the adult misunderstands what a child has said. For example, a child may utter a word that sounds like 'dog' where there is no dog present. In this case, the adult may interpret the word as 'dog' and seek clarification of meaning by asking 'What dog?' or 'Where's a dog?'. Finally, in some circumstances, the adult may not understand the child's word form at all, resulting in communication breakdown.

## Principle of Contrast

According to Clark (1983, 1988, 1990), the incomplete meanings of words hypothesized by young children and witnessed mainly in overextensions are slowly narrowed down. Clark refers to this as the Principle of Contrast, which she defines as 'every two forms contrast in meaning'. Contrast occurs as children's experiences broaden and they find out more about how words are used. One major source of evidence for the Principle of Contrast is found when children attach a new word to an object that was previously lacking a label. For example, the word 'dog' (or a childish variant) may be acquired by a child and used to refer to all animals. On acquiring a term for 'cat', the conceptual domain of animal is split between 'dogs' and 'cats', and the use of 'dog' becomes more restricted. As the child acquires yet other animal terms, the range of application of the original term becomes progressively narrowed. Ultimately, every word form is different and each word has a unique meaning that coincides with the adult or conventional meaning.

Clark (1990, 1991, 1995) discusses lexical development as following two principles – that of Contrast (discussed above) and that of Conventionality. These operate to constrain the options available for words and reduce the overgeneralized meanings as well as providing children with general principles that can be used to analyse the language. Conventionality relies on culturally defined or mutually agreed on meanings and, with the other pragmatic principle of Contrast, guides the selection and use of words, including new words, in the child's lexicon. Clark has conducted a range of studies examining the application of these principles to the acquisition of words, including the child's coining of neologisms when no suitable term is available. These innovative words are used instead of overgeneralizations and the use of simple deictic terms such as 'that', but are superseded once the conventional terminology is learned (Clark, 1991).

Other biases in children's early language that facilitate or constrain the mapping of form (syntax) onto meaning (semantics) or use (pragmatics) include the mutual exclusivity bias or the natural bias of children to construct mutually exclusive meanings for words as they acquire them (Merriman and Bowman, 1989), whole-object and taxonomic assumptions (Markman, 1991), and fast mapping (Heibeck and Markman, 1987). All of these approaches make assumptions about what might be influencing word learning, particularly in the early stages when children receive minimal exposure to a word or situation and have to respond. The experimental studies are believed to mirror real life in so far as the principles (assumptions, constraints, biases) are assumed to operate whenever an unfamiliar word is heard or the context demands an interpretation. The precise mechanisms whereby this happens however await further research and speculation.

## Single Words as Holophrases

Early psycholinguistic researchers believed that each single word represented a whole idea and argued then that the single words 'stood for' entire sentences. De Laguna (1927) labelled these single word utterances **holophrases**, to indicate that each word represented a full idea. For example, when a child produces the word 'dog', what he or she was expressing was 'Look, the dog is eating its dinner.' Each single word sentence uttered by the child requires a full adult sentence for the expression of its meaning. However what is the child actually using these one-word utterances for? If each word does express an idea, how does the child work out what aspect to talk about? One possible way of interpreting the single word speech of children is to hypothesize the words express **roles** rather than believing they are merely labels.

## Single Words as Roles

Greenfield and Smith (1976) argued that the single word utterances of children are identifying **roles** rather than labelling or naming objects and activities. By assigning roles to children's one word utterances, not only did Greenfield and Smith attempt to take the meaning of the child's language into account, but they also tried to link early language with the functions of later language.

What are the roles for one-word speech? If a child utters the word 'cat', the child may, as we have discussed, be simply labelling the family pet.

However, the cat can fulfil a variety of roles – the cat can be a **mover**, is **moveable** (it can be picked up and carried) and it might feasibly be a **place**. Clark (1979) believed that by assigning potential roles to one word utterances, it would be possible to describe systematic ways in which young children **use** and develop their language. So for example, amongst the early roles named by children were movers, such as parents, family pets, cars and trucks, and moveables including various toys and objects such as cup (which can be raised to the mouth or dropped). Greenfield and Smith (1976) further argued that the order in which various roles became named depended on their salience to the young child. So, potential movers and moveables were more salient than recipients of actions and places.

Nelson et al. (1993) discussed evidence why children apparently learn mostly nouns in the early acquisition period. They distinguished between nouns as names, between proper nouns and common nouns and between count and mass nouns, and argued that the functions or types of nouns are important to consider in any analysis of acquisition. Experimentally, they demonstrated that children use nouns in early language to describe actions or activities, locations or events; in fact, they used 10 different semantic categories. Nelson et al. believed this more sophisticated way of describing the language used by children reflects more accurately theoretical notions about the mapping of language onto pre-existing concepts as well as the intuitive assumption that children talk about things in their daily lives. That is, instead of a theoretical framework that postulates innate constraints on language learning, word learning occurs in natural contexts of everyday discourse. The actual words used were not all nouns, or object words, although the factors found to encourage language development also favoured noun production.

The identification of roles and other conceptual or semantic categories at the one-word speech period allows for continuities with later language to be described. Later language, with its increased vocabulary and more complex grammar, has also been characterized as describing roles. Roles take the intended meaning of the utterances into account in so far as conceptual categories operate within the child's social and linguistic world (whether or not they are innately specified). The major drawback in using roles is that there is little agreement amongst researchers regarding the definition and description of roles or of categories. Thus we have roles such as mover and moveable, actor and agent, recipient of actions and object, owner and possessor, and place and location. Although there may be some equivalence between some of the terms, they are not completely interchangeable. Definitions are usually provided to help the reader understand what is meant by the terminology. As long as we continue to impose adult-based categories for the description of children's developing language, this will remain a problem, and the debate is likely to continue. This issue will be raised again in relation to descriptions of multi-word utterances.

## Discrepant Labelling

Baldwin (1993) was interested in the extent to which infants actively consult an adult speaker for clues to meanings for words. Drawing on research that examined the extent to which infants are able to follow a parent's gaze or a pointing gesture, Baldwin wanted to examine the role of the infant in any such joint social enterprise as well as how joint reference might facilitate the learning of the referent of a new word.

An ingenious experiment was conducted, in which infants were shown two novel objects and heard a novel label applied four times to one of the objects, under two different training conditions, namely, follow-in labelling where the adult looked at and labelled the object that was the focus of the child's attention, and discrepant labelling, where the adult looked at and labelled an object that was not the child's current focus. Later, infants were given a comprehension task, to see which object they selected when given the label used earlier. Using infants from 14 months through to 19 months, Baldwin found that all infants noticed the discrepancy in focus in the discrepant labelling condition as they were more likely to look away from their own object to the other one or the adult experimenter's face when discrepant labelling occurred. Thus there was clear evidence that infants actively monitor and follow attentional cues.

In the comprehension phase, older infants after the follow-in condition consistently selected the correct object. This provided a baseline estimate of performance. Both younger infants in the follow-in condition, and all infants in the discrepant labd8ling condition, performed unsystematically. Only older infants in the discrepant labelling condition performed at greater than chance level, by selecting the correct referent.

. This study, and others conducted by Baldwin (Baldwin and Moses, 1994), showed that infants are able to use a speaker's intended referent as a clue to meaning, and conversely, that mapping errors do not occur. How children avoid such mapping errors during discrepant labelling is subject to debate, although Baldwin and Moses offer a mentalistic interpretation (infants understand that adults have intentions to refer) such that infants consult adults' attentional cues. Subsequent research (Baldwin and Moses, 1994) confirms this interpretation, with evidence that infants can distinguish referential from non-referential acts, irrespective of the redundancy of cues, and that they draw inferences from the social communicative behaviours of the adults.

## Syntactic Bootstrapping

A promising avenue of research for the development of word meaning has been the examination of syntactic bootstrapping which assumes some innate predisposition for language that constrains the mechanisms available and used in language development. In syntactic bootstrapping, it is hypothesized that children somehow use the grammatical structure of adult input language to help them work out the meaning as well as the lexical form of any new word heard (Naigles, 1990). Naigles and Kako (1993) conducted a validation of syntactic bootstrapping in relation to the acquisition of verbs. They examined the biases for action that exist for children aged about 2½ years in the absence of syntactic information, and how those biases can be altered by the type of syntactic framework offered. That is, they were interested in how a syntactic framework offers clues for the child's interpretation of verbs but in such a way as to constrain the possible interpretations available. Naigles and Kako conclude that the initial preferences for particular actions are determined by perceptual salience (of the experimental materials provided) to the child, but subsequently, that children use the syntactic information provided. They claimed this work demonstrated that young children use the syntactic information to constrain the meaning of novel verbs.

A challenge to this view came from Gleitman and Gillette (1995) who claimed that mapping or pairing (word with action) was too simplistic to account for the learning of meanings of verbs by children, and that efforts would be much better directed at examining relationships between sentences (as syntactic objects) and the world. Methodological improvements have led to refinements in theorizing; syntactic evidence can assist verb acquisition. The question then is: does this apply in real life? Gleitman and Gillette suggest not, but that broader real world exigencies exist that may constrain but not impede development. Constraints that do occur, they suggest, involve the relationship between the sentence spoken and its interpretation by the child, with an emphasis on the role of the extralinguistic context.

Finally, Barrett (1995) described his theory of word learning – the multi-route model – which assumes that words are learned one-by-one (and not by some general systemic principle) via two routes, the social–pragmatic and the referential. These routes reflect the nature of the mental representations onto which the newly acquired words are mapped. Barrett was interested in describing how early word learning takes place and also how other theories fail to capture the richness of developments. He also believed that children make use of the context in ascribing meanings to words and hence, they deal with each word individually. Social–pragmatic words are initially mapped onto representations of events and the words are then used in those contexts. Referential words, by contrast, are mapped onto representations of prototypes and are then used to refer to actions, entities, and so on, that resemble those prototypes. This view neatly encompasses two theoretical positions – prototype theory and event representation – and permits the explanation of a wider range of phenomena than other accounts. Developmental changes to the meanings attached to single words are evidence for changes (modification, reorganization) to underlying mental representations, although the word itself remains context-bound. Subsequent decontextualization occurs in the social-pragmatic route when an underlying event representation becomes disembedded and becomes, in effect, a prototypical referent. Both routes are then similar, in so far as further development requires identification of the principal features of the prototype, expansion of the referential scope, assignment of meaning and further differentiation of prototypes.

The model has wide applicability and encompasses many of the notions existing in the research literature to date, consolidating them into a single, but as-yet-incomplete, model of lexical development. The focus of the theory is predominantly on words that have concrete external referents, but can account for many of the phenomena described in this chapter, including overextension and use of words in limited contexts.

It is evident that lexical, grammatical or syntactic, and semantic knowledge are being acquired during the one-word stage. It seems as though lexical development and grammatical structures are fairly easy to trace. It also would be reasonable to assume that the meanings children are trying to express throughout the early language development phase are indeed linked. Undeniably children's experiences are increasing, as are their cognitive capacities, and it would make sense for the linguistic encoding of these experiences to be continuous with previous encoding and contiguous with other aspects of the developing child.

## Beyond Single Words

Once children begin combining words, we can start to look for rudimentary evidence that the grammar of the language is being learned. Description of the child's language can be made in terms of systems of grammar or syntax. Most attempts to describe the rules children are using to combine their words have been influenced by the linguistic theories of language. If we have an innate predisposition to learn the rules of grammar, then the first true manifestation of this ability should occur when words begin to be combined in multi-word utterances. While there have been various methods used to describe the child's increasing use of grammatical rules in language, we will concentrate on describing only those attempts that have been controversial, influential or both. Firstly, we will outline a descriptive method that is used to characterize children's increasing language ability, and then go on to describe methods that aim to predict children's subsequent grammatical development.

### Utterance Length as a Measure of Language Development

The increasing length of children's utterances is commonly taken as a measure of language development. The measure of the length of the spoken utterances is believed to gauge accurately children's linguistic progress. In fact, rather than using chronological age when describing a sequence of language development, a more frequently used measure is **Mean Length of Utterance (MLU)**. MLU captures not only the increasing length of children's utterances, but also their increasing complexity. It does this by using **morphemes** as the basic building blocks of language, rather than words. Morphemes are the smallest units of meaning in language and may be **free** or **bound**. Free morphemes include simple nouns, verbs, adjectives, articles and prepositions. Bound morphemes are verb and noun endings such as the plural -s or progressive -ing, which exist only in conjunction with the noun or verb to which they are attached.

The MLU is typically calculated by averaging the number of morphemes spoken per utterance by a child during 100 consecutive utterances of a recorded language sample. These utterances are usually selected from a longer transcript of the child's language. An utterance is defined as a string of language and is more or less equivalent to a sentence, the boundaries being ascertained through pauses between strings. In the case of single word utterances, only one word, or morpheme, such as 'dog' forms the string. It is isolated from any other utterance by having a gap or a pause (the length of which may be stipulated by the researcher) between it and any other utterance. The utterance 'dogs' would be two morphemes long, as it is composed of 'dog' plus the plural ending 's'.

The number of morphemes per utterance is counted and these are then averaged over the 100 chosen utterances. While it is not always an easy task to identify utterances and often even less easy to identify morphemes, it can be made manageable by specifying exactly the rules for counting. Brown (1973) provided some useful ground rules, such as counting ritualized compounds ('bye-bye') and diminutives ('doggie') as one morpheme since there is good reason to suppose children learn them as a single entity. Provided individuals or groups working on the same transcripts stick to the same rules and specify them clearly, consistency within and between children is easy to establish and maintain.

At the one-word stage of language development, each utterance is one morpheme long and the MLU = 1. The MLU then increases with additions to vocabulary and with the development of the more complex morphemes that enable greater clarity and specificity of meaning to be expressed. Children's linguistic progress is then accounted for by increases in MLU, a more useful indicator of language development than chronological age. While there is a positive correlation between MLU and chronological age, it is weak and subject to individual variation. MLU does, however, fail to capture the regularities of early child speech, in the sense that it does not focus on the specific morphemes constituting the spoken language. It merely counts those that are used. We will now turn to an examination of the developments that occur during the child's learning and production of multi-word utterances, which offer the opportunity for studying regularities and continuities in language development.

## Telegraphic Speech

Usually between 18 and 24 months, children start to combine words to form two-word utterances. Again, the use of two-word utterances is a recognizable phase in the development of language. One of the first attempts to characterize the regularities in two-word speech was undertaken by Brown and Bellugi (1964) who described such speech as **telegraphic**. Telegraphic speech was characterized by a high frequency of **content** words (nouns and verbs) and a low frequency of **function** words such as articles and prepositions. Like a telegram, the omission of the function words leads to no apparent loss of communication. So it was concluded that the omitted words were highly predictable and maybe even redundant. For example, it would be easier to predict the omitted word in sentence (1) than in sentence (2):

(1)   We sat down —— the table for dinner.
(2)   The boy jumped off the ——.

The difficulty with the notion of telegraphic speech is that while it describes rather neatly the form of two-word utterances, it is unable to explain either why or how the child chooses only content words. It is arguable that because content words have meaning, have concrete referents and may even receive heavier stress when spoken, they are easier to learn. Although selection of content words **may** relate to notions of meaningfulness, it is more likely that the words are chosen on the basis of the child's knowledge and experience of the world. However, how the selection mechanism operates is anyone's guess.

## Pivot Grammar

Braine (1963) described the rules used by children when they begin combining words in two-word speech. Braine was concerned with formalizing the grammatical rules children were apparently using with two-word utterances. He created what he termed **pivot grammar**. He claimed that there was a small number of words used frequently and in a fixed position in two-word utterances. These **pivot** words co-occurred with low frequency words from an **open** word class. So for example, if we take samples of a 2–year-old's utterances over a period of a few days and transcribe those utterances, we might begin to find some patterns of language use. By grouping these utterances, we can capture the regularities in the speech of the child. Thus a child might utter the following:

| | | |
|---|---|---|
| hi doggy | dolly fell | more milk |
| hi dolly | that fell | more bottle |
| hi Mummy | bottle fell | more doggy |

Braine further claimed that the only combinations of Pivot (P) and Open (O) words were P + O, O + P, O + O and O alone. P + P combinations or P alone did not exist in children's utterances.

Pivot grammar has not stood up to scrutiny and was heavily criticized. Firstly, pivot grammar is not the grammar of adult language. It is inadequate for describing the language used by adult speakers of English as it is unable to account for language development after the two-word stage. It cannot predict later grammatical developments, and certainly cannot characterize adult language competence. As a grammar, it is fairly weak, since it is unable to specify which sentences are and which are not permissible (that is, grammatical) in the language. A grammar describing structural relationships between elements in sentences must be able to make predictions about acceptable and unacceptable forms. It was further claimed that the fixed word position notion was too restrictive and as a consequence, the combinations proposed by Braine were not the only ones possible. For example, both Bloom (1970) and Bowerman (1973) presented evidence that children in the two-word stage may use pivot words alone and they also found high frequency (= P) words that varied their location within utterances. Thus children produced utterances such as 'no milk', 'daddy no', where the so-called pivot word could be in either first or second position. From such evidence, it was argued that in fact there was no basis for distinguishing pivot from open words.

Braine (1976) has acknowledged these, and other difficulties, with pivot grammar, but still maintained that children learned positional patterns in early word combinations. Using cross-linguistic data, Braine contended that children learn a limited number of formulae that map meanings onto positions in the surface structure of spoken language.

Both telegraphic speech and pivot grammar as characterizations of children's early combinatorial language failed to take account of what the child was actually doing with the language, namely using it to convey meaning in social interaction. It may also be conjectured that pivot grammar in particular represents a strategic attempt by children to systematize their language rather than regarding it as structural development. Viewing these early attempts by children to regularize their language use as strategic rather than structural also enables clearer linkages with subsequent language development. However, more recent attempts to describe the regularities of multi-word utterances have been derived from considerations of both the meanings the child is trying to convey together with the forms actually used. That is, focus has been on the uses and functions of language in communicative and social contexts, using this approach to demonstrate continuity between earlier and later stages.

## Other Characterizations of Multi-word Utterances

Other characterizations of the two-word period based on the *form* of the utterances include Nelson's (1973) referential/expressive distinction. Children who were predominantly referential tended to have vocabularies of nouns and names for objects, while expressive children's language was more varied and was primarily social and regulatory. Young children were not categorized as either referential or expressive on the basis of their language, rather some children were *more* referential and some, *more* expressive.

This contrast has been extended in the work of Bloom, Lightbrown and Hood (1975) who analysed the two-word combinations of four children. As well as finding various combinations of pivot and open words, they believed a better distinction between the different language forms produced by children was between 'nominal' and 'pronominal'. This distinction could be used to describe all the early language of children. Instead of dwelling on structural similarities and differences at the one- and two-word stages, the nominal/pronominal distinction, like the referential/expressive distinction, described tendencies of children to use certain parts of speech more frequently than others. Using the structures of language produced by children, they could be categorized as tending to be either nominal or pronominal. Again, this distinction was not dichotomous but was in fact a normally distributed continuum. Children did not always fall exclusively into one category or the other.

Nominal children used combinations of two content words (open words or nouns) as well as referring to themselves by name for example, 'Stephen walk.' By contrast, pronominal children tended to use pronouns and non-specific reference for example, 'I do'. This distinction between nominal and pronominal children based on their language was a rather transient phase (found between MLU = 2.00 and 2.50). The nominal/ referential vs. pronominal/ expressive distinction has further been linked to other aspects of language acquisition (Bates and MacWhinney, 1987), and it seems a useful way of categorizing children during the early period of language development at least.

## Semantic Relations Hypothesis

Brown (1973) proposed that instead of examining the structure of two-word utterances, we should focus on **semantic relations** which describe the range of adult meanings expressed by two-word utterances. For example, instead of using the traditional grammatical categories of subject and object of a sentence to describe which parts of grammar children are learning, the semantic relations hypothesis proposes that we consider the **role** each word plays in the sentence. Thus not only is the grammatical structure of the utterance considered, but the possible meaning the child is trying to express is taken into account. This links with the discussion of roles in one-word speech which also tried to capture not only the forms of language that were developing, but also the meanings of those forms. Semantic relations such as Agent, Action, Object, Location and Possession were proposed to account for the meanings young children were trying to express. At the two-word stage, Brown was able to find a set of eight relations. These are shown, with examples, in table 3.

*Table 3*  Semantic relations (after Brown, 1973)

| | | |
|---|---|---|
| 1. | Agent + Action | Boy kick |
| 2. | Action + Object | Kick ball |
| 3. | Agent + Object | Daddy ball |
| 4. | Action + Location | Sit chair |
| 5. | Entity + Location | Book table |
| 6. | Agent + Possession | Mummy hat |
| 7. | Entity + Attributive | Stove hot |
| 8. | Demonstrative + Entity | That dog |

The advantage of the semantic relations hypothesis is that it can account for the child's progress into three word speech and beyond. By adding together or combining relations, children can begin to produce phrases such as:

(Agent + Action) + (Action + Object)

becoming

(Agent + Action + Object)

seen, for example, in

(Daddy throw) + (Throw ball) = (Daddy throw ball).

As well as being able to account for the child's grammatical development, the semantic relations hypothesis takes the child's meaning into account. Granted, this meaning is inferred by adults based on their knowledge and on the contexts of the utterances. The semantic relations hypothesis makes it possible to draw up a description of language development from earlier stages through to the later multi-word utterances. Further, it is universal in its applicability, enabling general claims to be made about language development.

There has been widespread acceptance at a general level of the semantic relations hypothesis, although there has been debate in describing an appropriate range of semantic categories. Not only must the categories encapsulate the child's intended meanings, but there must be sufficient (though not too many) to do so adequately. Most of the research has been concerned with describing the emerging semantic categories in a small sample of children. This has given rise to methodological differences such as those that arise from using children's utterances from different situations, for example, data generated in the home versus language gathered in the laboratory. Different researchers have different labels for the various categories, to add to the complication. So it is still far from clear exactly what best describes the form and function of the child's developing linguistic system. Nevertheless, given that the use of language is about shared meaning, it does make sense to take account of the meaning when describing children's language.

### Semantic Bootstrapping

Like the syntactic bootstrapping hypothesis, semantic bootstrapping refers to use of adult semantic classes by children to make assumptions about the grammatical categories of the language (for example,

Macnamara, 1982; Pinker 1984). In particular, this theorizing links explicitly to the view that children first learn nouns as names of objects and classes of object, which then facilitates their later learning of language. Use of the semantic category permits the identification of a grammatical category and further extension and generalization of the categories to other words are supposed to be dependent on the earlier (and correct) identification of nouns in relation to the function of naming. Generalization occurs to other grammatical forms (such as verbs) and to other functions, via bootstrapping. Even if innate constraints were to operate, children would still be incapable of recognizing which words were nouns versus which words were verbs.

The semantic bootstrapping hypothesis assumes that once children can distinguish classes of words (or at least, nouns from other types of words), then they look for common grammatical features. This task is limited by the constraints that operate on the linguistic system (*not* the child) and so patterns can be identified and matched. Although the hypothesis has been called into question (for example, Nelson et al., 1993), there is a basis by which it provides a plausible and parsimonious account for the predominance of nouns in early language and for the way in which lexical forms acquire grammatical structure.

## Individual Differences in Early Language Development

We have sketched what seems like a universal pattern of language development from one-word to two-word grammatical speech during the early years. We have only touched on some of the research on individual differences in language development, research which is beginning to suggest alternative routes towards the development of language structures. Much of this research on individual variation has been aimed at linking differences in language development to other aspects of the child's development, especially social factors.

There are many ways in which the language experience of children varies, and these include variations both within the child and external variations. The range of experiences children have with spoken language is enormous, as is the extent to which they have active involvement in social interaction. Any of these could influence the rate of learning language as well as the size of the child's vocabulary, the range of meanings the child is capable of expressing and the contribution the child is able to make to conversations with others. There have been only a few studies looking at how individual differences may affect children's language learning.

Goldfield and Snow (1986) illustrated how the ways mothers respond to the differences in their children will influence the course of that child's subsequent language development. They used a categorization of children based on their productive language, namely the nominal/referential versus pronominal/expressive distinction and linked the differences in language to other aspects of development.

Referential children played more with objects and used objects in their interactions with adults, so they would give adults toys and books. Expressive children were more responsive to adults and adult talk, were more sociable and perhaps more imitative of adults. These differences, from wherever they originate, perhaps elicit different types of verbal interaction from an adult, the form of which might also be related to the adult's preferred 'style' of interaction in a broad sense. This adult input then modulates the child's 'style' and so on. As children interact with a variety of adults, each with their own 'style', they will encounter a range of reactions to their own individual style and thus language development proceeds. Although we are not dichotomizing children (nor adults), as most have both referential **and** expressive elements in their language, this distinction may well be a useful heuristic for further research on the growth of language. There is an interaction between linguistic input (see chapter 2), parental or adult 'style' and child 'style' that affects spoken language development, and perhaps other aspects of cognitive development, including written language development.

# CHAPTER FIVE

# Learning Spoken Language: Further Accomplishments

By 2 or 3 years of age, most children have begun to combine words according to some grammatical rules. They can communicate with others in a reasonable way. But they still have many challenges to face, and these will be examined in this chapter. Because we are emphasizing continuity and progression in language development, many of the linguistic accomplishments that are discussed have precursors in the prelinguistic and early language periods. However, their realization as correct adult forms does not occur until later. Some of the developments are changes in form, that is, grammatical (syntactic) developments, while others involve changes in function and meaning, or semantic development.

The development of negation or making sentences negative, is typically depicted as a later development, requiring a certain degree of linguistic sophistication before it can be used correctly. Nonetheless, we are all fully aware that one of the first words children acquire is frequently 'No'. So although the form of negation changes in later language, the function of stating the negative is recorded in one-word speech. Mastery of the forms of negation in a grammatical sense takes a fairly long time. Similarly, some of the forms of language that began to develop in the early language period still require further refinement and development, especially when we consider their functions. For example, the functions of the article system (the uses of 'the' and 'a') are not fully mastered until the child is aged about 9 years, although these forms first appear in the language of children aged between 2 and 3 years (Maratsos, 1976).

The mistaken assumption that all children have full command of their language once they begin to talk in sentences can lead to problems for the children themselves. Some people think that all that develops from age 2 or 3 is an extension and elaboration of existing linguistic capabilities. Any potential difficulties are not recognized, since the child has the basic skills and just requires assistance using them. In some cases, the difficulties children face with later language development are not immediately obvious. In order to appreciate them one really has to manipulate the situation experimentally to elicit use of the grammatical forms. Palermo and Molfese (1972) were amongst the first to describe many of the changes in language 'from age five onwards' and they drew extensively on research by Carol Chomsky (1969) and early studies dealing with semantic development (for example, Asch and Nerlove, 1960). More recent work includes that of Romaine (1984) and the collection edited by Durkin (1986). Karmiloff-Smith (1979a, 1986a) also reviewed many of the experimental studies of later language development. The use of experiments does not necessarily invalidate the conclusions in terms of their applicability to the 'real world'. Indeed, many experiments have been developed from careful, perhaps fortuitous, observations of children's spontaneous language use and misuse. In other cases, the experiments have been theory-driven, but they still reveal some of the problems children have with complex grammatical structures. Sometimes, once these difficulties have been teased out, they are then noticed in children's everyday language. It is clear that being able to talk does not ensure *all* aspects of language have been learned.

## Later Syntactic Development

### Grammatical Morphemes

Brown (1973) studied the child's acquisition of 14 grammatical morphemes during language development. These small but important words provide evidence of the child's developing grammatical knowledge. Brown identified a sequence of morpheme acquisition, which began around the point when the three children in his study (aged between 1 year 10 months and 2 years10 months) were beginning to produce three word utterances (MLU = 2.25). The morphemes not only increase the child's MLU but they also enable the child to 'modulate meanings' more efficiently through the use of articles, prepositions and noun and verb endings. The 14 morphemes and their order of acquisition are shown in table 4.

There was enormous individual variation in the age of appearance of these morphemes, but as a guide, the first appeared at around age 1 year 10 months in one child and 2 years 10 months in another (MLU = 2.25), and the fourteenth appeared for the first time after age 2 years 3 months in the first child and after age 4 years in the other (MLU = 4.00). However, the *order* of acquisition, and the MLU at which forms emerged, were relatively invariant. It is important to recall that MLU and age are only roughly related, and there will be wide variations in the ages at which

*Table 4* The order of acquisition of the 14 grammatical morphemes (after Brown, 1973)

| Order | Morpheme |
|---|---|
| 1 | Present tense progressive **-ing** |
| 2/3 | Prepositions **in** and **on** |
| 4 | Plural **-s** |
| 5 | Past tense irregular e.g., **went** |
| 6 | Possessive **'s** |
| 7 | Uncontractible copula e.g., **is, was** |
| 8 | Articles **the** and **a** |
| 9 | Past tense regular **-ed** |
| 10 | Third person regular e.g., he walks |
| 11 | Third person irregular e.g., she **has** |
| 12 | Uncontractible auxiliary verb e.g., they **were** walking |
| 13 | Contractible copula e.g., he's a clown |
| 14 | Contractible auxiliary e.g., he's singing |

certain linguistic forms appear and are used. As previously stated, MLU is a more accurate guide than age to linguistic level.

Brown and his colleagues analysed speech samples from three children. For each child in the study, they deemed a morpheme had been acquired when the child used it correctly on 90 per cent of occasions when it ought to be used, according to correct adult usage. These were termed 'obligatory contexts'. During analysis, for example, occasions where pluralization ought to have occurred in the speech sample were identified. Then the actual speech, or morpheme, used or omitted by the child on those occasions was examined. If on 90 per cent or more of the occasions, the child produced a plural -s form, then the child was said to have acquired that form. After the 90 per cent criterion had been achieved for each morpheme, the subsequent grammatical and semantic developments were studied separately, with full mastery of some morphemes taking until children reached 9 or 10 years of age.

The study of morpheme acquisition provides other interesting evidence for the development of language (Peters, 1995). Paradoxically, one of the ways in which children show that they are acquiring the rules of grammar is by the mistakes that they make. One of the clearest examples of this is the **over-regularization** of irregular forms of verb tenses and plural forms even though the irregular form may have been in the child's existing repertoire. So, for example, children who had previously produced the correct versions of past tense verbs and plurals now produce such words as 'bringed' and 'goed' instead of 'brought' and 'went', and 'mouses' instead of 'mice'. These errors are taken as evidence that children are learning the rules for the regular past ending **-ed** and the plural **-s** respectively and applying these to all cases.

Some investigators have examined the emergence of Brown's 14 grammatical morphemes across a range of children (for example, de Villiers and de Villiers, 1973), while other researchers have concentrated on investigating the acquisition process of specific morphemes. In particular the acquisition of the prepositions 'in' and 'on' (and 'under') has been researched extensively (for example, Wilcox and Palermo, 1974; Clark, 1973b; Grieve, Hoogenraad and Murray, 1977), as have the articles 'the' and 'a' (Maratsos, 1976; Warden, 1976; Garton, 1982, 1983, 1984b). Unlike the other morphemes in Brown's list, except the prepositions, the articles are free morphemes, whereas all the others are bound inextricably to nouns or verbs. Studies of the prepositions and the articles have not only focused on the grammatical properties of these small words, but have also looked at the semantic properties and the developing uses of these words. The study of such morphemes provides interesting insights into the development of language, and we will briefly consider the research into article acquisition.

## *Article Acquisition*

Researchers studying the acquisition of the article system have looked at the ways in which young children learn about the different functions of 'the' and 'a'. The children studied are usually between 3 and 9 years of age, as mastery of all the functions is not found until the upper age limit (Maratsos, 1976; Warden, 1976). The article system is generally viewed as a contrastive system, whereby either 'the' or 'a' is required with a noun depending on conversational constraints and the meaning intended by the child.

The definite article, 'the', can be used when the object (or person or event) is known to both the speaker and the hearer. Objects become known mainly either through previous experience or previous introduction into the conversation. So 'the' is used when the referent has been made specific for both speaker and hearer. The indefinite article 'a' is used by a speaker to introduce a new object or event into the conversation, for example, 'There was **a** man walking down the street'. The indefinite article means a certain man is intended. This utterance can then be followed up with 'And then **the** man turned the corner', the man now being known to both speaker and hearer; the corner being presupposed by the existence of the (previously known) street. The indefinite article can also be used to name an object, 'That's **a** duck', meaning that is one particular duck, and further to refer to any one object as in the sentence 'Please may I have **a** pencil?' where any pencil is required.

Developmentally we can study how children learn the uses of these words by charting the emergence of correct uses and by the errors they make. Both Maratsos and Warden found what they called an egocentric use of the definite article in young children. They found children under the age of 9 years tended to use the definite article when the object or referent in their utterance was known only to themselves and not to their hearer. Young children are seemingly unable to take their hearer's lack of knowledge into account and consider only their own knowledge or perspective. Other systematic errors were also recorded in the uses of 'the' and 'a' as the children's grammatical system developed and as the contrastive article system was learned.

However, while this early research drew heavily on Brown's (1973) conceptualization of the articles as grammatical morphemes, one of which was required with each and every noun, subsequent work (Karmiloff-Smith, 1979b; Garton, 1983, 1984b) has looked at the articles and their acquisition in terms of the functions these words fulfil. Instead of tracing the emergence of 'the' and 'a' and their correct and incorrect uses in a grammatical sense, both Garton and Karmiloff-Smith conducted experiments aimed at eliciting a range of different uses of the articles and other determiners, such as the demonstratives 'this' and 'that'. For Karmiloff-Smith, the changing use of such terms during development is indicative of the more general endogenous process of the growth of knowledge.

Rather than being constrained by an adult model of the article system, Garton argued for adopting the child's perspective on the developing language and examining what article forms were used (and not used) in what contexts. Her studies showed that 3–year-old children were sensitive to adult language directed to them and, for example, that their article usage reflected the form of the question. In one experiment (Garton, 1984b), two different question forms ('What did the farmer do?' vs. 'What did the farmer knock over?') elicited different article forms from children, regardless of the class composition of the array of model animals used. On some instances, children were required to name the animals before questioning (to increase the possible use of the definite article for subsequent mention to an already identified animal).

The main result from this experiment was that after a **Do** question, 3–year-old children predominantly used the definite article ('the farmer knocked over **the** cow'), while after a **Knock over** question, responses mainly contained the indefinite article ('**a** cow'). These occurred regardless of whether the animals had been named first or not. As can be seen, the form of the children's responses varied after the two question types. Indeed, it was proposed that the tendency to respond with a particular sentential form was influenced by the type of question asked which in turn led to the form and function of the article produced. Thus the children were actually responding to the language directed to them and were being influenced in their productions by the nature of the input.

Because 3–year-old children were not totally consistent in their patterns of article use, it was claimed that the articles being produced did not correspond to adult usages. Garton (1983, 1984b) argued further that children's language ought to be described not in terms of what they can and cannot do *vis-à-vis* an adult model of correct language use, but regularities in children's use of the articles should be identified. In this way, it is possible to assess what functions the child is hypothesizing the articles fulfil. By regarding children as active hypothesis-testing learners of language, the systematicity and regularities the children are imposing on their use of the articles can shed some light on the ways in which children learn language. The case of the acquisition of the article system is but one exemplar of how we should be conducting research into aspects of language development.

## Negatives and Questions

Both the development of negation and the development of question forms in children have been extensively studied. Most studies have concentrated on the developing *use* of such forms in older children, although their expression prelinguistically has also been studied (for example, Carter, 1974; Pea, 1979). The two are frequently examined together as the developmental progression in their use tends to be regarded as similar (de Villiers, 1984). In this section, we are going to trace the emergence of the grammatical forms of negation and questions. The mastery of these grammatical devices is an accomplishment that usually takes place during the child's third year.

Klima and Bellugi (1966) described three broad stages in the development of negation. These developments began once children were around age 2 years, with an MLU of between 1.00 and 2.50. In Stage I, the child merely adds 'no' or 'not' to the word or proposition. Thus at age 2 years (MLU = 2.42) our son, Stephen, produced 'No tato', 'No done no', and 'Not teddy bear.'

In Stage II (around age 2 years 6 months, MLU = 3.00), children begin to incorporate negative forms into their sentences – internal negation. For example Stephen then produced 'I no want teddy' and 'That('s) not Stephen.' Furthermore, during this stage, words such as 'don't' and 'can't' appear in sentences. As neither 'can' nor 'do' were evident in the sample of speech collected by Brown at the time these negatives were recorded, it was inferred that the negatives 'can't' and 'don't' were being used as unitary words rather than as negative forms of 'can' and 'do'. Therefore, we find utterances such as 'Can't get that off' and 'Don't want my egg' (Stephen, age 2 years 5 months and 2 years 6 months respectively). Finally, in Stage III (around age 3 years 6 months, MLU = 4.00), children begin to master the rules for negation and incorporate the negative forms into negative sentences. The words 'don't' and 'can't' are used as negative auxiliaries with the negative placed correctly after the auxiliary in sentences, for example 'You can't whistle it' (Stephen, aged 2 years 9 months, MLU = 3.95). 'Not' is also correctly used instead of the earlier 'no', and for example, Stephen (aged 2 years 8 months) said 'Stephen's not hungry.'

Klima and Bellugi also studied the development of the question form and came up with a developmental sequence that roughly paralleled that of negation. There are two question forms in English. Yes/no questions require inversion of the auxiliary verb and the subject of the sentence, together with rising intonation, for example, 'Did you go to the bank today?', where 'did' and 'you' are inverted from their normal order and the answer to the question would be either 'yes' or 'no'. Wh- questions require a wh- word (such as what, where, who) at the beginning of the sentence, inversion of the auxiliary verb and subject (like yes/no questions) and rising intonation. The use of rising intonation is frequently taken as an indicator of a question in very young children, although the use of intonation is far from consistent (Halliday, 1975; Crystal, 1978).

In Stage I of the developmental sequence of question forms (child's age = 2 years; MLU = approximately 2.00), yes/no questions emerge as simple sentences with rising intonation. At around the same time, simple **wh-** questions, typically with 'where' and 'what', appear, with the Wh- word attached to the beginning of the sentence, for example, 'What daddy doing?' and 'Where man go?' (Stephen, age 1 year 10 months and 1 year 11 months respectively). Interestingly, children ask many more 'where' questions than 'what' questions, possibly because they are understood and more easily answered than 'what' questions, which inversely, may be more difficult.

In Stage II (approximate age 2 years 6 months, MLU = 3.00), 'why' questions appear ('Why he get paid for?' – Stephen, 2 years 7 months), and there is little change in the use of yes/no questions. Finally, in Stage III (age 3 years 6 months, MLU = 4.00), there is inversion of the subject and auxiliary firstly in yes/no questions – 'Is budgie gone?' (Stephen, age 2 years 8 months) – and then later in **wh-** questions. So eventually, children produce such questions as 'What's this over here?', 'Which school am I going (to)?' and 'Where's the orange hat gone?' (Stephen, age 2 years 11 months).

Clearly, having the use of negatives and interrogatives increases children's communicative ability, although many studies show that words like 'no' have a range of functions from their first usage (usually during the one-word period). De Villiers (1984) compared emerging forms and functions of both negatives and interrogatives, analysing many previous studies to test several hypotheses regarding their development. She used a framework adopted from linguistics (speech act theory) to review how form and function inter-relate during development, and how communicative development is continuous. While it is possible to describe what functions are fulfilled by certain forms of both negatives and interrogatives, it is far more difficult to describe what forms are serving the functions of negation and questioning for the young child, particularly in the early stages of linguistic development.

Possibly due to methodological differences, very few consistent examples of form/function mapping in parental speech were found across the studies reviewed by de Villiers. That is, parents did not always use a question form where the intention was to question the child, nor did they use negative forms consistently. Other words such as 'rarely' were used to serve the function of negation. Therefore children are not being exposed to consistent forms for the expression of negation and interrogation. The variety of both negative and question forms reported seemed surprising to de Villiers, implying she had expected much clearer mapping between straightforward grammatical forms such as 'not' and their functions as negatives.

## Ask, Tell and Promise

When Stephen was aged 3 years 6 months, we were living in University accommodation that came complete with a gardening service. One day, the gardener was mowing the lawn and Stephen was watching. When Stephen came in from the garden he announced 'That man told me my name'. By this he meant 'that man *asked* me my name', which was what had in fact happened (and we assume Stephen answered appropriately). From utterances such as these we realize that children have difficulties with sentences with 'tell' and 'ask' in them, and may become confused between them. These grammatical constructions are fairly complicated and are the source of many errors in children's language. Carol Chomsky (1969) reported a series of studies she undertook to examine the understanding 5- to 10-year-old children had of some of the more complex structures of language.

Chomsky carried out detailed studies of 'ask' and 'tell' where she compared the following pairs of sentences (alternatives are given in parentheses):

1   Ask (tell) Fred what time it is.
2   Ask (tell) Fred what your name is.
3   Ask (tell) Fred what to feed the doll.

Children were required to respond to Fred (a puppet) according to the instructions given by the experimenter. Developmentally, the sequence of acquisition was firstly where children interpreted both 'ask' and 'tell' as 'tell' in all three sentence types, so they told Fred what the time was, their own names and 'bread and butter' respectively. Then sentence type 1 was sorted out, followed by sentence type 2 and finally sentence type 3. In the 'ask' version of the final type of sentence, children tended to ask Fred 'What are you going to feed the doll?' instead of 'What should I feed the doll?'. By the age of 9 or 10 years, children were able to respond correctly to both versions of all three sentence types.

Consider now the following alternative sentences:

1    Donald tells Bozo to hop.
2a   Donald asks Bozo to hop.
2b   Donald asks Bozo (for permission) to hop.
3    Donald promises Bozo to hop.

Chomsky employed the assistance of two puppets, Donald (Duck) and Bozo, that were required to perform the various actions as directed by the language. Chomsky used these and equivalent sentences to study how children interpret different complement structures. The children were instructed with sentences containing 'ask', 'tell' or 'promise'. Structurally all these sentences look the same, they all seemingly take an object (Bozo) and a complement verb (to hop). The following interaction then occurred during an experiment (and luckily the child spoke during the session!):

*Adult:*   "Donald tells Bozo to hop across the table. Can you make him hop?"

*Child (aged 6 years 9 months):*   "Bozo, hop across the table."

*Adult:*   "Bozo promises Donald to do a somersault. Can you make him do it?"

*Child   (making Donald do the somersault):*   "I promised you you can do a somersault."

(Chomsky, 1969, p. 40)

In the above example, the child interprets 'tell' correctly and manipulates Bozo, the complement of the first instructive sentence. But in interpreting 'promise' in the same way, the child makes an error and makes Donald perform the somersault not Bozo, while also producing an agrammatical sentence, showing the confusion. Children make this mistake up to around the age of 8 years.

Chomsky invoked the **minimum distance principle** to illustrate the differences between 'ask', 'tell' and 'promise' sentences and the sources of difficulty for children. This principle states that in sentences such as 'Donald tells Bozo to hop', the complement verb, to hop, relates to the nearest noun on the left of it in the sentence, in this case, Bozo. Thus, the verb 'tell' follows the minimum distance principle in so far as the complement verb relates to the nearest noun phrase to its left, namely Bozo. So Bozo, the individual, is being told to hop. 'Ask', however, may or may not follow the minimum distance principle – it does in example 2a, but not in 2b where 'ask' is used in the request form. Thus, any verb that is a **command** ('tell', 'order', 'compel') follows the minimum distance principle while a **request** verb such as 'beg' does not. 'Promise' is different from both these verb types because the complement verb relates to the subject of the sentence, never the object. Therefore in sentence 3, it is Donald who has to do the leaving, not Bozo.

Chomsky proposed four stages in the development of correct understanding of 'promise'. Firstly, the minimum distance principle is applied to all examples (of 'ask', 'tell' and 'promise') that are structurally similar. Secondly, children realize there are exceptions to the principle (like 'promise') but make errors on instances consonant with the principle as well as the exceptions. Thirdly, the minimum distance principle is applied correctly to those verbs like 'tell' correctly, but it is not until the fourth stage that there is correct performance on all words including 'ask' and 'promise'.

Other sentence types studied by Chomsky were those where the subject of the sentence on the surface is not the subject in the grammatical structure. Using a blindfolded doll, children were asked 'Is the doll easy or hard to see?'. Five-year-olds interpreted this as 'hard', and to make it 'easy', they removed the doll's blindfold. By the age of 9 years, children could understand this type of sentence correctly.

While replication of Chomsky's work on 'ask' and 'tell' has been undertaken, the results and their interpretation are not in complete agreement (for example, Carraher and Spinillo, 1984). An interesting debate between Warden (1981, 1986) and Chomsky (1982) centred on the basis – syntactic, semantic or pragmatic – by which young children interpret these words. Warden argued that the issue is fundamentally a methodological one. Until we can adopt a contextual perspective, where the child's knowledge of a word's meaning is tapped across a variety of situations and uses, then we cannot assume a misinterpretation or an error implies that the child's ability is insufficiently developed. Warden further argued that Chomsky's approach and interpretation were too narrow and limited, and risked underestimating the child's language ability. Researchers should examine how children understand and use, misunderstand and misuse the word(s) under scrutiny before making claims about language ability. This point echoes one made by Garton (1983, 1984b) in relation to the study of the acquisition of 'the' and 'a' in young children and which was discussed earlier in this chapter.

The studies that have looked at the development of complex language structures after the age of 3 years indicate that there are still aspects being acquired (see K. Durkin, 1986). It is inadequate to examine *only* syntactic, or structural, development, as many linguistic, social and cognitive factors are involved. Karmiloff-Smith (1986a) believed the most fundamental change in language after the age of 5 years is that linguistic categories change function. Instead of operating at the level of the sentence, linguistic categories span extended discourse, linking structures and themes across sentences and paragraphs. Before tying together all aspects of later language development, it is necessary to examine some of the research on semantic development alone, independent of grammatical development, in children after the age of 2 or 3 years.

## Later Semantic Development

While the meanings of words are not divorced from their structure, historically the two aspects were studied independently. Early attempts to study semantic development were made via an examination of vocabulary growth. As children's vocabulary increased and became more discriminating, researchers proposed 'dictionaries' to characterize this growth. Children's vocabulary development was likened to dictionary entries, whereby additional words are entered (that is, learned) on the basis of their similarity and difference in meaning to previous words.

Other researchers simply counted the rate of expansion of the child's vocabulary, although this technique does not allow much to be inferred about the way the child is interpreting the world. For example, synonyms such as 'seat' and 'chair' are included as two words, although they may have nearly identical meanings. Inversely, homophones (for example, 'pair' and 'pear') may be erroneously included as one word, not two. However, vocabulary size serves only as a gross indicator of language development.

One rather interesting way in which we can examine the meanings children attribute to words is to test their ability to relate double meanings.

For example, Asch and Nerlove (1960), in a classic study, examined double function words such as 'sweet', 'hard', and 'warm', which can be used to describe the physical property of an object *and* the psychological property of an individual. Asch and Nerlove claimed that there was a relationship between the two properties because when applied to a person, appropriate physical images, related to our senses, were conjured up.

In the experiment conducted by Asch and Nerlove, 3– to 10–year-old children were presented with objects and requested to say if they could be described as hard, or warm, or sweet. If the children answered 'Yes', they were then asked if such a word could be used to describe a person. If the children then agreed to this, they were asked to specify the relationship between the two meanings.

An age-related trend in levels of understanding was noted. At 3 and 4 years of age, children agreed that objects could be described with the adjectives, but many doubted and even denied that such words could describe people. Between 5 and 6 years of age, the children applied the words to physical attributes of people, for example, 'the lady has cold hands'. By 7 and 8 years of age, children agreed that the words could be applied to psychological properties of people (for example, 'the baby has sweet little toes'), but were unsure why. It was not until children were around 9 and 10 years old that they were able to use the double function words correctly in both contexts and to specify the relationship between them. The study of non-literal language, or double function terms, enables examination of the strategies used by children while learning word meaning by looking at both the correct *and* incorrect meanings attributed to such words.

From this work, it has been concluded that children firstly learn applications of double function words separately, then later realize the inter-relationship between them. That is, word meaning is firstly learned in isolation, with relations between meanings developing later once similarities between language structures and functions are recognized. This conclusion has found substantiation in the work of Karmiloff-Smith (1979b) who described the unifunctional application of words in French-speaking children (such as the indefinite and definite articles, *un/une* and *le/la*) prior to a system of plurifunctionality emerging, as children learn relationships between words and meanings. It is likely that such developments in a semantic system stem not only from the child's increased language development but also from the child's increased knowledge about the world, the child's increased cognitive development, and development of the child's awareness of the structures and functions of language (Karmiloff-Smith, 1986b). In this way, it is possible to speculate that children are learning to distinguish among people, events and objects in the environment (in the sense of a socio-historico-cultural context) when they are learning to use words meaningfully. Both the meanings attributed and the meanings understood are derived from and contextualized in the child's ever-expanding social world.

Further work on how children ascribe and understand meaning has been undertaken in some more recent studies of children's understanding of non-literal language, specifically double function terms, usually presented as metaphoric expressions (Wales and Coffey, 1986; Kogan and Chadrow, 1986; Vosniadou, 1987; Gentner, 1988; Gentner and Ratterman, 1991). Gentner (1988) considered the anomaly noted between young children's apparent fluent production of metaphoric language and their difficulties understanding experimentally presented similes which she refers to as metaphors. She believed that part of children's difficulty lies in the fact that those metaphors commonly produced are based on common *object* attributes and on appearance. For example, children will produce such metaphors as 'The hose is like a snake' because they are both long and skinny. Metaphors based on common *relational* attributes are more difficult, and are typically those used by adults and in experiments. The commonalities intended are not based on appearance, and an example would be 'Her happiness was like the sunshine', as both radiate out warmth.

Gentner conducted a series of experiments with both children and adults and found that relational interpretations for metaphors were increasingly given with age. Five- and 6–year-old children produced far more object attribution interpretations than relational interpretations for the metaphors, regardless of whether they were attributional, relational or double (both relational and attributional) metaphors. She concluded that for children what develops is a specific tendency to interpret metaphors relationally, as adults predominantly do. She hypothesized three accounts for this shift. Firstly, the child's cognitive competence might be increasing, or secondly, children are learning the pragmatic conventions of how to interpret metaphors. Both of these hypotheses she discounted in preference for an explanation that stated there is a shift to relational interpretations during development as children learn more about different domains. Thus familiarity with, for example, the spatial domain would mean metaphors in that domain would be interpreted relationally prior to metaphors in another domain.

Expansion and confirmation of the relational shift are claimed to add to its importance theoretically. The child's ability to process similarities based on object commonalities precedes the use of relational commonalities. This shift can account for experimental results in metaphor production and interpretation. Broadening the focus to the child's developing understanding of similarity (appearance, analogy, as well as metaphor), again three hypotheses are offered (Gentner and Ratterman, 1991) to account for the relational shift noted in children's productions and understanding of such cognitive organizing principles. The first, that it reflects a general developmental or maturational change, has received support from the work of others (see, Goswami's, 1991, work on analogies). The second hypothesis is that the relational shift reflects the acquisition of domain knowledge, as discussed above and favoured by Gentner in earlier accounts. Thirdly, learned mapping strategies may produce performance differences due to differences in experience and practice. This account is discounted as it is not widely supported. After a comprehensive survey and analysis of the experimental evidence, Gentner and Ratterman (1991) conclude that the acquisition of domain knowledge is the most powerful determinant of an understanding of similarity. However, they also add that the use of language to describe similarity (such as the words 'same' and 'different') may also be an important precursor to an understanding of the relations expressed in metaphor and analogy.

Wales (1993) also extended the work on metaphor – going beyond the literal – to focus on the relationship between syntax and semantics and the child's cognitive abilities, which might impose constraints on understanding. Drawing on the work by Vosniadou (1987), Wales claimed that while it is clear children can use and understand some forms of metaphor before others, this has no implications for claiming a relationship with the development of cognitive abilities. What now needs to happen, according to Wales, is a disentangling of the relative influence of the application of domain specific knowledge and/or inference rules applied across linguistic processes, before we can proceed to an explanation of the child's developing production and understanding of metaphor. Both of these (domain-specific knowledge and application of inference rules), viewed as constraints, may operate and Wales urged a multidisciplinary approach to tackle this issue and clarify how an understanding of children's developing use and understanding of non-literal language can contribute to knowledge of semantic development both theoretically and empirically.

## The Role of the Child in Later Language Development

If one is concerned with the processes involved in language acquisition and the child's active role in the development of language, then a number of the studies just described, particularly the earlier ones, are not addressing this issue. It is not very helpful to study either grammar *or* meaning in isolation. One should examine language where both the structure of the sentence, say, and the meaning contribute to correct understanding and use. Thus we now turn to consider studies where the child is regarded as an active contributor to language learning. Relevant studies are those that acknowledge (implicitly at least) that language use can be difficult or ambiguous on some occasions. The difficulties sometimes lie in the language structures used and sometimes in the meaning. The child must actively work on the language to extract meaning. The studies that are described also call attention to the fact that syntax and semantics are more intimately related than has been suggested up to now.

### Active and Passive Sentences

The study of children's understanding of active and passive sentences allows for the examination of the active processing of both syntax and semantics in language development (for example, Slobin, 1966; Herriot, 1969; Olson and Filby, 1972). Typically in these studies, an active sentence ('The dog chases the kitten') and a passive sentence ('The kitten is chased by the dog') were judged against an appropriate picture. For young children, the truth of active sentences was more often judged accurately since these sentences corresponded to the form depicted and are in the usual word order. The truth value of passive sentences was more difficult to establish.

Other studies (for example, Grieve and Wales, 1973) have pointed out that passive sentences can be **reversible** ('The cat is being chased by the dog') where the subject and object are interchangeable, **non-reversible** ('The kitten was carried by the girl'), or short, **truncated** ('The kitten was chased'). Young children, up to about age 5, have greater difficulty interpreting reversible passives since, as in the example given above, both the subject and the object are capable of performing the action. Thus, these sentences require understanding of the syntactic form (active vs. passive) plus understanding of the possible roles of the subject and object, itself related to the semantics of the verb (is it reversible or not?). The research studies have shown that it is not until children are aged about 10 years that they can fully understand the different types of passive sentences. Such constructions are similar to the 'easy to see' construction used by Carol Chomsky and discussed earlier, in that the first noun in the sentence is not necessarily the agent of the action in the verb.

These studies provide evidence that children are actively involved in extracting meaning from the language spoken to them and are using both syntactic and semantic knowledge, as well as pragmatic knowledge, to interpret the language. When faced with a passive sentence which presents some syntactic difficulty, the child turns to use semantic knowledge to gain access to the meaning. The child will then respond to the sentence according to current knowledge of the world. For example, the two sentences 'the man was carried by the fireman' and 'the ladder was carried by the fireman' are reversible and non-reversible passives respectively. In interpreting the latter sentence, children know that firemen carry ladders and not vice versa. So when faced with a sentence containing the elements 'fireman', 'ladder' and 'carry', children derive meaning for the sentence from their knowledge of the world, regardless of the meanings of individual words and regardless of the syntactic form. Reversible passives (such as 'the man was carried by the fireman' and 'the fireman was carried by the man') cannot be interpreted from semantic or pragmatic knowledge. The interpretation must be made at the syntactic level, specifically using clues based on word order. Under normal circumstances however, children will apply both their syntactic *and* pragmatic knowledge to get access to the semantics of sentences, that is, when trying to get the meaning.

Sudhalter and Braine (1985) studied children's understanding of passive sentences where the relevant verbs were either **actional** (for example, verbs denoting physical actions, such as spill, knock, hit) or **experiential** (for example, know, remember, see). Children ranging in age from 4 to 10 years of age were questioned about the actor and the experiencer in various passive and active sentences. They found that all children consistently found the actional passives easier than the experiential ones. Developmentally, they found that comprehension of the passive takes place gradually. It is not an all-or-none affair, but rather there is a slow increase in comprehension with the actional verbs leading the experiential verbs. Children's knowledge of the passive is therefore built up slowly, and Sudhalter and Braine suggested that mastery of the passive requires linguistic knowledge that is accumulated during childhood.

## Narratives

Another area of later language development that has been studied is how children understand and tell stories which require the linking of ideas and concepts across extended time (Karmiloff-Smith, 1985, 1986a). Sentences are rarely isolated from other sentences, and ideas are often developed in extended conversations or stories. There have therefore been studies of children's production of narratives and the linking of ideas across extended discourse. Karmiloff-Smith reported a study in which 4- to 9-year-old children were required to tell stories from sequences of pictures, presented without accompanying text. Some of the sequences had a clear central character with a lesser character of the same sex; some had two opposite sex characters and some three; some stories had no clear linking. The design was such that in some cases there was potential for ambiguity between pronouns (where two males were the characters for example), while in other cases, there was no ambiguity. Other manipulations were included to vary the means of linking the pictures. By examining how children link the pictures in their stories using their language, a developmental progression in the means available for establishing and maintaining **discourse cohesion** can be charted.

To begin with, at around age 5, children seemed to make clear, well constructed stories. However, Karmiloff-Smith argued the stories were not integrated as children described each successive picture independently. After age 5, there was evidence that some cohesion was being established, as children introduced pronouns correctly. She cited as an example 'There's a boy and a girl. He's going fishing and she's going to make sandcastles' (1986a, p. 470). As the children got older, the narrative developed as a single thematic unit, children choosing one character as the main subject. An example of a narrative as a structured unit is 'There is a boy and a girl. He's going to catch fish so he takes the girl's bucket and he runs off and catches lots of fish' (Karmiloff-Smith, 1986a, p. 470). While this story is lacking in detail, it is thematically cohesive and unambiguous. It is not until children are around 8 or 9 that they can link stories internally, obeying the thematic subject constraint but introducing detail and variation through differential linguistic markers such as noun phrases ('the boy') and pronouns, and using linking devices such as 'and' and 'so'. For example, 'There's a boy and a girl. The boy wants to go fishing, so he tries to get the girl's bucket, but the girl won't let him take it, so he grabs it out of her hand' (p. 471).

From these, and other similar examples, Karmiloff-Smith showed how we must not regard the 5-year-olds' seemingly correct use of language as being the endpoint of spoken language development. Rather, research should, as Karmiloff-Smith herself has done (and see also Spinillo and Pinto, 1994), examine how children deal with extended discourse, examine how they make reference, and look at their errors and corrections, so that we can indicate where older children might have difficulty with their spoken language.

More recent research has been examining the narrative skills of young children, in relation to elicitation of narrative by parents and in relation to corrections during narration. Parental elicitation of narratives has been claimed to be important because of the value of such narratives in the social transmission of cultural mores as well as their relation to later literacy acquisition (Peterson and McCabe, 1992). While cross-cultural variation is noted in the structure of narratives, differences in skill levels within cultural groups are also recorded. In order to account for such individual differences, research has been examining the role of parental elicitation. Peterson and McCabe's research has been investigating parental narrative style over both extended discourse and time periods and how variations in narrative style are linked to the structure and form of the narratives created by children. In general they found close correspondence between parental elicitation techniques (such as questions) and child narrative skill. So, for example, a mother who repeatedly requested information about people, events or places lead the child also to stress such specifications in the narratives produced. This research emphasizes the interactive nature of parent–child communication, reflected in similarities of discourse form from age 2 years upwards.

Trabasso, Stein, Rodkin, Park, Munger and Baughn (1992) investigated 3- to 9-year-old children's narratives, elicited by a pictorial sequence, specifically to examine how planning can be manifested by more cohesion in the narratives produced. Younger children apparently interpreted the task as one of communicating information about isolated characters or actions, while, with increasing age, there was greater evidence of adherence to a superordinate plan, linking the actions and objects. A second study, involving mothers telling stories to their children, was conducted, since the predominance of descriptions in the younger children's attempts at story telling may have been a function of the non-social nature of the task. However, results of the interactions between mothers and their 2½-year-old children revealed that the questions asked by mothers tended to elicit names of objects or actions or yes/no responses. A shift with increasing age of the child was noted in more sophisticated encoding of events and actions in both the questions used by mothers and in the children's responses. This suggested 'that mothers' questions took into account the cognitive and linguistic skills of their children in the task, that their descriptive and identification skills are fostered in such interactions, and that children's narrations reflect a history of interactive, communicative context with adults' (p. 153).

Hickmann and Schneider (1993), on the other hand, have investigated children's ability to recover from errors made during discourse, with a view to establishing how children are able to restore discourse cohesion during story telling. This work drew on the research conducted on both article use (see earlier section) and on narratives, and aimed to assess whether or not children's restoration of discourse cohesion (via correct use of articles) depended on conscious awareness. Self-repairs are claimed to reflect awareness of what children spontaneously perceive to be errors, while elicited comments about language use are usually extracted after

completion of the story. The work by Hickmann and Schneider examined the processing of stories where the target noun phrases were either
appropriate or inappropriate (in terms of article usage) and where children's monitoring was spontaneous or elicited. In general, they found
that children from age 5 years showed remarkable sensitivity to inappropriate references as evidenced through correct modifications of some
anomalous usages. Age differences were noted in the increasing reliance
on the discourse context with age, with on-line spontaneous correction
increasing after age 5 years. Finally, awareness of the cohesive functions
of noun phrases (specifically involving the articles) was a later development, consistent with previous work by Karmiloff-Smith (1986a, 1986b).

Awareness of discourse functions was studied by Karmiloff-Smith and
colleagues (Karmiloff-Smith, Johnson, Grant, Jones, Karmiloff, Bartrip
and Cuckle, 1993) who examined both children's and adults' knowledge
of the cohesive properties of discourse. Knowledge was equated with
metalinguistic awareness, that is, the development of an explicit theory
about language, specifically about the constraints that operate at a sentence and a discourse level. Repair data were the objects of study, specifically lexical, referential and discourse repairs to stories (narratives), both
spontaneous and elicited. An ingenious experiment involving both
reaction time and a structured metalinguistic interview was conducted,
with children from age 7 years to 11 years of age, and adults. Overall, the
experiment demonstrated that repair detection improved with age, although all age groups detected all three categories of repair with ease.
The metalinguistic awareness data, collected after the reaction time data
and after repeated hearing of the stories (albeit modified to some extent),
indicated whether the repairs were appropriate or not, based on the level
of sophistication of explanation provided. All subjects gave high levels of
appropriate responses to lexical and referential repairs; strikingly lesser
numbers gave appropriate explanations for discourse repairs. Karmiloff-
Smith et al. interpreted this latter result as showing that discourse, lexical
and referential repairs are distinguished, and that the differences are due
to two different linguistic functions (one at the sentential, propositional
level and one at the discourse level) being encoded by the same linguistic
marker simultaneously, thus competing for on-line processing resources.
A developmental perspective then allows for the acquisition of conscious
awareness of the two levels. Karmiloff-Smith et al. then discussed a
complex model to account for the developmental progression proposed,
enabling discourse-level processing to emerge only after sentential processing, the latter occurring in real time, the former when automaticity
has been reached in propositional processing. The importance of this research is noted in the use of repair data to demonstrate how narratives are

constructed by children, and how structural changes occur during development.

## Cognitive Verbs

Torrance and Olson (1985) found a clear association between structural aspects of children's spoken language development and learning to read. They found that children's use of 'cognitive' verbs such as 'know', 'think', and 'remember', correlated highly with subsequent reading ability. They believed that reading and writing (as school-based learning activities) actually encouraged children to distinguish the form of language as it is spoken and as it is used to convey meaning. This distinction is referred to as the say/mean distinction (Olson, 1977). The literal meaning of what we say is not always what we *mean*. This can be illustrated with the utterance 'It's cold in here' which can mean 'Please shut the door' in some contexts. The surface form does not correspond with what is intended, though the action of shutting the door will presumably prevent the room from getting any colder. We do not always mean literally what we say – there is sometimes an implied or inferred meaning intended. Interpretation of a speaker's intended meaning requires knowledge about language, as well as knowledge about social conventions and pragmatics. This will be discussed in the section on understanding the processes of communication in chapter 6. With the learning of written language, many of these issues in spoken language become more apparent, since the child learns how to read literal and non-literal text and learns about writing text. It is claimed that written language development therefore facilitates an understanding of the say/mean distinction.

In their study of children's use of cognitive verbs and early achievement in reading, Torrance and Olson proposed three hypotheses to account for the existence of the link. Firstly, they speculated that good readers might use more cognitive verbs because, in general, they used more complex syntax anyway. A good reader might simply have a greater level of competence with complex structures of the language. While descriptively this may well be so, it does not make any predictions however about how such an accomplishment might be associated with better reading. Secondly, they proposed that cognitive verbs might reflect greater knowledge of vocabulary in general, as vocabulary development has been associated with early reading. Again, descriptively this hypothesis is tenable, but it makes no predictions about the nature of the relationship.

Finally, Torrance and Olson presented what they believe is the best explanatory hypothesis to account for the link between use of cognitive verbs and good reading. In this hypothesis they claimed cognitive verbs are regarded as part of a conceptual system for decontextualizing language and thought. Understanding of the say/mean distinction is a prerequisite to reading because as children come to appreciate that there are ways of saying things that are perhaps better representations than others of what is meant, then they can choose the appropriate psychological commitment to express what was said. These psychological commitments are expressed through metacognitive verbs such as 'believe', 'know', 'think' and 'doubt'.

The acquisition of cognitive verbs (sometimes referred to as metacognitive words when applied to nouns), that is, words that signal beliefs, desires, thoughts and so on, reflects the child's mental state. The language both monitors and permits access to internal states as well as allowing the understanding of communication about the internal states, or cognitive processing, of others. Children acquire the terminology because they want to express these internal states (of thinking, knowing and believing) as well as allowing them to define and distinguish between them.

The study of cognitive verbs is also important because of the insight into children's semantic development (Booth and Hall, 1995; Tomasello and Merriman, 1995). Verbs are quite different to nouns since they represent quite complex syntactic information as well as requiring agreement with the grammatical and relational aspects of the sentence in which they are contained. Research has therefore examined children's understanding of mental state verbs in relation both to theories of lexical acquisition and of knowledge acquisition as well as to the development of theory of mind, that is, an ability to explain and predict the mental states of the self and of others. Cognitive verbs label such acts and signal in some ways children's capacity to recognize and act on such things as 'knowing', believing' and 'thinking'.

Distinguishing between cognitive verbs and behavioural verbs not only requires that children understand the distinction between what is meant and what is said, but also that their knowledge can be represented at the mental level and the overt, behavioural level. Researchers debate over exactly when the distinction between mental state knowledge and overt knowledge, between meaning and saying, appears developmentally and what are its manifestations (see Astington, Harris and Olson, 1988; Wellman, 1990). It seems that the overt distinction as marked by appropriate use of cognitive verbs occurs quite late, sometime during the early school years, even though the use of such verbs has been found in early vocabulary of children (Shatz, Wellman and Silber, 1983). Experimentally, Wellman and his colleagues have found a distinction between 'know' versus 'think' or 'guess' by 4 years of age (Johnson and Wellman, 1980), while the latter distinction (between 'think' and 'guess') may not be fully appreciated until around age 8 (Moore, Bryant and Furrow, 1989) but with some understanding developing around age 6 years (Ziatas, Durkin and Pratt, 1998).

Because these language structures do not emerge (or at least are not distinguished satisfactorily) until children are over the age of 5, it has been claimed that there is a link between their acquisition and learning to read. It has been claimed that is precisely mastery of the syntax and semantics of these mentalist or cognitive verbs that enables the detachment of language as it is spoken from language as it is intended. Such detachment is then crucial for reading development. However, so far the evidence has largely been retrospective as in the case of Olson and his colleagues who tried to uncover the special skills of good readers. A prospective study would enable closer scrutiny of the emergence of cognitive verbs and beginning reading, taking into account the influence of schooling if necessary.

Not only are structural advances in language development necessary for reading development, but it may be that communication skills are also essential. Torrance and Olson claimed that the conversational, discourse aspects of language use were not related to reading ability. It was argued that the social, interactional uses of language were not necessary for later reading success. In the next chapter, we intend to show that this dismissal might be premature. It may be both a semantic and syntactic component *plus* a pragmatic, communicative component are needed, before literacy is achieved.

## Synthesis and Implications

Charting the development of spoken language, both grammar and the meanings of words, in children from around age 2 through to the early school years has important implications for the broader study of literacy if only because it has enabled us to realize that children's spoken language development is not complete on their entry to school. Children between the ages of 3 and 8 years still have many of the structural aspects of language to master. The research reviewed here, in conjunction with the fact, as we shall see in the next chapter, that children have not yet learned all the skills of communication, would indicate that they have much to learn about the forms and functions of language. Although we marvel at the magnitude of children's language use at the point of school entry, as clearly they have learned a great deal about language in a relatively short period of time, they still have a great deal more to learn. The years from age 5 onwards must be regarded as a time when language skills are consolidated and expanded.

What are these additional developments, viewed especially from the learning of the forms of language, in general theoretical terms? It might be that children's cognitive strategies (language, perception, memory) are increasing so that additional information can be dealt with more efficiently. Or it may be that children develop an increased ability to *apply* already existing strategies more widely. It may well be difficult or even undesirable to separate these two issues, and perhaps each is partly true.

There are two important developments in addition to the child's achievements with spoken language. One of the major developments that *does* occur is the child's increased ability to think and talk about language. The child's increased ability to use language not just for spoken communication but as a representation system for reading and writing enables the child to become a more sophisticated user of language. This ability will be discussed in chapter 7. Further, the child's social communicative skills are increasing, enabling conversations to take on a more adult-like quality. The next chapter will consider this latter aspect in greater detail as there are many different ways of looking at communication and the strategies involved in making and breaking conversations.

# CHAPTER SIX

# Communicating with Language

This chapter considers the **pragmatic** aspects of spoken language, that is, the ways in which language is used in social communication. The focus will be on the child as a **communicator** and an active conversationalist. The previous chapters have described the development of the skills of talking in an understandable manner in children up to about the age of 8 years. Emphasis was placed on the *social* nature of language, especially during the acquisition process. Children are regarded as having completed or nearly completed their language learning when their speech is adult-like in terms of the words used and correctness of the grammar, at least in a formal sense (which ironically is often judged by their reading and writing skills, not their colloquial use of language in everyday situations). This social perspective is maintained when we consider children as communicators or conversationalists, in interaction with others – parents, peers and teachers – while being observed in natural environments or while participating in experimental research.

Children, particularly very young children, probably understand much less of the language spoken to them than we actually assume. We are often impressed by the extent of young children's comprehension of the language spoken to them. They understand key words and phrases and they do this by relying heavily on the context to try to work out what is being said to them, often subsequently and not surprisingly, producing errors of interpretation. Clark and Clark (1977, p. 486) reported, among other examples, a child announcing that germs are 'something the flies play with', as a result of hearing her mother saying 'We have to keep the screen door closed honey so the flies won't come in. Flies bring germs into the house with them.' The child, on the basis of this information, tried to work out the meaning of the word 'germ'. Examples such as this one show clearly how children actively try to interpret the language they hear and to make sense of it. Children use the context of the language to work out its meaning. At the crux of this interpretative process is communication between the child and another person.

In focusing on communication, this chapter examines conversation, in which individuals talk to share and exchange information. Communication can take many forms, including face-to-face conversation, teaching or lecturing, using the telephone and morse code. A distinction between the **skills** and the **processes** of communication should be made. The skills of language are those linguistic abilities children develop as they become increasingly competent at talking, while the processes of communication refer to how children become active conversationalists, obeying the social conventions governing appropriate language use in different situations. Although the present focus will be exclusively on spoken language, there are several important implications for reading and writing. For example, the development of appropriate conversation skills (including question and answer routines, and the markers of colloquial style) and an understanding of communication processes (for example, the negotiation of shared meaning) will influence a child's later understanding of and ability to write (for example, a narrative story with dialogue).

In many ways, the child is continuing to learn those social conventions regarding the uses of language that began in early infancy. In previous chapters, we described the development of early communication skills in children up to around 2 years of age. We described the functions of infants' cries, the functions of formats as interactional structures that facilitate language and how mother–child interaction can assist in language learning. We now describe the development of communication skills in children from 2 or 3 years of age to 8 or 9 years of age. The emphasis will be on the types of language used in effective conversation, where 'effective' refers to the social, playful or educational (in both its broadest and narrowest senses) functions of such verbal exchanges. Communication skills will be considered in three contexts, the home, the preschool (or nursery school), and the primary school classroom. The different demands of these three contexts will be compared and contrasted. The areas of research interest are parent (usually mother)–child interaction (some of which has already been touched on in the research on the processes of early language acquisition); the transition from parent–child to peer interaction and communication; the comparison between language at home and language in educational settings; and language in the primary school classroom.

The second part of the chapter will deal with the child's understanding of the processes of spoken communication and some important research areas will be described. These will not necessarily be described in relation to children's age or developing linguistic abilities. We are going to consider children's developing ability to deal with communication failure and, not unrelated, the distinction between *saying* something and *meaning* something. We will further examine how children negotiate shared meaning in conversation with others. Some recent work that takes account of the social aspects of communication will also be discussed. We will then examine children's developing ability to use different language forms (such as direct versus indirect requests for information), and the relationship of these different forms of language to the child's developing knowledge of interpersonal and social conventions. Finally children's language use in social problem solving will be described and the importance of communication for language and cognitive development discussed (Garton, 1992).

## Early Communication

### Parent–Child Interaction and the Development of Communication

It is clear that once children begin talking, they are already active participants in social interactions. They actively contribute to the interaction, using their existing communicative resources. They employ particular strategies for communicating with adults, strategies which lay the basis for future language use. Wells (1981) emphasized the importance of **conversation**, the normal type of linguistic interaction that one can describe. By focusing on conversations between mothers and their young children, Wells tried to unravel some of the mysteries surrounding the development of communication.

Wells believed it was vital that we look at some of the more subtle aspects of conversations that children must learn. Some of these characteristics are learned prelingually, enabling subsequent conversations to become more focused on the language. For example, children have to learn about turn-taking. That is, they have to know when it is and when it is not appropriate to make a contribution to a conversation. Children can learn the nonlinguistic cues that are used to signify the start or end of a turn in a conversation, or even of a conversation. These can be learned **before** actually learning the language.

French and Woll (1981) suggested that the role of language in conversations is **constitutive**. By this they meant that language and the context in which it is spoken are very closely related and each is created by the other. By saying that the context constitutes the language, they meant that during conversation, the participants rely on the use of context to work out the meaning of each other's utterances. In other words, the meaning of the language is worked out in and by the situation in which the conversation was taking place. They also meant that the context is constituted by the language of the conversational participants. That is, the conversation and the situation of its occurrence take on meaning from the language used. Using conversations between parents and their children as their data base, French and Woll examined how social interactional relationships are constituted through and by the conversations. They argued that it was via such interactions, where linguistic and nonlinguistic contextual cues are used by both participants, that children came to learn about language.

French and Woll provided examples of how children used strategies in conversations for gaining access to the conversation, engaging another's attention for conversation and terminating conversations. Many strategies for gaining access involve the use of the question form, for example, 'You know what Mummy?', a strategy French and Woll argued was appropriate for a child conversational participant, but which may not be for an adult participant. They believed children first learned **child-like strategies** for conversation and the use of the question form is an acceptable way for a child to gain entry to a conversation. If the child asks a question such as 'Know what?', the adult responds with a question ('What?'), thus returning the conversation to the child and allowing the child to participate. Further, question forms usually eventually lead to the adult responding, rather than ignoring the child, so it is an initiating strategy that almost guarantees success, especially if the child persists for long enough! As the child's linguistic resources develop, the conversations change and the child's strategies must of necessity also change. Conversation thus becomes the context for the constitution of language.

Studies such as these demonstrate how very young children use both their language and their knowledge of the relationship between the world of objects and the world of people to become proficient conversationalists. Not only does the child's language develop in terms of increasing vocabulary and increasingly complex grammar, but the child also learns more about the world. Children constantly seek to express themselves and to comprehend the language of others. The medium through which children can best achieve language development is **social interaction** – with an adult, usually a parent (Garton, 1992). The parent provides the necessary contextualization for the child's developing language while being sufficiently sensitive to the child's need to use increasingly sophisticated ways of communicating.

### Transition from Parent–Child to Peer Communication

French, Boynton and Hodges (1991) and Ely and Gleason (1995) both comment that there is little in the literature that examines how children move from parent–child exchanges to learn how to talk with peers. This is despite the large body of work focusing on parent–child interactions and their importance for early language development. It is also despite the extensive work on language as used in classrooms, usually between teacher and children.

Peer communication usually comes *after* children have learned to interact and communicate with an adult (Ely and Gleason, 1995), although it is worth noting that children who spend much of their early years with other children such as twins or children in full-time care actually acquire language at a *slower* rate than children who predominantly spend their time with adults. Child–child discourse, as French et al. (1991) term it, is delayed relative to adult–child discourse. However, peer communication is qualitatively different to adult–child communication since there is no recognized conversational 'expert' in the dyad. There is also the added difficulty of establishing and negotiating shared presuppositions (that is, establishing common knowledge) as well as sending and interpreting subtle and appropriate conversational cues.

French et al. cite a range of research that demonstrates that peer communication is sensitive to contextual cues and children can adjust their conversations to the age and communicative status of the other child and to accommodate topics displaced in time and space. However, such conversations are still limited to the immediate setting, at least for children under the age of 5 years. French et al. examined the free play interactions of preschool aged children and again, consistent with previous research, demonstrated that the physical setting determined to a large extent both the actual activities and language use. For example, play between children in the 'home corner' mirrored domestic activities of cooking, eating meals and so on. These activities are appropriate to the setting and provide a recognizable context for sharing of experience. This work has been extended to structured observations of 2– and 3–year-old children, paired with a similarly aged child. French et al. report that the experiment replicates the previous reliance by young children in conversation on the physical environment to elicit and support the establishment and maintenance of shared knowledge. Early peer communication apparently requires the context of the physical environment to provide the means for establishing some joint activity and joint conversation. French et al. discuss the importance of shared event representation as the vehicle to encourage communication between young children, and how this relates to both to language and to cognitive development.

Peer communication, like the adult–child conversations which lay the foundation for language development, uses the immediate context. Whereas the adult can be regarded as the skilled communicative partner, this is not so for two young children talking to one another, although in part this can be compensated for by the use of enactment and sharing of common and familiar events. The research in general shows that children are adept at communication with both adults and other children before they start school.

While there is clearly a variety of influences on a developing child's spoken language learning, it has now been recognized that there may be important differences between the types of conversations children are having at home or with peers and those they are having at, for example, school. It is popularly assumed that children from lower socio-economic or non-English speaking backgrounds are disadvantaged on entry to school because their linguistic experience to date has not prepared them sufficiently for the language used in formal education. This claim implies that one major contributory factor for educational failure (or success) is that the language of the home differs from that of the school, either in its grammatical structure or the uses to which it is being put. Research has therefore been undertaken to compare conversations at home and at school.

## Comparison between Conversations at Home and Conversations at School

At around age 5, children make the shift from home to school. For many, this transition from home involves first of all a move to preschool or nursery. Psychological and educational research studies have attempted to describe similarities and differences between the linguistic environments of home and school by analysing the conversational patterns between children and parents in the home and between children and teachers at school. In order to make comparisons between the language used at home and school, it is necessary to describe the social conditions that exist in both environments, conditions that influence the nature and type of conversations possible. Firstly, we will examine research that has compared communication patterns between home and preschool, before looking at research comparing home and school. While the comparisons will be directed towards the language children use and experience in the different settings, the nature of the different types of social interaction will be described. Finally, a discussion of the differences between home talk and talk in educational establishments will end this section.

*Home and preschool*   Ely and Gleason (1995) highlight some of the major issues for children when they enter school, whether from home or preschool, continuous or discontinuous. Both direct socialization and indirect socialization occur, the former relating to what the child should say in school (mainly to teachers) and the latter to variations in interaction at school, including such things as gender and racial stereotyping, often noted in educational contexts.

Tizard and Hughes (1984) conducted a study in which they directly compared talk of 4–year-old girls at home and at preschool (or nursery school, as they term it). While the description of the nursery school leads one to believe it is preschool, the authors referred to it as 'school'. The main thrust of the study was in fact to highlight the important role mothers, compared with preschool educational establishments, played in the linguistic and cognitive development of their children, and Tizard and Hughes concluded that 'the home provides a very powerful learning environment' (p. 249). During the course of everyday living, these 4–year-old girls communicated and conversed with their mothers and in so doing, were learning a great deal about the world. Tizard and Hughes believed five factors contributed to the home being such an effective learning environment, in comparison with the nursery school.

Firstly, in the home context, a varied range of activities takes place. These include household chores such as cooking, washing, gardening, going shopping, going to the library, visiting friends and relatives, going to the cinema, the swimming pool, and so on, travelling by car, walking, talking on the telephone, watching television, and listening to the radio. All these activities allow children to experience aspects of the culture to which they are being socialized. Such activities are also the bases for talk, either concurrently or at a later point in time. Tizard and Hughes listed this as the second provision of the home context. Children and mothers can talk about their shared world experiences and, through such talk, children can integrate their increasing knowledge about the world and its people.

Thirdly, with the decline in the birthrate, most families have decreased in size and there is a smaller number of children making demands on the mother's time. Extended one-to-one conversation between a mother and her child is possible in such a context. The activities in the home learning environment are meaningful for the 4–year-old child in so far as the purpose of activities such as going to the library, making shopping lists, using the telephone, are clear to the young child. Often mothers will embed their activities in a context for their children by talking about what they are doing and why they are doing it. Such activities become interesting for the preschool child and their relevance apparent. This is in contrast to the school environment, where the meaning of teacher-directed activities is often less than clear to the child (Donaldson, 1978).

Finally, Tizard and Hughes believed the intense emotional relationship between a mother and her child characterizes the home learning environment, and may indeed even hinder learning at times. In general, however, this close relationship enables a mother's concerns over her child's accomplishment of skills to be translated into effective expectations and achievements.

While these characteristics are not necessarily true for all homes, many mothers are providing more than adequate learning environments for their young children. In contrast, the nursery school environment is a grounding for school. Tizard and Hughes claimed that nursery teachers see their role as socializing young preschoolers into aspects of school, such as daily routines and how to communicate with other adults and other children, while preparing the child educationally. Unlike the more formal world of school, the focus of the nursery school is on child-directed play. In Tizard and Hughes's study, this meant that the adults were not directing or setting goals for the children, so were not supporting or scaffolding the children to any substantial extent. The teachers were, however, adept at using the question and answer routine (see next section) as a means of fostering language development. There was, according to Tizard and Hughes, a gap between home and preschool, a not insurmountable gap, but one nonetheless that exists and will continue to do so as long as the learning experiences of young children are divided. A comparison between home and preschool highlights many social differences that could contribute to different language learning experiences, and these differences become even more apparent when we compare home with school.

*Home and school*  MacLure and French (1981) compared the structure of adult–child conversations both at home and at school. They compared conversations recorded in early primary school classrooms with conversations recorded between young children and their parents in their homes. MacLure and French focused on the structure of conversations based on the question and answer routine. The question and answer routine is a readily identifiable sequence at school and its structure consists of the teacher asking a question, a pupil answering and the teacher evaluation of this answer, as illustrated in the following example:

*Teacher*: What is the capital of Japan?
*Child*: Tokyo.
*Teacher*: That's right.

This structure was also prevalent in the home talk recordings of preschoolers and their mothers. MacLure and French thus argued that *structurally* the children are familiar with this type of conversation before they go to school but point out that there are important differences between home and school question and answer routines.

Firstly, teachers tended to ask many *pseudo*-questions, namely those questions to which they already know the answer. These are typically the questions used in teaching, for example, 'What do two and two make?', 'What can you see in this picture?' and 'What does this word say?'. It is argued that teachers ask such questions because children's contributions to conversations can be monitored in relation to the teacher's defined frame of reference. Pseudo-questions are much less common in mother–child conversations. In school, 'real' questions, to which the teacher does not know the answer, are asked only in a restricted range of contexts. MacLure and French cited the management of the day's activities, (for example, 'Have you washed your hands yet?'), turn allocation for question answer, (such as, 'Who hasn't given me an answer today?'), and for setting up topics for further activities, ('And what is your favourite song, Johnny?'), as being the most common contexts where teachers are actually seeking information.

Secondly, and more importantly, it was the teachers who did most of the questioning. Not only do teachers do most of the talking in the classroom, they also ask more questions. Children ask relatively few questions at school and most tend to be procedural, (for example, 'Can I use my yellow pencil here?'), rather than spontaneous requests for knowledge. This was in contrast to the home where children asked the most questions, some of which reveal a remarkable degree of curiosity – as shown, for example, by a 4–year-old who asked his parents 'What [would happen] if all the ambulances had a crash on the way to the hospital?'. However, at both home and school, the third part of the question–answer sequence is sometimes omitted by children or is regarded not as evaluative but as repetitive. In the example below, the child repeats the mother's answer ('Clapperboard') to a question. Mother and child are watching TV (from MacLure and French, 1981, p. 213):

*Child:* Mummy, what's those?
*Mother:* Clapperboard.
*Child*: Clapperboard.

Most of the differences between conversations at home and conversations at school arise because of the educational significance of talk at school – the child is at school to be **taught**. At home, conversations are not predominantly didactic, although they can be occasionally, when a mother is teaching her child something. These teaching situations at home do not involve the question and answer routine so popular with teachers in the classroom. Further, at home, there is one-to-one interaction between a parent and child. Sometimes the interaction involves more participants, such as at meal times, but even here the social situation generally involves a small number of people. With question and answer routines in the home, the meaning of the question (and of the response) can be negotiated over several rounds of conversation if necessary. Children listen to the question or the answer as they are active participants in the conversation and continue to be so throughout the interaction.

In contrast, a teacher is required to engage a class of around 30 children in conversational interaction. This places different demands on the participants than do the one-to-one parent–child conversations at home. In the question and answer routines observed in classrooms, the number of participants varies from one teacher and one child to one teacher and all 30 children within a single interaction. The teacher directs the initial question to all 30 children, and then selects one child who provides an answer. The child is then given feedback, which is often inadequate or ambiguous, regarding the response. While this one-to-one interaction is going on, the other 29 children are expected to attend. The teacher then shifts to a different child, either to get another answer to the original question if the first answer is incorrect, or to extend the topic, and expects the newly selected child to enter the conversation. Again, the teacher engages in one-to-one interaction with this child while the remaining 29 are expected to attend. Thus in school, children enter and leave conversations as the active participant and spend the rest of the time as a passive participant. Interactions in classrooms are frequently of this type, and some children may rarely engage in one-to-one interaction.

Despite these differences, MacLure and French emphasized the **continuity** in the nature of the conversational interactions at home and at school. Young children have learned a great deal about the structure of conversation (both adult–child, as described, as well as child–child) before they go to school. What does change however is the relative frequency of certain types of conversational structure in the two settings, the relative contributions of the two participants (the adult and the child) and the significance of certain interactional structures at home and at school.

Wells (1983) examined the 'complementary role of parents and teachers' in talking to children by directly comparing the same children at home and at school, in conversational interaction with adults. His observations revealed that at home, conversations tended to be centred on events and happenings pertinent to both participants, although the extent to which these become the topic of conversation varies from one household to another. Many parents talk extensively about what they are doing, why they

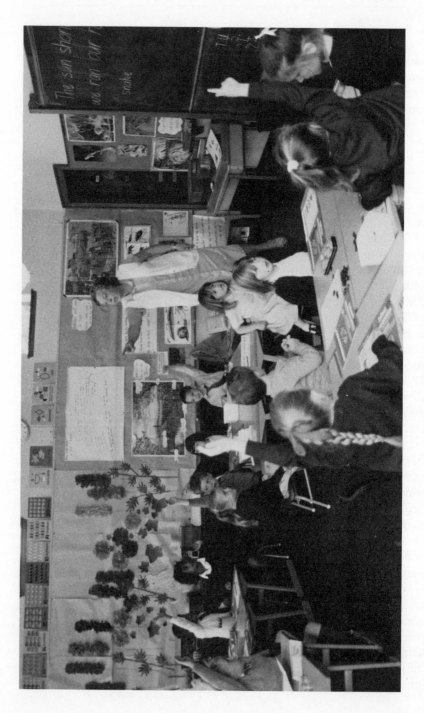

Language in the classroom

are doing it, what they are feeling, and so on, while in other families, such topics are never raised. Obviously, the experiences to which the children are exposed and to which they are making a contribution must affect subsequent language use and participation in conversations. A child who is only allowed to 'speak when spoken to' at home would have a different contribution to make to a conversation than a child who has been encouraged to talk at every opportunity.

There are tremendous differences in the attitudes of parents towards children's participation in conversations with other adults. Some parents encourage their children to talk to adult friends while others expect children to leave the adults alone when adult friends visit. Clearly such major differences will affect the number and quality of conversational interactions to which children are exposed and in which they have the opportunity to participate. Such differences in early experience with language will influence conversations at school. All children at home, however, participate in conversations that are meaningful in the context of either implicitly or explicitly shared information. That is, parents and their children talk about shared knowledge in conversations that are by and large symmetrical, each participant making a contribution. These conversations are therefore similar to peer communication where shared events and representations provide a context for and support the conversation.

Therefore, the language experience of children at home is for the huge majority of children rich and varied, but problems may result at school because, as Wells said 'the uses they habitually make of language *may be different from those most valued in school*' (Wells, 1983, p. 134, our italics). He stressed the view that language differences should not be equated with linguistic inferiority or superiority. Differences in language *use*, however, will lead to problems at school if children are regarded as deficient when they have not mastered the full range of language teachers expect of a 5-year-old. It must also be recognized that teachers now have a greater awareness and knowledge of language development than previously and probably hold reasonable expectations about the language capacities of 5-year-old children.

It has been argued (for example, by Wells) that because many of the communication problems between teachers and children are not seen in the home (even given the structure of the conversation may be identical) nor between peers, it would be inaccurate to label children as lacking in language skills. Rather, the children do not know how to deploy their skills appropriately at school because of an inability to meet the conversational demands of the classroom. The types of conversation expected at school may not be found extensively elsewhere. Teachers, however, may view an inability to communicate on their level as an inherent linguistic deficiency on the part of the child rather than a particular problem of dealing with the conversation of the classroom.

The intention of school talk is usually instructional, but it should be broadened to enable children to become more equal contributors in the conversations. This can be done by encouraging spontaneous contributions from children, and by the teacher following up child-initiated questions, in the same way as conversations at home occur. The talk should be relevant, which can be achieved through negotiation by both conversational participants. There are institutional limitations that constrain the types of conversation in classrooms, but greater opportunity could be afforded for children to engage in other forms of communication either with the teacher or with each other in structured activities.

In summarizing the research on differences between talk in the home and talk in different educational establishments, it is worth noting the differences children must face between home and school (cf. the overall tone of the chapter by Ely and Gleason, 1995). The educational aims of the school system require that teachers teach children and in order to achieve this didactic goal, teachers frequently adopt conversational styles that are different to those usually encountered in the home. For very many children nowadays, there is an intermediate step between home and school – nursery, or preschool. There are however substantial differences between primary school classrooms and preschools which may influence the talk in these settings (Pratt, 1985). Rather than being adult-centred with pedagogic intentions, the preschool tends to be child-centred with an emphasis on spontaneity and playfulness. There are frequently more adults in attendance at preschool or nursery school, providing the opportunity for more time to be spent with individual children. One way of overcoming some of the difficulties young children have on entering school (whether from home or from preschool) is to foster communication skills, especially at the preschool level. The preschool teacher can act as some sort of a bridge between the types of conversation held at home and those found in the more formal school classroom. Furthermore, the supporting contexts of playful activities in the preschool can facilitate the development of communication skills, particularly between the children themselves. Such settings allow children to negotiate shared meanings and roles, to argue, and to establish joint understandings – all useful conversational skills for later life.

However, although there are different educational approaches in preschool compared with school, it seems that there are few major differences in the type of adult–child conversations between the two. In both, there is a much smaller number of adults than children, and these adults perceive their role as didactic. While there may be more opportunities for

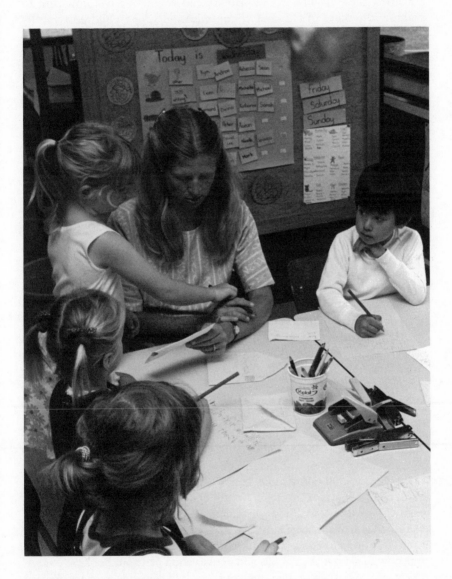

Language in the preschool

children to communicate and initiate conversations in the preschools and nurseries, these decline in the primary classroom. We will now turn to examine the types of talk and communication young children typically encounter in their early years of primary schooling.

## Language in the Primary School Classroom

In looking at language in the classroom, some researchers have examined what sorts of language problems children have that might cause them difficulties in school learning. Other researchers have studied the communication processes between teachers and children as they occur spontaneously in the classroom. We will examine research from these areas in relation to children's spoken language development.

There are obvious benefits to teachers of understanding children's spoken language development, especially if we consider the different demands school places on young children. As noted previously, there are different expectations and certain myths surrounding school. It is often popularly believed that school is there for children to learn, in particular, for the inculcation of reading, writing and arithmetical skills. However, it is important especially for teachers to remember that the language of children beginning school is not yet fully developed. Notwithstanding the differences in home support and encouragement given to spoken and written language activities, spoken language itself is not yet a fully mastered system when children begin school. Children may produce imperfect utterances, sentences might be ungrammatical or structurally incorrect, or their meanings obscure. All children's language should be listened to and understood where possible by the teacher. Just as importantly though, young children may have difficulty understanding the teacher. Teachers as adult users of the language (and usually their native language) speak as adults and may forget that 5-year-old children do not have the same level of understanding as adults do.

Teachers should not use long convoluted sentences, as children will not understand what is being said. Young children are unable to follow extended sentences containing patterns that are unfamiliar to them. Teachers should also avoid using language that is ambiguous. They should always be as clear and concise as possible. For example, the sentence 'It's maths time now so get out your books and pencils and open your books at page 4' is long and potentially ambiguous to a 5-year-old who may not have grasped the link between maths as a subject, the need for a particular book and the use of a pencil to complete the work in the book. It would be far better for a teacher to say 'We're going to do some maths now. Please get out your maths workbook. It's the green one with red writing on it. You will also need a pencil. Please get one out. We're going to do the sums on page 4', as she demonstrates the workbook and opens it at the appropriate page. Although it might take longer to say, the language used is much simpler and clearer, and is well supported by the context.

Figures of speech, which are surprisingly common in teachers' talk in the classroom, should also be avoided in the early years. For example, one of us was observing a class of 6–year-old children being given a 'printing lesson'. The teacher was demonstrating how to form the letter 'p'. She said to the children, 'Now I want everybody to make sure that their eyes are on the end of this piece of chalk.' How they all achieved this is anyone's guess. Another common phrase is 'Pull your socks up.' How does this help you keep your desk tidy or prevent you from being late again?

The vocabulary of teaching and learning tends to be technical and hence possibly difficult for young children to understand. The problem of unfamiliar words in teaching and learning continues throughout education, as subject areas get more specialized. Teachers should be aware that many 'jargon' terms may require explanation, sometimes repeatedly. For the young child, terminology used in mathematics teaching requires careful and thorough explanation. Some terms such as 'addition' and 'subtraction' may be new, while others will be familiar words that take on different meanings, for example 'big number' and 'little number' (Durkin, Crowther and Shire, 1986). Such ambiguity in application of everyday words such as 'odd' and 'table' to mathematical concepts is often resolved by seeking the most familiar meaning (Durkin and Shire, 1991). Even common vocabulary such as 'recess' or 'break' may not be understood until the teacher explains the meaning.

The study of classroom language often assumes that the misunderstandings that occur are due to the child's inadequate language skills. As we have discussed, the misunderstandings may arise because the teacher has possibly not taken into account children's limited, but still developing, language (Durkin, 1993). The inability to answer the teacher's questions is usually regarded as the child failing in some way. The child may be regarded as having a low ability, not having attended to the teacher, not being motivated or as having poor language skills. There have been many studies aimed at examining just where the problems might lie, and both teacher talk and pupil talk in the classroom have been considered. One of the major problems is the fact that classroom talk is often unrelated to 'normal' talk. Classroom talk may be divorced from a context that allows children to interpret the language. In classrooms, teachers may expect to stand at the front of the class and impart knowledge to children by *talking*, because this is what they believe teaching is. This provides no place for the child learner as an active participant in this type of teaching process.

One ubiquitous method teachers use for the assessment of children's knowledge is the asking of questions. As we have discussed, children are familiar with the question and answer routine, although in home conversations, they tend to be the initiator, the questioner. In school, it is mainly the teacher who does the questioning. Teachers frequently ask questions to which there may be several answers. Often the children's task is to work out which answer the teacher actually wants.

Pratt (1985) gave an example of how a child is expected to work out the answer required by the teacher when she asks 'What day is it today?'. There are several answers to this question that can be correct (for example, 'Tuesday', 'Susie's birthday' or 'Shrove Tuesday'). However, which of these correct responses is *appropriate* depends very much on the child judging which answer the teacher is actually seeking. In order to do this the child must try to take account of the teacher's intention in asking the question. This may be done by evaluating the context in which it is asked. So, for example, if the teacher was in front of a chart used to indicate the day, date and weather, then the appropriate response would most probably be 'Tuesday'. If the teacher was standing close to a chart listing the birthdays of the children in the class, then the response 'Susie's birthday', would be appropriate. Finally, 'Shrove Tuesday' would be appropriate if the teacher was standing at her desk with a bowl of flour, some eggs and some milk, preparing to make pancakes! Children have to learn the contextual cues used by the teacher in order for them to work out the intended meaning. The children must 'guess' what the teacher intends in order to provide an appropriate response and some become adept at doing this. Some children however have difficulty answering teachers' questions appropriately.

If it is believed that effective teaching requires the inculcation of knowledge to children, then there is no room for the negotiation of shared understanding. Allowing children to take a more active part in classroom communication (and hence the learning process) may be perceived as threatening because the use of questioning by teachers gives them considerable control. Teaching should allow for **shared meanings** to be established, communicated and assessed. Teachers should endeavour to make this as easy as possible for the child, and avoid creating difficulties. Teaching can create barriers to effective learning if it is assumed that the cause of all difficulties is the child who is slow, stupid, does not speak English fluently, or is simply just not listening. Teachers should take account of the fact that some children may be experiencing difficulties with classroom language through no fault of their own. These children simply may not have learned or mastered the language and how it is used nor had sufficient experience with different types of conversation. Children's language skills continue to develop throughout the early school years, and it is prudent to be mindful of that fact.

## Understanding the Processes of Communication

We have regarded both knowing (about language) and learning (how to talk) as psychological processes that are social in origin. We now turn to examine how children begin to understand the processes of conversation and communication. As we have described, especially in the classroom, communication may not always be straightforward. The source of the problem in communication may not always be the child, although there is evidence that children still have a lot to learn about the skills and processes of communication. This has implications not only for classroom talk, but also for everyday conversations and the interactions children have with other people.

### Communication Failure

What happens when communication fails? Or more precisely, why does communication fail and what can be done to repair the conversation? The answer to these questions depends in part on whom one believes is responsible for the breakdown. Is it the **speaker** who has failed to communicate unambiguous information, information that is either inadequate, insufficient or just plain muddled? Or is it the **hearer** who has misunderstood the speaker, because of inattention? Whom you deem responsible for communication breakdown seems to be related to your age. Further it follows that whoever 'caused' the failure should also be responsible for correcting the 'error'.

Robinson and Robinson (for example, 1977, 1978, 1981) found in general that children under the age of about 6 years tended to blame the hearer for communication failures, while after age 6, they blamed the speaker. They claimed that young children are unable to realize that messages can be ambiguous or incomplete. Robinson and Robinson used communication tasks in which two participants (for example, an adult and a child or two children), each with identical experimental materials, were separated by an opaque screen. The materials were sets of six cards with drawings which varied systematically. For example, the drawings might be of either happy or sad faces, some wearing red hats and some wearing green hats. This task is regarded as the standard approach in the study of referential communication (see figure 3).

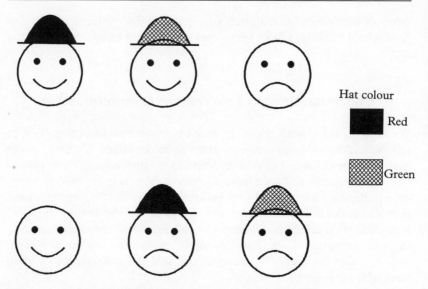

*Figure 3* Examples of drawings used in communication tasks

The aim of the task is for the two participants, the speaker and the hearer, to select the same cards from their sets. The speaker begins by selecting a card which is described verbally to the hearer. The hearer is then expected to select the card with the same picture on it from the set available. If the participants select different cards, then a mismatch occurs because the communication has failed. The participants can then be asked about the reason(s) for this failure.

Various experimental manipulations have been investigated including the sending of ambiguous messages by the speaker. Ambiguous messages do not specify the speaker's intended referent precisely, making the hearer's job rather difficult since several items may fulfil the described criteria. For example, the speaker may say 'the sad man wearing a hat', where there are two cards that fit this description – a sad man wearing a red hat and a sad man wearing a green hat. Interestingly, young children as hearers tend not to query the content of such ambiguous messages and simply select one of the cards. If this results in a mismatch, they then blame themselves for not hearing the message correctly.

These young hearers tended to believe that if they 'thought harder' then all would be clearer (Robinson and Robinson, 1982). Both young hearers and speakers believed that the hearers had been given sufficient information to make a match even when faced with an obvious mismatch. This tendency to blame the hearer is very reliable and robust across different experimental manipulations. Young children will blame the hearer regardless if it is themselves, another child, an adult or even Donald Duck. Older hearers (aged around 8 years), on the other hand, queried messages that conveyed ambiguous information so they were unable to choose a card to carry out the matching task. They would question the speaker and sometimes ask for clarification. They realized the ambiguity of the speaker's message, blamed the speaker and requested disambiguation (Pratt and Nesdale, 1984). Although it is sometimes assumed that younger children act as if ambiguity does not exist, it cannot be concluded that they are unaware of ambiguity. It might be proposed that young children are aware that a description applies to more than one card but they select one anyway (perhaps due to social circumstances of the experimental task). Adults would not select a card given ambiguous information; rather, they would ask for more information. As Pratt (1984) has shown, this represents a difference in communication strategy. Adults, and to some extent older children, use a verbal strategy, seeking clarification by asking, while younger children use a non-verbal strategy, selecting one card, and if judged incorrect, selecting another.

Lloyd, Boada and Forns (1992) characterized referential communication, as assessed by the type of task described above, as dealing with the following five issues which may pose difficulties for young children. Firstly, messages and meanings may not coincide and messages may have more than one meaning, and meaning may be conveyed in two or more different ways. Secondly, young children assume the message is 'good' if the outcome is correct while they assume it is their fault if the outcome is incorrect; and thirdly, children need to distinguish the roles of speaker and hearer as they may or may not have characteristics in common. Fourthly, various explanations have been offered for both the communication failure and for how performance might be improved, including the acquisition of literacy (see next section); while finally, educational attainment and school success depend on evaluating teacher communication appropriately. This was discussed earlier in relation to language in the primary school classroom.

Lloyd et al. discussed limitations of the standard approach and task used in studies of referential communication. In particular, they noted the exclusion of any social interactional component to the task. The task, they claimed, does not permit any negotiation between participants nor any way of assessing the extent of the cooperation or conflict. Lloyd et al. believed that such restrictions to the speech allowed must constrain the interaction and render it quite atypical as far as normal communication is concerned. Furthermore, the constitution of the pairs in the standard task (usually an adult experimenter and a child, or two children) is potentially problematic as Lloyd et al. claim that no consideration was given to

the social status of the participants and how this might affect performance. Lloyd et al. acknowledged the huge contribution the research in
this area has made to our understanding of the development of communication skills particularly in relation to language used in the classroom
(which the traditional experimental paradigm closely mirrors) but
believed it timely to re-evaluate progress and to consider the theoretical
implications and explanations of the work. In particular, attention was
drawn to the relevance of Vygotsky's theory for an account of the social
interactional components of referential communication.

One way in which performance on the referential communication task
has been interpreted is discussed below, because it is pertinent to the
theme of the book. This is the distinction between what is said and what
is meant in terms of how the relationship between the message and the
referent is understood, and how this can be related more generally to the
development of literacy. A second explanation looks at how meaning is
negotiated in communication, and how this may be applicable to
performance on the task. Finally, modifications made to the task as a
result of the criticisms of Lloyd and his colleagues are presented in the
section following, where the social contexts of communication, including
negotiation, are discussed.

## Communication and the Say/Mean Distinction

It is important to appreciate that the sending and receipt of both ambiguous and unambiguous messages may be a problem for younger children,
a problem which has relevance for the study of literacy. Torrance and
Olson (1987) tested children from kindergarten age up to around age 8
on their ability to differentiate the literal meaning of a sentence from its
intended meaning. They examined this by testing children's understanding of ambiguous messages. Short stories were used, involving a speaker
(Lucy) and a hearer (Linus), and the child's task was to assess whether
Linus had acted according to what Lucy had said or what she had intended. For example, Lucy requested 'red shoes', meaning 'new red shoes'
(as opposed to 'old red shoes'). Linus then fetched the 'wrong' red shoes.
As the message was ambiguous, and Lucy did not specify which shoes
she wanted, Linus had acted as she said, not as she intended.

On questioning the children about how Linus knew which shoes to
fetch, young children claimed Linus did not do as Lucy said because he
did not bring the shoes she intended. They ignored the fact that the shoes
produced did in fact match the description given. Children aged 8 years
and older admitted Linus acted as Lucy said, but not as she intended.
From this, and related research (for example, Robinson, Goelman and

Olson, 1983; Bonitatibus, 1988), it is evident that young children have difficulty with language when the intended meaning is not made absolutely clear. As children do not understand the distinction between **say** and **mean**, when they are then presented with an ambiguous sentence, they do not realize that the meaning they have extracted from what is said may be different to the meaning intended by the speaker.

## Negotiation of Meaning

Children also have to learn the strategies that can be used when a misunderstanding occurs and how to negotiate conversational meaning. They have to learn the sequence of a conversation and how to sustain meaningful conversation. Wells (1981, 1985a) described how an adult and a child can come to achieve successful communication based on the negotiation of shared meaning. The shared meaning not only comes from the form of the language used, but also from the functions of language and the contexts in which the language is used.

The matching tasks described previously may underestimate children's abilities because only one round of conversation is permitted. Pratt (1984) explored the negotiation of meaning using the matching task. Rather than curtailing the communication sequence immediately after the hearer had selected a card, it was allowed to continue until a matching card was found. In this situation, when in the role of hearer and receiving an ambiguous message, the child will select a card that fits the description and hold it up to see if it is the correct one. If the speaker then signals that it is the wrong card, the hearer will proceed to pick another one that also fits the description and wait for feedback about the choice. This succession of rounds continues until the hearer finds the correct card. Adults, in a similar situation where they have detected an ambiguous message, will try to disambiguate it using a verbal strategy and ask for clarification, for example, 'Is it the red one or the green one?'. Children, however, use a different strategy and negotiate the meaning over several rounds.

Pratt also examined children's reactions as speakers when their messages were either misheard or were ambiguous. He found that if the hearer holds up the wrong card, children from age 4 as speakers will disambiguate their message in conventional ways. Thus if the card selected by the speaker is of a 'sock' and the one chosen by the hearer is of a 'clock', then the speaker will repeat the message with emphasis, 'No, *sock*'. If the card selected by the hearer following the speaker's message 'sock' is of a (green) sock and this is a mismatch, then again the speaker will provide the relevant information for disambiguation – 'No, it's a red one' or 'A *red* sock'.

Thus, given the opportunity, young children are capable of negotiating shared meaning in a matching task.

Children can therefore use increasingly sophisticated strategies for negotiating and collaborating with adults. Both adults and children have to use these strategies which must be pitched at an appropriate level, be it the child's age, the child's linguistic maturity, the appropriateness for the context, the correct level of politeness, or a combination of all aspects of the social situation. Children further have to learn to be both speaker and hearer.

Generally children's conversation is typically embedded in the here and now, both in terms of time and place, and this renders negotiation much easier. Conversations are not necessarily directed by the adult present. Mothers allow their children to initiate conversations and can then usually quickly cue into the correct context. If not, they are able to ask appropriate questions to elicit additional information from the child. Peers act as more equal partners in the conversation. In both cases, meaning is negotiated through the common ground shared in the context – shared activities, people, relatives and pets known to the family and so on. Language is the means by which shared meaning is established and is a critical step in the development of sophisticated communication skills. A supportive physical context greatly enhances the creation and negotiation of such shared meanings. An extension of this notion can be seen in the recent experimental work conducted by Lloyd and colleagues, where some of the issues raised in the previous sections are specifically addressed.

## Social Context of Communication

In countering the criticisms he raised against the use of the standard referential communication task, Lloyd and colleagues devised an ingenious task which overcomes some of the difficulties. The task does not require the use of screens to separate the participants visually, both speaker and hearer contribute to the outcome by negotiating and collaborating with one another, and comparisons are made between participants of different status (child–child versus adult–child). The use of the verbal medium of language is facilitated through the telephone, a device which is well-known to children, restricted to two participants and encourages the spoken word. A task with similar communicative characteristics was also devised in a lab in Barcelona (Lloyd et al., 1992).

Lloyd (1991, 1993) described studies using the task, which was essentially a route-finding, or map, task, whereby the participants had to give and receive directions with the aid of a model, which had roads and familiar landmarks on it (such as churches). The participants were located in two separate rooms. Both participants knew the starting point but only one knew the particular route to the final goal. Model cars assisted in moving across the model. Participants were instructed to ensure the route was followed accurately. Obviously, the potential for ambiguity was included in the map, this time by having multiple identifiable landmarks, such as the churches, each with a subtle distinguishing feature, such as one with a pointed spire. Furthermore, alternative routes were possible from each successive landmark.

The outcome measures of interest related to success on the task as well as the strategies used in terms of the dialogue used in negotiation of the route. Younger children (7-year-olds) were not as good as older children or adults in terms of the adequacy of the message sent nor of the referent selected in response to a message. The types of strategies varied with age, with adults using directional terminology (such as 'turn left') more than children. Older, 10-year-old, children used strategies that tried to distinguish the features of the landmarks to be passed while 7-year-old children used minimal information to distinguish features on the way (Lloyd, 1991). A further study (Lloyd, 1993) found that kinship relationships affected the types of strategies used, and the distribution of strategies of related pairs (mother-own child) was more closely correlated than those of non-related pairs (unrelated adult–child). That is, management of the task was different depending on the relationship of the adult to the child. There was no difference in actual performance of related versus unrelated pairs, in terms of routes identified.

Interpretation of the results from these studies has been made in light of Vygotsky's theory (Lloyd, 1993, Lloyd et al., 1992) whereby adult guidance is regarded as the mechanism for the shift from other-regulation to self-regulation in the child. Detailed examination of the processes during the interaction or communication sequences has looked at the roles of the other person during the task and how performance is affected by having a mother or adult work with the child. The painstaking analysis of turn-taking during communication has shed further light on the processes at work in the referential communication task. It is clear that the interaction is more dynamic than previously claimed, and that the ongoing interpretation and evaluation of messages is more complex, and more subtle, than believed. Again, this work can also be linked to classroom communication where there is a recognition that children are faced with messages that have little contextual support, are potentially ambiguous, but are within a tutoring situation where guidance is being provided to the children. Ways in which adults (teachers) can enhance understanding of these messages can be explored through application of the results of experimental work such as that of Lloyd and colleagues, and can only serve to increase awareness of difficulties children may encounter with speaking and listening skills.

## Uses of Different Language Forms in Different Contexts

One way of studying the use of different language forms by young children has been to examine how they learn to use indirect requests. When adults make requests of another person, they tend to do so indirectly. This is because it is regarded as more **polite** to be indirect rather than direct (Clark and Schunk, 1980). For example, it is regarded as more polite to ask someone 'Would you mind passing me the salt?' than to say 'Pass the salt.' The former request is indirect, the latter, direct. The structure of the request is different in each case. There are various forms of indirect request and children must learn conventions about when and to whom it is appropriate to use these different forms.

Linguistically there are several devices that signal politeness such as the use of the question form, the use of the verb form 'would', 'might', and 'could', and the addition of 'please'. However, there are also social conventions that govern the use of indirect requests. In making a request, the requestor is asking another person for something – some action or some information. This entails that the requestee respond and provide the necessary information or act accordingly. For example, the requestor could demand 'Tell me the time' to which the requestee could either refuse ('No') or provide information ('Three o'clock'). However, the requestor is more likely to ask 'Would you mind telling me the time?'. Again, the requestee could refuse (in this case, 'Yes'), although this is unlikely. The reply is more likely to be: 'Not at all. It's three o'clock.' The requestor has framed the request to maximize the chance of receiving the information. It also enables the requestee, unable to respond, to save face (for example by saying, 'I'm sorry but my watch is broken').

In deciding which indirect form is appropriate, the requestor has to take various social aspects into consideration. These include the context of the request (formal versus informal social situations) and the status of the requestee (Is the request being made of someone of higher status, lower status? Is the requestee familiar or unfamiliar?).

Both the understanding and use of different forms of indirect request have been studied in young children of different ages (Bates, 1976; Wilkinson, Wilkinson, Spinelli and Chiang, 1984; Axia and Baroni, 1985; Baroni and Axia, 1989; Garton and Pratt, 1990). These studies show that children as young as 4 years of age can manipulate politeness, initially with the 'please' device and then by changing the sentence form. However, it is not until they are much older that they use and understand polite forms appropriately in terms of social conventions. Older children can use a greater range of indirect requests probably due to their increased capabilities with spoken language and their awareness of the need to take the other person into account when conversing (and when making requests).

Axia and Baroni (1985) studied some of the social factors, including the status of the participants, influencing the degree of politeness in requests. They found that children of all ages used more polite forms with adults of higher status, particularly if the adult initially did not act on the request (either did not 'hear' or ignored it). The 'cost' in terms of the speaker's and addressee's relative statuses and of the requestee's reaction to the request influenced the politeness level of the request, especially for 9–year-old children. Five-year-old children seemed less aware of the linguistic and social conventions governing the use of polite forms although they were able to use the forms appropriately in the experimental tasks.

Baroni and Axia (1989) studied the attribution of request forms (both polite and impolite) according to the degree of familiarity of the participants in the interaction. As well as examining children's understanding of different forms of request, they asked the children to state explicitly the rule they were using to make the attribution. So, if children correctly attributed the linguistic form, they were asked to explain why. Five- and 7–year-old children were required to attribute various polite and impolite requests to child participants in scenarios. The scenarios involved participants who varied in their degree of familiarity, and the request forms to be attributed differed in their levels of politeness, through the inclusion of 'please', the use of the interrogative and the use of the verb form 'would'.

Baroni and Axia found that the older children were more able to attribute request forms correctly than younger children, attributing polite requests to less familiar speakers and impolite requests to more familiar speakers. In explaining their attributions, 5–year-old children seemed unaware of any linguistic rule that might have cued their correct attribution, while 7–year-old children showed a beginning awareness of the linguistic rule governing the selection of polite forms. So, for example, after correctly attributing a polite request to an unfamiliar speaker, a child might say 'because he said "please"', showing awareness of the linguistic marker. A more sophisticated explanation would involve awareness of both the linguistic structure and the social convention surrounding familiarity, for example, between a mother and her son, by remarking that 'Mummy will you give me . . .' is more polite than 'Mummy, I want . . .'.

Wilkinson et al. (1984) studied different types of requests made by children in the classroom. Distinguishing between direct and indirect requests, and requests for action versus requests for information, they examined both the understanding and production of request forms in 6-, 7- and 8-year-old children. They found that with increasing age, children used more indirect forms for requests for academic information ('Please can you help me do this sum?') and were more aware that a question form was appropriate for a request. Younger children were overall more concerned with the politeness of the request, that is, the use of 'please', especially when making requests requiring action. Between the ages of 6 and 8 years, children became more aware of the need for indirectness in requests and were able to distinguish between requests for information and requests requiring action. Wilkinson et al. (1984) related the age differences to a developmental pattern of increasing knowledge about the uses of language, knowledge available at the commencement of schooling that is 'refined and elaborated' (p. 2140) during the early school years.

Finally, Garton and Pratt (1990) examined the politeness, effectiveness and likelihood of use of 12 request forms by 8- to 12-year-old children. All request forms were rated in relation to their use to four different aged addressees (a younger child, a child of the same age, an older child and a teacher). In general, request items were rated by all children as more polite or likely to be used than effective, suggesting some differentiation of the functions of the polite forms from other functions. However, there were positive correlations between all three dimensions regardless of the age of addressee indicating that the dimensions were related to each other. It was concluded that the children were able to distinguish between the dimensions of use of different request forms but were not making any distinctions in relation to the age of addressee.

## Language Use in Social Problem Solving

One important area where the processes of communication have been studied has been in children's use of language during problem solving tasks (Garton, 1992, 1993). The research has looked at both communication strategies during problem solving (for example, Cooper, 1980) and more specific uses of language (for example, Cooper, Ayers-Lopez and Marquis, 1982). In the latter research, some of the focus has been on the language used during conflict resolution in problem solving (Eisenberg and Garvey, 1981; Lindow, Wilkinson and Peterson, 1985; Phelps and Damon, 1987; Garton and Renshaw, 1988). In particular, researchers have sought to examine the relationship between the children's communication and subsequent progress on the problem. It has been claimed that the language used in social problem solving influences the solution of the task. This research draws heavily on Vygotsky's theory (see chapter 3).

Garton and Renshaw (1988) asked 7- and 9-year-old children to work together in pairs to solve a goal-directed problem using attribute blocks. The children collaborated to varying extents, and on the basis of their initial interactions, were classified as **joint** or **disjoint**. **Joint**, or collaborative, dyads were pairs who quickly negotiated a mutually acceptable interpretation of the task enabling solution of the problem. The children showed evidence of planning and of monitoring each other's behaviour. **Disjoint**, or non-collaborative, dyads failed to achieve a common interpretation, entailing subsequent difficulties with the solution of the task.

The occurrence and resolution of disagreements during the solving of joint problems was predicted to be an important marker of the extent of collaboration. As hypothesized, the **disjoint** dyads, who were unable to collaborate (that is, work together to their mutual benefit and solve the problem) disagreed more often and took longer to achieve subsequent consensus. The disagreements were described in terms of their **antecedent, opposition** and **resolution**. Because collaboration is a continuum, the only difference between **joint** and **disjoint** pairs of children was in the nature of the opposition to the disagreement. **Disjoint** pairs were more likely to challenge the antecedent event ('You can't put that one there'), while for **joint** pairs, the opposition was more likely to be negation of the antecedent ('No, not the blue one') or a request for a moratorium by saying 'Hey, wait!'

Garton and Renshaw also found developmental differences in the language used in disagreements. Older children were more adept at managing the social interactions and used different ways of resolving the disagreements than did younger children. Younger children were more likely simply to accept the dissenter's position, while older children required more explicit acknowledgment that both participants accepted the resolution. The 9-year-olds sought confirmation of their opinion from the other participant ('Yes, that's right now'), and that the interaction would only continue once the disagreement had been resolved to mutual satisfaction. Like the research on message adequacy, the older children in this study were more able to acknowledge and communicate with their hearers in conversation.

Garton and Renshaw (1988) believed that the social context created in the problem solving task forced the children to communicate, to talk about what they were doing. In so doing, their otherwise implicit solutions for the problem became explicit. This enables setting up strategies and solutions for debate and disagreement, allowing the use and control of the strategies in a meaningful way. The important aspect is the social communication and how it affects and influences cognitive development.

This notion is expanded in Garton (1992, 1993) where communication is regarded as fundamental to the achievement of successful problem solving and for the attainment of learning more generally. More recent work (Garton and Pratt, 1996), pursued this line by examining collaborative problem solving in relation to the differential knowledge status of the participants (through experimental manipulation) and how this is taken into account by the child. Again, recognition of such differences in knowledge status must be established (overtly or covertly) and interest lies in how children acknowledge this and then use the information during task completion. Social or collaborative problem solving requires communication to establish a shared perspective and shared meaning, to negotiate, to argue and disagree, to share, monitor or evaluate, and to ascertain the extent or limits or the knowledge of the other participant. Social interaction permits such a partnership and highlights the importance of the development of communicative skills in young children.

# CHAPTER SEVEN

# Reflecting on Language

In this book we are concerned with various aspects of spoken and written language development. Yet this book, and many others, would not exist if we did not have the ability to focus attention on language and reflect upon its nature, structure and functions. This ability which plays an important role in the development of literacy is generally referred to as **metalinguistic awareness**.

When we use language to communicate with others we seldom have any cause to reflect deliberately on its structure and functions. With regard to our processing, language is to all intents and purposes transparent. We move directly from the idea we wish to communicate, to the production of the speech to represent that idea without any conscious awareness of the structure of the speech we have used. Similarly when listening to speech, we extract the meaning without focusing any conscious attention on the actual sounds that constitute the utterance. Although at some level the individual sounds must be processed, we are not consciously aware of this.

Thus in accordance with the views expressed by Vygotsky (1962), using language is analogous to 'using' glass in a window to see the view. We do not normally focus any attention on the glass itself. Instead we focus our attention on the view. The glass serves the purpose of giving us access to the view. But we can, if we choose, look at the glass and may indeed do so for intrinsic interest or for a particular reason. Differences in the thickness of the glass or other blemishes may distort the view and lead us to focus attention directly on it.

Similarly when we use language, we normally extract the meaning without paying any *conscious* attention to the structure of the language or to any parts of it. Again if we choose we can turn our attention to the language itself. Cazden (1976) has described this as making 'opaque', the language forms that are normally 'transparent'. We may do this spontaneously at times for intrinsic interest or perhaps because an utterance has failed to convey a meaning adequately.

More importantly, however, is that those who work with language must be able to focus attention on it. That is, they must be metalinguistically aware. Consequently the development of metalinguistic awareness is essential if children are to succeed at school, as much of school time is devoted to working with language, in both the written and spoken modes. It is for this reason, and the related cognitive benefits (see Pratt and Grieve, 1984), that the development of metalinguistic awareness in children has received so much attention in the past three decades.

## The Concept of Metalinguistic Awareness

It is necessary to consider what metalinguistic awareness is before going on to examine its development in children. In particular, it is important to consider what is involved in being able to reflect on language and how this ability may manifest itself in practice.

In order for some ability to be labelled as involving **metalinguistic awareness**, it is essential that it consists of reflection at a level at which the individual is explicitly focusing attention on the language. The monitoring of language which occurs automatically as part of the speech production mechanism does not require metalinguistic awareness unless it also involves conscious reflection on the language. Moreover, as Bialystok (1993) points out, most definitions of metalinguistic awareness include a second component, namely, the ability to manipulate linguistic units.

Further, according to Perner (1988), for an ability to be considered metalinguistic the individuals must not only be able to reflect on language and focus attention on it, they must also have some appreciation that it is language they are reflecting upon. Perner illustrated this point with an example that draws in part from his own experience. While out one evening with a Greek visitor they became involved in an argument about the number of letters in the word 'bar'. The visitor thought it was spelled 'mpar'. Perner resolved the argument by pointing to a sign above the entrance to the bar and saying 'Look, it has only three letters.' As he pointed out this is a metalinguistic statement since he was referring to letters as linguistic entities.

This is contrasted with the case of two non-literate workers who are installing such a sign and are told that the plastic objects which are to be mounted on the wall are called letters and that these letters must be put up in the correct order. If the workers have no understanding that these letters are representations of language, then the comment 'That sign was easy to put up as it has only three letters' would not constitute a metalinguistic statement. The word 'letter' is being used to describe plastic objects rather than linguistic entities.

In line with these claims is the position initially set out by Bialystok and Ryan (1985a, 1985b) and further developed by Bialystok (1991a, 1993). According to these authors, metalinguistic awareness involves high levels of two components, the ability to analyse linguistic knowledge into categories and the ability to control attentional procedures that select and process specific linguistic information.

The first of these components, the ability to analyse linguistic knowledge, is responsible for making explicit, aspects of language structure such as the units of speech (such as phonemes and syllables) and syntactic constructions. The second involves the ability to consider intentionally the aspects of language that are relevant in a particular context. This component enables the individual to look beyond the most salient feature of language, namely the meaning it conveys, and attend to the underlying structures (such as the sounds or grammar of the language). Bialystok (1993) argues that metalinguistic tasks, that is tasks which require metalinguistic awareness to complete correctly, typically require high levels of both components, and certainly always require a high level of at least one of the components.

We turn now to consider some views about when and how metalinguistic awareness may develop. Following this we consider the application of metalinguistic abilities to four areas of language. As we have discussed in previous chapters, language consists of sounds that combine to form words which combine to form sentences which combine to produce conversations and discourse. Consequently, in considering the application of metalinguistic awareness, we examine each of these levels of language to determine the nature of the application of metalinguistic abilities. That is, we consider phonological awareness, word awareness, syntactic awareness, and pragmatic awareness. In considering these aspects of language, it will become clear that although the knowledge involved is different in each case, each involves increasing control over reflecting upon language.

## The Development of Metalinguistic Awareness

In this section we examine three different accounts of the development of metalinguistic awareness and then offer our own model. The three accounts differ both with respect to when metalinguistic awareness develops in children and to the causes of its development. In presenting these different accounts, we acknowledge the contribution made to this topic by Tunmer and Herriman (1984) in their conceptual analysis of metalinguistic awareness.

## Metalinguistic Awareness Develops in Parallel with Language Development

This account is set out in most detail by Clark (1978) in a comprehensive survey of different types of evidence for language awareness in children. According to Clark, awareness of language is an integral and essential part of language acquisition and develops at the same time. She stated that 'from the start they [children] seem to be aware of both form and function [of language]' (p. 35), and that 'children start out with a very elementary version of language and, to move on to the next stage, must realize that it is inadequate or "wrong". They must therefore become aware of when language fails' (p. 36).

To substantiate her view that awareness of language is apparent from an early age, Clark reviewed several different types of evidence. These included speech repairs, language play (such as rhymes, puns and riddles) and explicit judgements about the appropriateness of particular linguistic forms in different contexts. Of special interest is the evidence she cited from speech repairs as these provide the earliest and perhaps the most controversial evidence for metalinguistic awareness.

Speech repairs of different types occur quite frequently in children's language productions and include repairs to the pronunciation of words, to word endings or to the word order in an utterance. Clark gave examples of these drawn from different sources. With regard to pronunciation she cited an observation by Scollon (1976) of a 19–month-old girl who repeatedly tried to say 'shoes' (/š/; /šI/; /š/; /šIš/; /šu/; /šu?/), until she produced an approximation (/šuš/) that her mother recognized. An example of word order correction was drawn from Snyder's (1914) description of the language of a 30–month-old boy. In this example the boy changed the utterance 'Down sand I been' to 'I been down sand beach.'

The existence of speech repairs establishes without doubt that language production is monitored at some level by the speech production mechanism. This is hardly surprising, since speech production is by no means infallible and needs to be monitored. Speech repairs do not however provide any conclusive evidence that young children are able to reflect on their language consciously. Although Clark acknowledged this problem, it is difficult to determine precisely what her view was. Whereas she claimed that awareness can be at many different levels from 'the automatic, virtually unconscious monitoring of their own speech' (p. 17), she later discussed errors as evidence for 'children being able to reflect on their utterances so as *to work out* what has to be repaired' (p. 23, emphasis added) suggesting that deliberate reflection is involved. Indeed it is more likely that in the majority of cases the detection and correction of errors in language production occur without reflection.

Nevertheless the existence of these corrections may in some cases provide the basis for the child to reflect on language. An example of this is provided by a friend's child, Kate, aged 2 years 6 months, who was sitting on an adult's knee playing a game. The adult pointed to one of Kate's feet and asked 'What's that?' to which she replied 'A footsie.' When the same question was asked about the other foot, Kate again replied 'A footsie.' The adult then pointed to both feet and asked 'What are these?' to which Kate replied 'Two footsies – no, two feetsies, *I mean*.' Kate's judgement, 'No', of her utterance and her comment 'I mean' indicated that at some stage in the production Kate had become aware that she had made an error and was correcting it.

This fortuitous observation points to some of the difficulties that exist in this area. First of all it is fortuitous because the adult involved happened to be one of the authors who, with an interest in metalinguistic awareness, took careful note of the interaction so that it was not forgotten. Secondly, the child involved came from a home where there was a lot of interest shown in language and a great deal of emphasis was placed on it. Consequently she was able to use words such as '*I mean*'. If she had not said this then the example would not have been so convincing, relying only on the judgement 'no' to distinguish it from a spontaneous repair in the eyes, or ears, of the psychologist.

This raises an interesting point. Whereas we would argue that the existence of speech repairs do not in themselves constitute evidence for metalinguistic awareness as many of them occur spontaneously, we certainly cannot conclude that all speech repairs do not involve awareness. In many cases it is likely that either the production of an error or the act of correcting it, although triggered at a subconscious level, will cause the individual to reflect on the language. Frequently however this reflection will not be explicitly commented on, either because the child does not have the necessary vocabulary or because there is no reason to do so. It is likely therefore that speech repairs will serve as the basis for some conscious reflection on language but the fact that it is conscious will not necessarily be evident to observers of these errors.

### The Development of Metalinguistic Awareness is Governed by the Phase of Development of Particular Linguistic Forms

Karmiloff-Smith (1979c, 1984, 1986b) suggested an alternative account of the development of metalinguistic awareness. The model she proposed is a complex one covering a broader spectrum of development than metalinguistic awareness (for a full explication see Karmiloff-Smith, 1992). In Karmiloff-Smith's terminology, development occurs in domains, each of which is a set of representations sustaining a specific area of knowledge such as language, mathematics and physics. Here we confine ourselves to the general features of her model as they apply to the language domain and hence are of relevance to the development of metalinguistic awareness.

Karmiloff-Smith claimed that there are three distinct phases in the mastery of linguistic forms. During phase 1 the child develops mastery of the various instances of a particular linguistic form. The production of these forms depends on implicit procedures that operate in their entirety. The components of each procedure are not accessible and cannot be operated on separately. They are according to Karmiloff-Smith, implicit, or Level-I representations.

An example of the mastery of a particular form studied by Karmiloff-Smith is the production of the indefinite article by French speaking children. In French the indefinite article '*un*' or '*une*' has several different functions. It may be used for non-specific reference (for example, '*un crayon*' [a pencil], when any is required), for its numerical function (for example, '*un crayon* [one pencil], when only one is required), or for a naming function (for example, '*c'est un crayon*' [that's a pencil], when labelling an object). In phase 1 children master all of these functions, but using a separate *implicit* procedure for each. These implicit procedures all result in the same linguistic form as output (that is, '*un/une*') but they operate independently of each other.

Once these procedures all lead to correct productions, then behavioural mastery is achieved. This is detected by an internal monitoring device which initiates the representational redescription of the implicit procedures into a form that is accessible to internal processing. This redescription marks the passage into the second phase and because the components of the different forms can be accessed, they can be linked. In the case of the indefinite article, the separate procedures are linked and it is recognized that one common form exists but with several functions. The cognitive demands of phase 2 are considerable and as a result mistakes may occur in productions. The child may make use of cognitive props (for example, the addition of a partitive for the numerical function of the indefinite article – such as *un de mouchoir* – one of handkerchief). During phase 2 these errors, once detected, are corrected. This is carried out at a metaprocedural level involving Level-E1 representations. While these representations are important for further developments which will provide access to conscious reflection, Karmiloff-Smith points out her research indicates they are not themselves accessible to conscious reflection. They are explicit only in the sense that they are accessible to other components of the cognitive system. That is Level-E1 representations can be manipulated by the system and related to other representations.

When metaprocedural success is attained, the transition to phase 3 begins. This involves a further representational redescription of the procedures into a form that provides the individual with conscious access to the components of the redescribed procedures. The representations are now at Level-E2/3. The theory distinguishes between E2 representations which are available to conscious access but not to verbal report and E3 ones which are available to both conscious access and verbal report. It is not necessary however, for redescription to move from E1 to E2 and then to E3. Karmiloff-Smith certainly allows for the possibility of E3 representations arising directly from redescription of E1 representations. With reference to consideration of metalinguistic awareness, research has been concerned with E3 representations as these allow verbal report. **Conscious** access to the representations is the basis of metalinguistic awareness. That is, with respect to the particular linguistic form in question, the individual can reflect upon it deliberately and make linguistic judgements about it. Consequently with reference to the indefinite article, its production in speech in phase 3 will appear equivalent to that in phase 1. That is, productions will be error free. There is however a difference in the procedures underlying these identical behavioural forms. Those at phase 1 are **implicit** and inaccessible whereas those at phase 3 are **explicit** and **consciously accessible**. Thus the child in phase 3 can explain why the indefinite article is used in a given context and can also judge whether examples of its use are correct or not.

One important contribution of Karmiloff-Smith's model is that the development of metalinguistic awareness is not tied directly to a particular age or stage of development. With regard to the general theory, children may be in different phases of development in different domains. Moreover, the theory also recognizes microdomains as subsets within domains. Different linguistic structures will constitute different microdomains. Thus as she pointed out 'the child will be simultaneously at phase 1 for one aspect of language, phase 2 for another and phase 3 for yet another' (Karmiloff-Smith, 1986b, p. 115). Awareness of different aspects of language will be dependent on the phase with respect to each particular linguistic form rather than being tied to a stage of cognitive development. According to her model, children cannot reflect upon a particular form until they have a set of procedures that lead to correct productions and these procedures have undergone two levels of redescription.

### The Development of Metalinguistic Awareness is Determined by More General Changes in Cognition That Occur in Middle Childhood

This account of metalinguistic awareness is set out by Tunmer and Herriman (1984). They argued that metalinguistic awareness does not develop until middle childhood and involves control processing. According to this view, the development of metalinguistic awareness is dependent on the child's cognitive stage of development. Essentially metalinguistic awareness requires cognitive processes that are characteristic of the concrete operational stage of development and as a result, children are not able to reflect on language until they are in middle childhood. Tunmer and Herriman cited as evidence the fact that most research into metalinguistic awareness does not find children making explicit judgements about language until they are at least 5 years of age. They dismissed speech repairs suggesting that these merely involve automatic processes rather than control processes.

Further support for their position came from a study by Hakes (1980). Children were given three metalinguistic tasks, (judgements of the acceptability of sentences, judgements of the synonymy of sentences and segmentation of words into phonemes), and a Piagetian-type test of concrete operational thinking. They found that children's performances on the four tasks were highly correlated suggesting that all were related to the same underlying cognitive ability.

Tunmer and Herriman therefore saw the use of control processes as being the key to the appearance of metalinguistic awareness. Rather than proceeding at an automatic level which may lead to spontaneous corrections, control processing enables the individual to choose to focus attention on the language and carry out conscious operations on it.

There are two main difficulties with Tunmer and Herriman's account. They did not adequately deal with instances in early childhood where children's comments indicate that they are reflecting deliberately on language. They correctly pointed out that most of the research into the development of metalinguistic awareness indicated that children are unable to complete most metalinguistic tasks presented to them until at least 5 years of age. There is nevertheless a considerable amount of anecdotal evidence of instances of metalinguistic awareness at much earlier ages.

Secondly, they did not give any indication of the cause of what seems to be a fairly sudden and major cognitive shift from automatic processing to control processing. Although they hypothesized that there is an underlying cognitive change which is responsible, they did not offer any indication of the mechanisms that are responsible for this change nor why it should occur around 5 or 6 years of age.

## An Integrated Account of the Development of Metalinguistic Awareness

The three accounts of metalinguistic awareness involve conflicting claims about when and how metalinguistic awareness develops. Despite these differences, it is possible to combine much of what has been claimed into one model of the development of metalinguistic awareness. This model is based on that suggested by Bialystok and Ryan (1985a, 1985b) but extends their views to include conscious reflection on language that does not involve intentional control to gain initial access to language. In presenting this model it is important to consider very carefully what is implied by control. We stated earlier that metalinguistic awareness must involve reflection on language that is available to consciousness. We also pointed out that although we normally do not focus any attention on language we can do so if we choose. It is the second of these that is important when looking at the development of metalinguistic awareness. **Choosing** to look at language involves **deliberate control**. We believe that much of the disagreement about when metalinguistic awareness develops centres on this issue.

When children make speech repairs then, as stated above, this may occur without any awareness. At times though, the repairs do lead to reflection on language but it arises spontaneously. A speech error has triggered the reflection rather than the child deliberately focusing attention on the language for intrinsic interest.

There are many other examples where some aspect of language will spontaneously reach consciousness and will not require control processing to raise it to this level. One such example is again provided by our friend Kate, this time aged 3 years 1 month. Kate was sitting at the table when she asked 'Can I have a bit of cheese please? – *cheese please* – that's a rhyme.' Here the sounds of the words were sufficiently salient to lead Kate to comment on them. There is no doubt that underlying Kate's comment is a conscious reflection on one aspect of language. But this reflection did not require a deliberate and controlled focus of attention to bring it to a conscious level. That is, Kate was not being required to focus on the language and make an explicit comment about it. Instead the language led to spontaneous consideration of it and subsequent comment.

Other similar examples of this spontaneous, yet conscious reflection on language are given by Clark (1978) and include young children's comments on the speech of others. An example of this was given in chapter 4 where one child corrected the pronunciation of another child saying 'It's not dar, it's *c*ar.' Similarly Karmiloff-Smith quotes a 4-year-old child, Yara, who upon being told by her mother that the object for which she wants a name is a typewriter spontaneously comments, 'No, you're the typewriter, that's a typewrite.'

In addition, there is a great amount of print in the environment – a form of language that is much more durable than the transient nature of spoken language. It is thus likely that the young child's attention will be drawn to aspects of the printed language spontaneously. Print is there, right in front of children's eyes, and as they cannot yet read, they cannot go directly to the meaning as they do with the spoken word. They may however enquire about the reason for its existence or ask why there are spaces between some bits (letters) and not others.

This type of behaviour involving spontaneous comment on salient aspects of language, is similar to what Gombert (1992) has referred to as epilinguistic behaviour. According to Gombert, there exists a set of behaviours or activities that are strongly related to metalinguistic awareness, but are not sufficiently open to conscious reflection and deliberate control to justify being referred to as metalinguistic. He referred to these as epilinguistic and claimed that such behaviours are characterized by the low levels of knowledge they presuppose, and their interweaving in rich situational contexts.

The spontaneously triggered reflection on language, which is at a conscious level, will occur before deliberate reflection that requires high levels of control processing. The latter type involving control processing is required in the myriad of experimental tasks presented to children to determine their metalinguistic abilities. In these tasks, rather than some intrinsic property of a piece of language capturing the child's attention spontaneously, the experimenter expects the child to focus attention on a particular aspect at her request. Even with experimental tasks, one must take care to distinguish different degrees of difficulty as Bialystok (1991a) has pointed out. Some tasks will require the child to analyse the language in a context where the degree of control processing is low, whereas others will involve much greater control. Thus in a task where the child is asked to judge whether each of a series of sentences is grammatical, less control processing will be required if the sentences make sense to the child and do not contain semantic anomalies. Given the salience of the meaning of sentences, much higher levels of control are required if the sentences that are to be judged for their grammaticality contain semantic anomalies as well. Consequently when examining the development of metalinguistic awareness, we must take account of the nature of the task and the extent to which it involves control, in addition to considering the phase of development with respect to the linguistic forms being studied.

This model also explains the position adopted by Tunmer and Herriman. In their definition of metalinguistic awareness, they emphasized the importance of control processing and the requirement that one must be able to direct attention to the structure of language deliberately. Furthermore the research findings that they cited in support of their view all involved tasks that required high levels of control, levels that are unlikely to be found in children until 5 or more years of age.

In summary, then, we argue that metalinguistic abilities will develop gradually and that the level of the ability demonstrated by children will also depend on their mastery of the linguistic forms being considered. The growth of this awareness will have its roots in intrinsic properties of language that lead children to reflect spontaneously on aspects of language. Such properties will include the existence of speech repairs in one's own speech, the existence of errors such as mispronunciations in the speech of others, words that are difficult to pronounce, words that rhyme with each other and characteristics of the written word which, given its more visible and permanent form, will be more salient than the spoken word.

As the child further masters the different forms involved in language use, then increased levels of reflection will develop. The spontaneously triggered reflections will provide a basis for more controlled reflection. Consequently the child will make a gradual shift to reflecting deliberately on aspects of the language. It is likely that this shift will be enhanced by the developing mastery of the written language and that this mastery will lead to much higher levels of control. This issue will be taken up in more detail in the last section of this chapter.

## Phonological Awareness

The development of phonological awareness, or phonological sensitivity as it is sometimes referred to, is concerned with the developing awareness of the sounds of the language. This area has received much research attention in recent years because of its importance for reading. If children are to master the reading and writing processes, they must be able to learn the correspondences between the individual sounds of the language, the phonemes, and the letters that represent these sounds, the graphemes. In order to do this they must first be able to focus attention on the sounds.

Although phonemes are the most basic units of the language, combining to form words, focusing attention on them presents a particularly difficult task for the child. Liberman, Cooper, Shankweiler and Studdert-Kennedy (1967) have shown that although we perceive phonemes, they do not exist as separate entities in the flow of speech. There is no clear divide between the end of one phoneme and the beginning of the next. Liberman (1987) has described this as **coarticulation** of speech because there is substantial overlap, with the acoustic information for adjacent phonemes being transmitted at the same time. Consequently when we break up a word into its constituent sounds and say these sounds individually, for example 'cat' into **cuh ah tuh**, we are only able to produce approximations to the underlying phonemes. In appreciation of this, the reader should try saying **cuh ah tuh** as quickly as possible. You will note that however quickly you say it, the three sounds do not blend together into the word 'cat' unless a distinct jump is made that involves distorting the sounds.

Given the difficulty in identifying the individual sounds of speech how then do children develop this ability? Peter Bryant and his colleagues (for example MacLean, Bryant and Bradley, 1987; Bryant, Bradley, MacLean and Crossland, 1989; Bryant, MacLean, Bradley and Crossland, 1990) claimed that phonological awareness in children develops initially through an awareness of rhyme and that early experience with nursery rhymes will enhance the development of phonological awareness. In one study they found that some children as young as 3 years of age could classify words on the basis of whether they rhymed or not indicating the ability to recognize the common sounds that occur in some words (such as **ad** in 'lad' and 'sad').

Bryant et al. (1989) as part of a larger study looking at phonological awareness and reading, examined the relationship between children's knowledge of nursery rhymes at age 3 and phonological awareness at both 5 and 6 years of age. Knowledge of nursery rhymes at 3 years of age was assessed by asking each child in the study to recite five popular nursery rhymes and noting whether, for each rhyme, the child knew the whole rhyme, part or none of it.

Phonological awareness was assessed when the same children were 5 years of age using two phoneme oddity tasks – the opening phoneme test and the end phoneme test. The opening phoneme oddity task involved presenting children with sets of four words. In each set, three of the words started with the same sound while one did not (for example, peg *land* pin pot). The child had to detect the odd one out in each set. The end phoneme task was the same except the sets of words were selected so that the final phoneme of one of the words differed (for example, pin gun *hat* men). The opening phoneme task was again given to children when they were 6 years old.

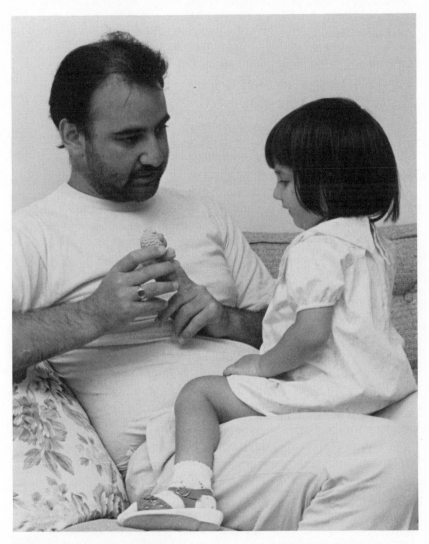

Early experience with nursery rhymes

The results indicated that there was a strong positive relationship between knowledge of nursery rhymes and phonological awareness at 5 and 6 years of age. Whereas a positive correlation cannot be taken as definitely showing that experience with nursery rhymes enhances the development of phonological awareness, their carefully controlled study does suggest a definite connection that merits further research attention.

In another study, Kirtley, Bryant, Maclean and Bradley (1989) pursued the possibility that it might be easier to detect some phonemes in words than others. In particular they argued that it would be easier for children, when presented with monosyllabic words, to make oddity judgements based on the initial phoneme than ones based on the middle or end phonemes. This prediction was based on the fact that there is a natural divide in monosyllabic words between the opening consonant or consonant cluster and the remainder of the word. These parts of the words are referred to as the **onset** and the **rime** and of course if the two rimes are identical (for example, **at**) then the words rhyme (for example, 'cat' and 'rat'). The tendency to break words naturally at this point had been referred to previously by Mackay (1972). He cited as evidence the fact that when speech errors occur that involve producing a combination of two semantically related words (such as 'shout' and 'yell'), then the onset of one (**sh**) is combined with the rime of the other (**ell**) to produce the combination (shell). The other possible error involving splitting each word after the vowel, producing for example 'shoull', is not heard. Consequently given the natural break that occurs, it is likely that children will find it easier to attend to the single onset sound than to attend to one of the two sounds bound together in the rime. The results of the study by Kirtley et al. (1989) confirmed this prediction. The 5-year-old children experienced more difficulty with the oddity tasks that involved basing judgements on one of the phonemes in the rime than those involving the onset phoneme.

Whereas the task used by Bryant and his colleagues required that children reflect on the sounds of the language in order to identify the odd word out, it does not involve the explicit awareness of single segmentation of the words into separate phonemes. A range of other tasks has been used to investigate this ability in children. The problem with some of these tasks however is that the child is required to say the sounds in the words and as mentioned above it is not possible to verbalize individual phonemes.

Liberman, Shankweiler, Fischer and Carter (1974) avoided this procedural problem by using a tapping task. Children were presented with a series of words, usually consisting of one to four phonemes, and required to indicate the number of sounds in each word by tapping once for each sound with a piece of wood on the table. Because it is very likely that the child will not have encountered such a strange task before, it is usually introduced with a series of examples given by the experimenter along with, at times, corrective feedback on the first few trials. The argument is that if children have the ability to segment words into phonemes, then the examples and feedback will be sufficient to convey the task requirements.

If they do not have the ability, then they will be unable to complete the task successfully. The results of the Liberman et al. (1974) study showed that preschool children were unable to determine the number of phonemes in words but the majority of first grade children were able to segment the words into their constituent phonemes.

Although this task seemed to avoid the difficulties encountered by others where the child has to verbalize the segments, Ehri and Wilce (1980) and Tunmer and Nesdale (1982) have shown that it may not be an unambiguous measure of phoneme segmentation ability. It is possible that children who are readers may invoke an alternative strategy to solve the task. They may respond on the basis of the spellings of the words.

Tunmer and Nesdale investigated this using the phoneme tapping task with preschool and first grade children aged between 4 and 6 years. They presented a set of 24 words half of which contained digraphs (pairs of letters that represent a single sound such as **sh** representing the /š/ sound in **sh**ut and **oo** representing the /u/ in roof). Their prediction was that if children used the spellings of the words then the number of taps would be equal to the number of letters and not sounds in the words. For example with 'book' they would tap four times, once for each letter instead of three times, once for each phoneme. In contrast their performance on non-digraph words would appear correct as the number of letters in 'bat' for example is equivalent to the number of phonemes.

There were two interesting aspects to their results. Firstly, although many of the preschool children performed poorly, about one-quarter of them could do the task successfully. These children had not received any formal reading instruction. Secondly, there were distinct patterns of responses that emerged in the older children with some correctly segmenting both non-digraph and digraph words while others performed less well on the digraphs, often tapping once for each letter. This suggested that these children were using the number of letters in the words as their strategy for the task.

The findings of this study raise the question of whether the children who used a letter strategy were unable to segment the words into phonemes. This seems unlikely because if these children can spell words, it is likely that they can read and consequently will be able to identify individual phonemes. (See the later section in this chapter and chapter 9 for a full discussion of this point.)

It is more likely that these children are able to segment words into phonemes but that once they can spell the words, the number of letters becomes a more salient cue and so they make use of this strategy. Essentially they do not have the high degree of control processing required to focus attention on the phonemes which are less salient than letters.

Recent work by Martin, Fraser and Pratt (1996) certainly suggests young readers are at least as able to manipulate the sounds of words as they are the letters. Although the study was investigating the basis of reading disability, data from comparison groups of average readers are of relevance here. Martin et al. based their study on a different measure of phonological awareness, namely the deletion task originally developed by Bruce (1964). This task involves orally presenting the child with a word and asking the child to say what is left when a sound is deleted from the word, for example what is left when the /s/ is removed from stop, or the /n/ from snail. Using this task and taking account of a modification reported by Stuart (1990), Martin et al. presented groups of children aged 8 and 11 years with two variants of the task, in counterbalance order across children. One of the variants required the child to say what word sound was left when a particular *sound* was deleted from a word. For example the child was asked "If I remove the /r/ sound from bread what word is left?". The other variant required the child to say what word the letters spelled when a particular *letter* was deleted. The example in this case would be "If I remove the letter 'r' what does the new word spell?". Children were given two practice words for each type of presentation. In addition, there were two modes of presentation, spoken and written, with the latter including the presentation of the items written in large font on cards. The results of this study revealed that in the spoken mode, the performance of the younger age group was much higher on phoneme deletions than letter deletions. The difference for the older group was in the same direction but not so marked. For the written mode of presentation, the younger group performed at similar levels on both phoneme and letter deletion tasks, while the performance of the older group was superior on the letter deletion task.

Of particular importance here is the performance for the spoken mode as this is the mode of presentation used in most phonological awareness tasks. As stated, this showed that when a deletion task is used children experience more difficulty with responses that rely on the deletions of letters and consequent spelling of the new word, than those relying on the deletions of sounds and the consequent sound of the new word. Thus the type of task presented may well influence the extent to which children rely on or are influenced by the spelling of the words.

Consideration of tasks investigating the development of phonological awareness raises an issue of importance to much work investigating linguistic and cognitive abilities in with children. It is essentially very difficult to design a task that provides a pure measure of the ability being investigated, which is not affected by other factors. With regard to the phoneme tapping task, which avoids the need to say individual sounds,

Goswami and Bryant (1990) point out that it does require an understanding of one-to-one correspondence (one tap corresponds to one sound) which is not fully developed in children until age 5 or 6. Consequently children's performance on the deletion task may not accurately reflect their phonological skills as it may be affected by an understanding of one-to-one correspondence, as well as by their early orthographic knowledge. Similarly, the deletion task involves holding the word presented by the investigator in memory while the child carries out an operation on that word and determines what word is derived from it. As pointed out by Rohl and Pratt (1995) the ability to do this will clearly be linked to working memory capacity, and again children's performance on the task may not be an accurate reflection of their phonological awareness. In this context, research by McBride-Chang (1995) has shown that children's general cognitive ability, working memory capacity and speech perception all contribute to performance on a range of phonological awareness tasks.

In recognition that single tasks may not provide an accurate and comprehensive measure of phonological awareness, many researchers now include several measures of phonological awareness in their work so that they can develop a more accurate picture of when it develops. Yopp (1988), and Høien, Lundberg, Stanovich and Bjaalid (1995) have both examined the inter-relationships between a range of different tasks. Unfortunately, the results of these two studies are not directly comparable for a number of reasons including being conducted in different languages (American English and Norwegian respectively), the use of group testing methods in the Høien et al. study and problems in the same study with ceiling effects as a result of many children getting all or close to all items correct. Nevertheless both studies would suggest that not all phonological awareness tasks are measuring exactly the same underlying abilities.

Some researchers have argued that the differences are ones of degree, with, for example Stanovich (1992) discussing phonological sensitivity as ranging from shallow to deep, with deeper levels requiring greater degrees of awareness. In contrast, Høien et al. argue that there are different components of phonological awareness corresponding to the different levels of language analysis required. With regard to phonological awareness tasks these authors distinguish between *rhyme awareness*, as measured by tasks such as those used by Bryant and colleagues discussed above, and *phonemic awareness*, as measured by deletion and tapping tasks which require manipulation of individual phonemes.

Overall, the research into the development of phonological awareness suggests that children initially become aware of the sounds of language as they notice some words sound similar – that is, they rhyme. As suggested earlier, the occurrence of rhyming words in close proximity to each other in speech may well trigger spontaneous reflection on the sounds of the words. This will lead the child to focus on both the similarity between the words and the difference. When monosyllabic words are considered, it is easier to attend both to the parts of the words that are the same (that is, the identical rimes) and to the parts that are different (that is, the onsets) as a result of the natural division between rime and onset. Thus the child has gained access to single phonemes, the onsets. From this point deliberate reflection may be extended to other phonemes in words until the child is able to carry out phonemic segmentation of the level required in tapping tasks and other similar tasks. It may be however, that the development from awareness of rhyme to individual phonemes relies on additional input that is for most children linked to reading instruction.

## Word Awareness

The research into the development of word awareness has focused on children's understanding that a word is a linguistic unit distinct from other units (such as phonemes and phrases) and that it is an arbitrary symbol which does not bear any direct relationship to the object it represents.

In a series of studies reported by Berthoud-Papandropoulou (1978), Swiss children aged between 4 and 12 years were asked a number of questions designed to investigate their understanding of the word concept. They were asked to define the term 'word' ('Do you know what a word is? – What do you think?'), to say whether they thought various exemplars were words or not, to count the number of words in a spoken sentence and to give examples of long, short and difficult words.

The results of this research indicated that the younger children did not make any distinction between the word and the object to which it refers and therefore did not regard words as separate linguistic entities. When defining the term word their justifications often referred to the properties of the object (for example, 'Strawberry is a word, because it grows in the garden').

Four- and 5-year-olds also frequently rejected many words as not being words, particularly if these were short function words such as prepositions and articles. They did however accept phrases as examples of single words. Bowey and Tunmer (1984) have suggested that this is another example of children both underextending and overextending their use of a word, in this case the word 'word'. In the development of the meaning of words, over- and underextensions normally occur because the child focuses on one attribute of the concept being referred to. For example, a child may extract four leggedness as the defining attribute of the term 'dog' (see chapter 4). With the metalinguistic term 'word' though, young children do not focus on a characteristic of the linguistic entity itself. Instead they focus attention on the meaning or the idea that is represented by the word. Thus the difficulty children experience in defining the domain of reference for the term 'word' is a result of the difficulty in focusing attention on the linguistic unit. They do not have the degree of control required to achieve this.

Children say that content words such as nouns and verbs are words earlier than function words, not because they have a more salient linguistic form, but because they have an identifiable unit of meaning for the child. Similarly short noun phrases such as 'the big man' are accepted because they convey a single meaning for the child. Function words however are not accepted either because they do not represent a separately identifiable meaning or because the meaning of the word in isolation is too abstract for the child to grasp.

Children's replies to the other questions posed by Berthoud-Papandropoulou generally confirmed that they have difficulty separating the linguistic entity from the meaning and focusing attention on it. When asked to give examples of long words they gave words such as 'train' and 'cupboard' (because there is a lot of stuff in it), and for short words they volunteered 'eye' and 'primrose' (because they are small).

For the majority of children this confusion between the object and the word itself continues until they start to read and write at school. In print, the existence of words as entities separate from their referents is much more salient. Frequently for children who are facing the challenges of learning to decode the text, the meaning of the words is far from salient. The influence of the written word in helping children understand the concept is evident in the definitions of words given by children in the Berthoud-Papandropoulou study. Once they had begun to read, 56 children aged 6 to 12 years made reference to the letters that make up words, while only six children referred to the sounds that are in words. Consequently many children will be assisted in their task of developing an understanding of the 'word' concept following their introduction to print. They will not only find it easier to focus attention on individual words as separate linguistic entities but they will also develop an understanding that words are arbitrary units that do not have any direct relationship to their referents. They will see long words written that represent small objects (like 'millipede') and short words that represent big objects (like 'whale'). They will also see that words such as articles and prepositions exist as words in their own right.

The work of Berthoud-Papandropoulou, along with other research using similar techniques, has provided important insights into the development of the word concept in children. It should not necessarily be interpreted however as suggesting young children do not have some concept of this linguistic entity that is independent of its meaning. It is now well established that children will strive to make sense of questions posed by adults and that even if they are not familiar with some of the terms used by adults, they may make a guess about what they are being asked, often an inspired guess based on salient aspects of the context, and answer on this basis (Donaldson, 1978).

So although it has been shown that young children confuse properties of the object with the word itself, it may be that they do have *some* concept of the linguistic entity 'word' and can reflect on it at some level. Their confusion might arise because they are not familiar with the term 'word', and, given the importance of meaning for children, they may infer that they are being asked about this more salient aspect. Consequently, it may be that children are able to reflect on words as linguistic entities earlier than these studies suggest.

The possibility that young children have some concept of a word was investigated in a study by Bowey, Tunmer and Pratt (1984). Using a modification of a technique developed by Downing (1969, 1971), they examined the ability of children aged between 5 and 8 years in preschool and Grades 1 and 2 to discriminate words from phonemes and words from phrases. Children were presented with a series of stimuli and were asked in each case whether it was a word or not. The word stimuli always consisted of familiar one- and two-syllable words that were contrasted in separate tasks with sounds that did not constitute English words (such as /ɛ/, /f/, /tə/, /kə/) and with short two word phrases (such as 'the storm', 'cold wind').

To take account of the use of the term *word* in the instructions, half the children at each age level received a short training task. The training was essentially the same as the test trials with children being asked to say whether each stimulus they heard was a word or not. During the training corrective feedback with explanations was given. Depending on the particular task, the explanations consisted of telling the child that a sound was a little part of the word and that words were made up of more than one sound (the word–phoneme discrimination task) or that, for example the phrase 'cold wind' was made up of two words and that 'cold' is a word and 'wind' is a word (the word–phrase task). It can be assumed that if the children were not able to reflect on the linguistic units involved, then they would not benefit in any way from the training as they would not be able to attach the explanations provided in the corrective feedback to any concept they had. If they could focus attention on these entities though, but did not know the term 'word' then those receiving the short training would benefit. Their performance would be better than the group of children who did not have any training. The children who received training would benefit because they would have had the opportunity to determine exactly what they were being asked.

The results indicated that the 6- to 8-year-old children in Grades 1 and 2 had a reasonable grasp of the word concept and could discriminate words from sounds and phrases, particularly when the words were content words (nouns, verbs and adjectives). These children were able to do this whether or not they received training. This suggested that they had some understanding of the term *word* and did not require training to convey its meaning when working with content words. Function words presented more difficulty and both the year 1 and 2 children benefited from training when function words were involved.

In contrast, the 5–year-old preschool children who did not receive any training were not able to discriminate content or function words from other linguistic units. Those who received training however were able reliably to discriminate content words from sounds and phrases indicating that they were able to attend to these linguistic units when required to do so. This did not extend to the function words, suggesting that the ability to direct attention to arbitrary linguistic units is not fully developed by this age.

Karmiloff-Smith, Grant, Sims, Jones and Cuckle (1996), using a different technique have probed children's awareness of what counts as a word. They read paragraphs to 4- and 5-year-old children and at predetermined points in the paragraph paused and asked the children in the study to say what was the last word. The pauses all followed words that were likely to be familiar to the children, and were inserted so that half immediately followed an open class word (nouns, verbs and adjectives) and half a closed class word (determiners, conjunctions, prepositions and particles). In addition the pauses followed both one and two syllable words, with the two syllable ones providing scope to determine whether children might adopt an incorrect strategy of giving the last syllable when asked.

Children were not given any explicit information about what the experimenter meant by 'word' but all were given a practice paragraph with corrective feedback and, if required, modelling of responses. The results of their work confirm that young children do have some concept of a word. Overall, the 5-year-old children were correct over 95 per cent of the time and the 4-year-old children around 75 per cent. In a second experiment, the researchers investigated the extent to which children may be repeating the last word without appreciating that it was in fact a word.

They asked 5-year-old children in one group to repeat 'not the last word, but the last thing' and those in the other group to repeat 'not the last thing, but the last word'. The performance of the two groups was markedly different. Children in the word group correctly identified the last word 87 per cent of the time, whereas children in the thing group identified the last word only 4 per cent of the time, providing a clear indication that children's high performance on the word task was not simply a result of them happening to repeat the last word without awareness or understanding that it was a word.

Interestingly, in contrast to the work of others, the study reported by Karmiloff-Smith et al. indicates there was no significant difference in performance between open and closed class words. This is of particular interest given the practice paragraph was restricted to words following concrete nouns such that children had not been given any training on closed class (or function) words. It may be that the pause following a preposition or conjunction which is embedded in the flow of text leads to it being more easily identifiable as a word than in the Bowey et al. (1984) procedure. Certainly, in Karmiloff-Smith et al.'s (1996) study if a pause came immediately after a preposition or other closed class word, that word would have been preceded by a content or open class word. This might have the effect of increasing the salience as it falls between a more easily recognizable word and a pause.

However, it also worth noting that children in the Karmiloff-Smith et al. study were in the second term of school. Although children at the same stage of schooling were older in the Bowey et al. study, their performance on the two classes of words following feedback was not that discrepant from those in the Karmiloff-Smith et al. study. Karmiloff-Smith et al. conducted a final experiment in which they presented the task to younger 4–year-old children who had just begun attending school. In this case the performance was not only lower overall (42 per cent correct), but there was a difference between the open class words (58 per cent) and the closed class words (37 per cent). Taken in conjunction with other work these results suggest that school experience is an important determiner of performance on word awareness tasks.

In summary therefore it can be concluded that prior to school, children have some awareness of words although this may well be limited to content words. Furthermore it is likely that they do not attach the label 'word' to their somewhat vague notion of the linguistic unit. They are more likely to interpret 'word' as referring to properties of the objects or actions represented by words. Thus if words do not represent objects or actions and therefore lack concrete properties, as is the case with function words, then they will not be regarded as words.

Once children attend school and embark on the process of learning to read and write, the linguistic unit becomes more salient and they are then able to apply their initial awareness of words as separate entities to their more permanent existence in written language. This will enable the concept to be further refined and extended to include function words while also being narrowed to exclude phrases.

## Syntactic Awareness

The study of development of syntactic awareness, or grammatical awareness as it is often referred to, in children has mainly been concerned with their awareness of sentence grammar. Although children are able to produce grammatically correct sentences in their speech from a relatively young age, this cannot be taken as evidence for syntactic awareness. Correct productions normally result from tacit knowledge of grammar in a form that may not be available to deliberate reflection. Consequently the tasks that are used to investigate syntactic awareness have been designed to ensure that successful performance requires deliberate and controlled reflection on the grammaticality of sentences rather than the tacit knowledge involved in speech production and comprehension.

Two main tasks have been used. These are the **judgement** task where children are required to judge whether sentences are grammatically correct and the **correction** task where they are required to correct sentences containing syntactic violations (see Blackmore, Pratt and Dewsbury, 1995, for a review of research using these tasks). As with the research into word awareness, the salience of the meaning conveyed by language can influence performance with children tending to evaluate sentences by their meaning. Tunmer and Grieve (1984) reported that children in the 4- to 7-year age range may reject a sentence that is acceptable grammatically because the meaning of the sentence contradicts their experience. For example, the sentence 'Yesterday Daddy painted the fence' was rejected by a 4-year-old on the grounds that 'Daddies don't paint fences; they paint walls' (Tunmer and Grieve, 1984, pp. 99–100). Equally they accept sentences with grammatical violations in them if the meaning is still evident and acceptable to them.

Pratt, Tunmer and Bowey (1984) used a procedure that minimized the influence of meaning on performance to determine whether young children could correct syntactic errors. They presented 5- and 6-year-old children with a correction task where the sentences were carefully selected so that the meanings of them, once corrected, would be acceptable to the children. It was explained to the children that every sentence they heard contained an error and that they were required to 'fix up each one'. Two types of grammatical violations were used – word order violations (such as Teacher the read a story) and morpheme deletions from obligatory contexts (such as Yesterday John bump his head). The two types of violations were presented by two puppets who were introduced to each child as not being able to speak properly. The child was asked to correct each puppet's utterances.

For the morpheme deletion sentences, both the 5- and 6-year-old children were able to correct most sentences and attained mean scores of over 90 per cent correct. In contrast, the word order task was more difficult, with 5-year-olds getting less than 50 per cent correct on average while 6-year-olds scored over 75 per cent correct. The lower performance in the word order task was most likely the result of these syntactic violations leading to greater disruptions to the meaning of the sentence. In the word order task, the meaning is often not apparent and the sentence has to be remembered as separate chunks that need to be reordered to provide a correct and meaningful sentence. This places great demands on the processing that is required and probably involves much more reflection on the grammatical structures involved than the morpheme deletion task.

The possibility that processing capacity limits children's performance on syntactic awareness tasks was investigated by Blackmore et al. (1995). They compared performance on the standard correction task to a condition in which toy props were used to provide contextual support that reduced the processing demands. The props were selected such that they provided concrete examples of the main referents in each ungrammatical string but were not sufficient in themselves to provide the meanings or correct syntactic forms of the sentences. Deriving the correct form still required focusing on the ungrammatical string presented. As predicted performance in the condition with props was superior to the standard condition.

Whereas the correction task offers certain advantages, it has also been criticized because it may not be providing a sufficiently clear indication of children's syntactic awareness. Bowey (1994) argued that the higher performance on the morpheme deletion task in the Pratt et al. (1984) study may not simply be a result of it requiring less processing capacity because the changes had minimal effect on the meaning compared with word order violations. She claims it is likely that many of the corrections would have been made by children spontaneously without them even realizing the sentence they heard was incorrect or therefore that they had corrected it.

Bowey (1994) cited evidence from her earlier research (Bowey, 1986) in which she examined this possibility. In a large study with children aged between 5 and 10 years, she presented children with a sentence memory task and a sentence imitation task in addition to a sentence correction task. In the sentence memory task, the children were required to repeat sentences of different lengths. Some of these were grammatically correct, while in others a random word order was used. Children's memory for the correct sentences was superior to that for random order ones with many failing to recall any random order ones correctly.

The results indicated that correcting word order violations might be more difficult for children because they have difficulty remembering the words in the sentence that they have to correct. However, of greater interest to her claim regarding spontaneous corrections was the performance on the sentence imitation task. The imitation task was similar to the memory task as children were expected to repeat the sentences they heard verbatim. Both the imitation and the correction tasks included morpheme deletions and minor word order violations. The results showed that the 5-year-olds frequently had difficulty repeating sentences with the errors still in them and would often produce a corrected version. They seemed unaware of the error when presented with the sentence. This occurred even when they were explicitly reminded following spontaneous corrections that they were to repeat it as they heard it. The remaining groups were all able to repeat the sentences with the errors still in them. Performance on the correction task was also lowest for the youngest children but increased more gradually across the different age groups.

As Bowey pointed out, her results show that even when children are told that sentences do contain errors, 5-year-olds may have difficulty detecting these. At times they may spontaneously correct them as found on the imitation task. This will lead to them appearing to be able to correct these sentences deliberately in a correction task, resulting in a falsely high estimate of their abilities on correction tasks. Nevertheless while qualifying the findings of these studies, Bowey's argument should not be taken as suggesting that all corrections by 5-year-old children are spontaneous and lack awareness. Many children when making corrections use contrastive stress to emphasize the morpheme that they have inserted and in so doing are demonstrating that they have detected the error and corrected it.

Rather than trying to avoid the influence of sentences that do not have acceptable meanings for children, Bialystok (1986) deliberately exploited the influence of meaning to examine changes in the degree of control children bring to the task. Her study involved both a judgement task and a correction task and she included both bilingual and monolingual children. We will restrict consideration here to the monolingual children's performance on the judgement task. In this task children were required to judge the syntactic acceptability of four different sentence types. Sentences were either grammatical and meaningful, grammatical but anomalous, ungrammatical but meaningful, or ungrammatical and anomalous. Bialystok's argument was that, because of the salience of meaning, the sentences which were anomalous would require higher levels of control processing and would therefore be more difficult to judge for syntactic acceptability.

The results generally confirmed this prediction with children making more correct judgements when the sentences were grammatical and meaningful or ungrammatical and anomalous, than when the sentences were grammatical and anomalous or ungrammatical but meaningful. It seemed from their performance that all children experienced considerable difficulty in controlling their focus of attention solely to the grammaticality of the sentences. Consequently, they performed very poorly on the sentences where judgements based on meaning were in conflict with judgements based on grammaticality.

Although of theoretical interest, the ability to make grammatical judgements independently of meaning is probably of little practical value to children. What is important is that they can, if required, evaluate the grammatical aspects of sentences. This is of particular importance both when children are learning to read and once they have mastered the process. When children are learning to read, they often encounter words that they cannot decode. They will be greatly assisted in the task of trying to find out what the word is if they use their knowledge of syntax as well as semantics and pragmatics (see chapter 9). Once they have mastered the reading process, their knowledge of syntax will continue to play an important role in monitoring and detecting errors of comprehension. For example, if one reads 'they was going to the fair', the detection of a disagreement between the subject and the verb suggests a reading error. It is important therefore to re-read the sentence to ensure that the correct meaning is obtained. Hence the development of syntactic awareness plays an important role in the development of literacy.

## Pragmatic Awareness

The study of pragmatic awareness has encompassed a wide range of topics including children's awareness of communication processes, their understanding of the social influences on language and their ability to evaluate the consistency of incoming linguistic propositions. As the first two of these have been considered in chapter 6 where we examined children's understanding of communication failure and their ability to evaluate request forms and match these to different social situations, we will consider the ability to monitor incoming information in this section.

This ability is an important one as it enables individuals to monitor their comprehension of incoming information. We assume that in normal circumstances information we hear in a conversation or lecture, or that we read in a book, will be consistent. If we notice an apparent contradiction from one sentence to the next or from one paragraph to the next, then this signals a possible comprehension failure. Action can then be taken, either in the form of seeking clarification from the speaker or re-reading a passage in the book.

The question at what age do children develop this ability was first studied by Markman (1979, 1981). She read children passages that contained inconsistencies. For example one passage that described different types of fish contained the following information:

> Fish must have light in order to see. There is absolutely no light at the bottom of the ocean. It is pitch black down there. When it is that dark the fish cannot see anything. They cannot even see colours. Some fish that live at the bottom of the ocean can see the colour of their food; that is how they know what to eat. (Markman, 1979, p. 646)

Markman found that even when the inconsistency was stated explicitly, as in the above extract, many children failed to notice it. Typically children up to 11 years of age did not detect any problems with the passages which implied that they were not monitoring their comprehension of them. In discussing her findings, however, Markman acknowledged that her task was quite a difficult one and that the results should not be taken as indicating that children of younger ages cannot monitor incoming information for consistency in other situations.

To determine whether younger children could detect inconsistencies, Tunmer, Nesdale and Pratt (1983) presented children with much shorter passages that described events which would be within most children's experiences. Each passage contained only three sentences and the children were told beforehand that some of the passages would be silly and not make sense while others would be okay and would make sense. The child's task was to evaluate each story. Some children received versions of the stories where the inconsistency was explicitly stated in the passage. Others were given versions where the contradiction was implicit and could only be detected if the information contained in the passage was evaluated with respect to one's existing knowledge of relevant information. A typical example of a passage containing inconsistent information is: 'When bikes have broken wheels, you can't ride them. One morning a car ran over Johnny's bike and broke the wheel. Johnny then picked up his bike and rode it over to a friend's house.' The equivalent implicit version of the story was produced by replacing the first sentence with the sentence 'Johnny got a new bike for his birthday.' The results indicated that by age 5, many children were able to evaluate the consistency of such stories. Although performance was generally higher on stories that contained explicit contradictions, some children were able to judge the implicit stories with a fair degree of accuracy. Consequently when children were given short passages that were based on events within their own experience, they could monitor these for consistency.

Pratt, Tunmer and Nesdale (1989) extended this work to examine children's ability to detect inconsistencies in passages that varied according to the extent to which they were based on experience. As Bruner (1986) has pointed out, one very important function of language is that it can be used to create and describe imaginary worlds. In stories, worlds are often created where the events that occur, although internally consistent within the story, will contradict children's own experiences. The Mr Men books, such as *Mr Silly*, written by Roger Hargreaves, provide an excellent example of such stories. Consequently if children are to monitor their comprehension of such stories they must be able to evaluate the consistency of passages independently of the relationship between the information contained in the stories and their own experience.

Pratt et al. investigated this using three different types of passages. These were **experienced-based** containing information that was within children's experience; **neutral** containing information which expressed arbitrary relationships; and **contra-experience** that presented information which contradicted children's own experiences. For all passage types both inconsistent and consistent versions were produced and again children were required to evaluate the consistency of each passage. The experience-based passages were the same as the ones used in the previous study. Examples of the other passages are:

**Neutral**
If it is the red stick, then it is the longest one. John looked at the different coloured sticks and picked out the red one. It was the shortest stick.

**Contra-experience**
In upside-down land fruit juice gets very hot in the fridge. One day Bob got the juice out of his fridge in upside-down land. His juice was very cold.

The results again indicated that by 5 or 6 years, children are developing the ability to detect inconsistencies in short passages. Further they are equally able to do this for neutral passages and experience-based passages. More difficulty was experienced with the contra-experience passages although some 6–year-olds were able to evaluate these accurately.

Dias and Harris (1988) found similar results when they examined 4- to 6-year-old children's reasoning ability. They presented children with syllogisms, some of which ran counter to their own knowledge. For example, children were presented with the following:

> All snow is black.
> Tom touches some snow.
> Is it black?

They found that children were much more likely to give the correct answers if the syllogisms that ran counter to their knowledge were given in a 'make-believe' context, using 'make-believe' intonation, than if they were presented in a 'matter of fact' manner.

These studies reveal that children can monitor incoming information. It is likely however that in their everyday interactions they will be less efficient in their monitoring than in experimental conditions where they are encouraged to do so. Consequently when comprehension failures arise children should be encouraged to reflect on these and discuss the reasons for misunderstandings and failures to follow the intended meanings of utterances. This is particularly important in the classroom where children may experience difficulty with much of the language used and fail to evaluate their comprehension properly. They will benefit greatly if the opportunities are provided for them to develop their metalinguistic skills further .

## Metalinguistic Awareness, Reading and Literacy

In this section we examine the relationship between metalinguistic awareness and reading, and then consider the broader issue of metalinguistic awareness and literacy. There has been considerable disagreement about whether the ability to reflect upon language is an outcome of learning to read or a prerequisite for mastery of reading. Donaldson (1978) has suggested that the process of learning to read in school is responsible for the development of metalinguistic awareness. She believed that reading is the trigger which leads children to develop metalinguistic control, control that in turn extends to other cognitive domains. In contrast, Tunmer and Bowey (1984) stated that 'the metalinguistic ability to reflect on language should . . . be an important prerequisite for being able to read, since without this ability the child would not be able to discover the properties of spoken language that are central to the correspondences between its written and spoken forms' (p. 152).

Although these two views are opposing, both probably contain elements that are correct. As we stated earlier in this chapter, the capacity to reflect on aspects of language exists before the child encounters reading instruction. This reflection frequently arises spontaneously and does not result initially from deliberate control. For the majority of children who come from homes that do not place a lot of emphasis on language, any reflection on language prior to school entry may have been spontaneous. Being faced with the task of learning to read will focus more attention on language. As we will describe in chapter 9, children must be able to focus attention on words and sounds in order to master the decoding of text. Children will not be able to work out letter–sound correspondences if they cannot focus attention on phonemes.

Furthermore as the teacher in the class will be talking about words, sounds and other linguistic units, children must learn to focus attention on these deliberately, in a manner that requires higher levels of control. These units of language will become the topic of communication sequences between teacher and child. A teacher may ask a child, 'What sound does the first letter of that word make?'. Initially many children will have great difficulty with such questions and teachers need to be aware that such deliberate and conscious reflection poses a challenge for children. Nevertheless the permanent form of written language and the fact that children cannot go directly to the meaning when they first encounter this form, does help them take on the challenge. Gradually as they master the printed word, they will develop higher levels of control over focusing attention on language and they will develop a wider spectrum of knowledge about different linguistic units.

There will of course be large individual differences between children that will influence the process of learning to read. For some children the capacity to reflect upon language will be more developed than others. Olson (1984) has pointed out that children who grow up in homes where literacy is valued are often explicitly taught words by their parents. The parent will sit with the child on his or her knee and as they look at a book together, will proceed to teach the meanings of individual words. They will start by considering nouns with the child being told it is a picture of a dog. The parent may repeat the word several times and then encourage the child to say the word, (for example, 'Jessie, say dog'). This pattern of interaction becomes well established in the first two years and the content of the interactions is extended to cover other words including adjectives and verbs. The parent may, for example, point to a picture of a man with a spade and say 'Look – digging – the man is digging – Sebastian say digging.' In addition to these interaction sequences extending children's vocabulary, they focus joint and explicit attention on language units. Children who experience such sequences become more aware of language. These children also become more familiar with a format for teaching that they will encounter in the classroom when, for example, the teacher is instructing children to say the word that is written on the blackboard.

Many children will not have had these experiences during the preschool years and for these children the limited ability to reflect on language that has arisen from spontaneously motivated instances must be developed deliberately by the teacher. There are many ways this can be done including encouraging children to develop an interest in trying to write, as described in the next chapter.

The broader issue concerning the relationship between literacy and metalinguistic awareness is a complex one and we certainly do not claim to provide a definitive account of this relationship. Rather we offer a few pointers that give an indication of what might be involved. In this context we wish again to make it clear that we do not take as our definition of literacy a narrow one concerned only with the ability to read and write. Rather we believe that literacy should be and frequently is interpreted more broadly to refer to a mastery of the language, in both its written and spoken forms, which enables an individual to exercise control over its use. In essence we think of a literate person as someone who uses language fluently and can exercise choice over how the intended meaning is conveyed. This can be extended to describe literate societies that have developed a high degree of control over their language. They have translated it into written forms and can move back and forth between the two forms exercising choice about which form to use and how to use each form.

Viewed in this manner, we believe that metalinguistic awareness and literacy are intricately interwoven and historically have developed together. It is also the case that developmentally for the child the two intermingle in development. The development of metalinguistic awareness mainly involves looking beyond the salient meaning conveyed by the language to the linguistic units that are involved. It does in turn provide much greater control over meaning. Whereas the young child tends to go directly to a particular meaning that he or she sees as the obvious one, the 'metalinguistically aware' child appreciates that the language we use does not have a one-to-one correspondence to meaning. Words are arbitrary sets of sounds that take on meanings through their use in shared social domains. Normally this domain will be the culture or subculture within which the word is used.

Further the syntax of the language enables us to represent the same or similar underlying meanings in different ways. For example, the sentences 'the cat chased the dog' and 'the dog was chased by the cat' have the same meaning. Also the existence of homonyms (such as 'sun' and 'son') and overlapping surface forms of the language leads to the production of utterances that can have identical surface forms but different meanings. Examples of the latter include ambiguous sentences such as 'Visiting relatives can be boring' and 'The robber took the money from the bank' ('and then rowed away', or 'and then jumped in the getaway car'). Consequently, one major outcome of the development of metalinguistic awareness is the more controlled extraction of meaning. The individual can deliberate over the meaning and reflect upon the most appropriate interpretation of an utterance or text.

Similarly when producing language, children become more able to choose how they want to say something. They can choose between a selection of words and syntactic structures to convey subtleties of meaning or to match an intended meaning to a particular situation. Children also learn that some constructions are more appropriate in written language while others are better suited to spoken language. Initially, as Olson (1988) claims, it is likely that the exercising of choice involving reflection on the various possibilities will occur when writing rather than speaking, for the act of writing is a much more deliberate activity. This in turn will lead to greater reflection on language, reflection that will generalize to spoken language and provide greater control over language use.

Chaney (1992), whose research reveals strong links between early metalinguistic abilities demonstrated by 3–year-olds and their overall language development, has suggested that many children of this age are already developing a mental framework for analysing language structure. For her, this provides children with the ability to solve key problems they encounter with language ". . . such as 'Where are the word boundaries in Humpty Dumpty satonawall?' and 'Do I say spaghetti or pasketti?' " (p. 512). In asking such questions children are demonstrating the ability to talk about and reflect on language as well as an understanding about choice. In these cases of course the choice is between a correct way to do or say something, which is what the child wants to know, and one or more incorrect ways. However, it is not a great step to move from this type of consideration about choice to choosing between two or more acceptable forms and deciding which is the most appropriate for the context, be it a written or spoken context.

Consequently we believe that much of what we regard as literacy when referring to a command of both spoken and written language forms is based on skills derived from metalinguistic knowledge. It is these skills that enable choice and control, and it is the exercising of choice and control that is central to literacy. Learning to read and write will play an important role in the overall development. The activities involved will enhance the further development of reflection on language and will also lead children to use their diverse range of metalinguistic knowledge in an integrated manner when speaking, listening, reading and writing.

# CHAPTER EIGHT

# Learning to Write

This chapter and the one following are concerned with the development of children's understanding of the written word. In this chapter the focus is on the processes involved in learning to write, while the next chapter deals with children learning to read. Clearly there is a great deal of overlap in the skills that children must master when learning to read and learning to write, and much of what the child learns while engaging in one of these activities will be of relevance and benefit to the other. Consequently although we focus on each of the two activities, learning to write and learning to read, in turn, the reader should be aware that there are important links between them and that the learning that occurs while engaging in one, benefits the other.

## Approaches to Writing

Before considering the processes that are involved when children learn to write, it is necessary first to examine the approaches that have been taken in the teaching of writing. There is no clear agreement in the literature about how children learn to write and as a result there are many approaches which differ on points of detail. For our purposes, however, the majority of these may be grouped together under the general heading of the **traditional approach**, as they involve the same basic assumptions about how children learn to write. According to this approach, which dominated people's thinking in the area for many years, children do not and indeed should not learn to write until they attend school. It is argued that writing is a very complex activity and that it must therefore be taught by qualified teachers. Essentially children learn to write as a result of formal instruction.

Many educators who adopted this position extended the argument to claim that learning to write should follow on from learning to read. That is, children should first be given the basic skills in reading and then they will be able to make use of these skills when learning to write. Because it is assumed children will have acquired a basic knowledge about letter–sound correspondences through their early reading, a heavy emphasis on teaching children to print the letters is frequently associated with this approach. As Dyson (1985a) has pointed out, this often requires that children spend large amounts of time copying writing that the teacher has written on the board. This can lead to children developing rather strange notions about the reasons for writing, a point clearly illustrated by the reply of one child in her study when asked why adults write. 'Big people', she said, 'got to write to show the people – the little people – what to write. . . . They write the alphabet that we folks write, little folks' (p. 498).

Once children have accomplished the basics of copying letters, then they can be given additional help with the spelling of more difficult words and with learning about the different forms of writing involved, for example, in writing stories or making diary entries.

We, along with a number of other researchers (for example, Clay, 1987, 1991; Dyson, 1985a; Hall, 1987), reject this viewpoint because it fails to take adequate account of children's active involvement in the learning process. It also fails to take into account the knowledge that many children have already acquired before they start school. Instead we adopt a developmental perspective, according to which it is argued that children who are given appropriate opportunities and encouragement will learn a lot about writing and the processes involved *before* they begin school.

We also claim that, when one considers children's encounters with the written word from a developmental perspective, there is no reason why learning to read should precede learning to write. Indeed, as Clay (1991) has pointed out, given the opportunity, many children will show an interest in trying to write before trying to read, an order of acquisition that has four major benefits for children.

The first of these benefits is because writing involves the active production of marks on the page, when children are writing their full attention is engaged in the activity. Children who are trying to write because they want to are, without question, actively involved. Active involvement in a task benefits children's learning.

The second benefit arises as a result of children trying to write down what they say. This leads them to becoming aware of the **relationship** between the written and spoken word, a key concept in the development of literacy. While there are indisputable differences between written language (for example, in books read to children) and spoken language, young children gain initial access to the written word by discovering links between the two forms of language.

A third benefit that leads on from the second is that, when children begin to work out that writing on a page consists of letters and so use letters when representing words in their early writing, their attention is directed to the individual letters because these must be written one at a time. This provides an excellent basis for learning about the alphabetic principle, that is for learning that in languages with alphabets, letters represent the individual sounds or phonemes, which in turn forms the basis for learning specific letter–sound correspondences that are fundamental for both reading and writing.

A final benefit is that children will often 'read' their own writing, that is, they will read back what they have just written. They realize that writing and reading are intimately related activities. Once children understand that they can read what they have just written, despite idiosyncratic letter and word formation, this understanding will continue to hold as they learn to write and to read more conventional texts.

## Print in the Environment

In the last few decades there has been a tremendous upsurge in the amount of print in the environment and young children's exposure to this print. Clearly when we reflect on the situation historically, it is evident that young children in the past would have had much less access to print. Consequently many children had to go to school in order to come into contact with print and the traditional view that children knew nothing about writing before school may have been more defensible.

The picture today is very different as there is an abundance of print in our environment. Although there will be large variations in the extent to which individual children's attention will be drawn to print, it is difficult to imagine a child in a westernized society who will not encounter print and who, for whatever reason, will not be motivated to pay attention to it at some point. Therefore it is extremely likely that all children will develop some understanding of the written word prior to being taught at school.

Some of the many forms of print that the child may encounter are listed in table 5. (The table does not provide an exhaustive list and we are sure that the reader will be able to think of many other examples.)

The amount of contact children have with the different types of print will vary greatly, though it is evident that most children will encounter some print, be it television advertising or a cereal packet on the table.

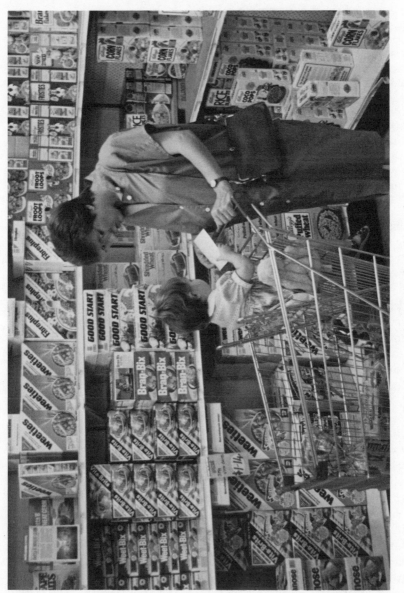

Print in the environment: the supermarket

*Table 5*   Print in the environment

Packaging – food, toys, sweets
Shop signs/names
Road signs
Advertising – on buses, trains, billboards, television
Reading material around the house – books (fiction, reference), magazines, TV
guides, racing form guides, newspapers, comics, mailorder catalogues
Labels – on clothes giving size/washing instructions, on cars giving the make
and model
Slogans – on T-shirts, on the walls of buildings
Lists – shopping, jobs to do in the garden, people to be invited to a party,
menus (in fast-food chains or restaurants)
Messages – to the milkman, to another family member not there at the time
Computers – use of keyboard, selection of game from menu on screen

This print can provide children with a basis for learning about both reading and writing, particularly if they have the opportunity to observe others interacting with the print in the environment, or better still if they are
involved in the interactions themselves. With regard to writing, children
may watch a parent writing a note for the other parent, noting down a
telephone message, making a shopping list, writing out a cheque or withdrawal form, or a doctor writing out a prescription. These activities can
provide the basis and stimulation for children to try writing, particularly
if adults have involved them in the writing process by talking to them
about it or positioning them so they can watch what is being written.

## Discovering the Writing Process

In chapter 3 the processes by which children learn new skills through
social interaction were described. Reference was made to the existence of
formats that involve highly routinized interactions between an adult and
the child (such as peekaboo). These interactions recur frequently. Many
preschool children will experience similar interaction sequences where
the content involves another person (adult or older child) writing
something on a piece of paper. Strictly speaking it would be incorrect to
call these formats as they involve more variations than the ones found very
early on in the course of spoken language acquisition. However their structure is sufficiently similar for them to serve as a basis for children to learn a
great deal about the content. Let us examine two such sets of sequences –
constructing a shopping list and withdrawing money from a bank.

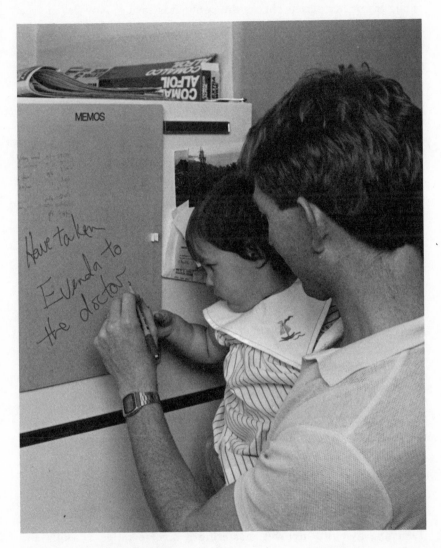

Leaving a message for mother

A familiar activity in many homes is making a shopping list before going to the shops. In many cases this will be done while children are engaged in other activities and so they will not have the opportunity to take
part. Some parents however involve their children in homemaking activities and so will talk to their children about what they are doing. Thus a
typical interaction sequence may involve the child sitting on the worktop

while his or her parent checks the cupboards saying 'Now let me see, what do we need?' and naming each item as it is written down on the list. In time, if given the opportunity, the child may wish to make his or her own list and will make some marks on the paper. Indeed our son's first explicit attempt to write involved constructing a shopping list. It contained one item – bananas – that was represented by a scribbled line on the page. This familiar activity can serve as the basis for some children's first attempts at writing. As the same activity may well occur frequently in the home, children have the opportunity to develop their skills further.

The second example, that of withdrawing money from the bank, is also one where children frequently watch a parent writing. Again young children, perhaps as a result of protestations about being left standing on the floor where they cannot see, may be sat on the counter of the bank while a parent writes out a withdrawal slip or signs a form. With time, as children watch these activities the protestations frequently transfer to wanting to have a pen to write on a withdrawal slip themselves. In this situation many parents will give their children a spare slip and pen and let them amuse themselves while the transaction is being conducted. Indeed, even with the increasing use of automatic teller machines, it is not unusual to find a child in a bank 'completing' a withdrawal slip, or to find such a 'completed' slip lying around on the counter.

There are many other common situations where children will experience writing activities being repeated frequently. Such activities stimulate children's interest and, through a desire to engage in the same activities as others, lead to them learning about the writing process. As we proceed to examine what children learn it will become clear that they are not simply imitating the activities of others but are actively involved in trying to form their own mental representations of the activities so that they may increase their understanding of what is involved.

## What Do Children Learn about Writing?

Learning to write involves mastering a diverse range of skills and understandings. For our purposes we have grouped these under four headings – early distinctions; letter formation and printing skills; the functions of the written word; and putting the message in writing. For the young child, these are not neatly separated areas that will be mastered independently of one another. There will be considerable interrelationship between the developing understandings in each area. Also there is no universally ordered sequence of acquisition. Children are developing a network of understandings. Whereas all children will finally acquire an

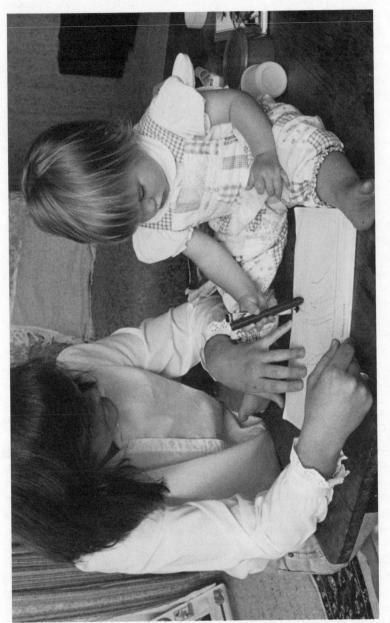

Children take an interest in writing on paper from an early age understanding of the principles involved, the route by which they do so will vary. Furthermore it is quite usual for children to hold mistaken beliefs about some of the principles in the course of finding out about writing. These mistaken beliefs will be corrected when the child receives additional information.

We are concerned with the period when children are making attempts to write and discovering the principles involved. These understandings typically develop between the ages of 3 and 7. Whereas we acknowledge that the child cannot write in the adult sense at this point, we prefer to call it **early writing**. As early writing blends into more conventional forms without any distinct divisions between the two, we have chosen to use the term early writing rather than distinguishing different stages.

### Early Distinctions and Understandings

At the time children first show an interest in writing they are usually also exploring other systems of representation such as drawing. One of the tasks facing them is to learn about the differences between the systems. If we examine the early attempts at writing, we find that children initially appear to fail to distinguish between drawing and writing and will mix these forms of representation on the page. It is, of course, not clear if they are mixing them on the page because they do not make any distinction between the different forms or because they have not learned the conventions that we usually adopt to keep them on separate parts of the page. There is some evidence to suggest that initially children simply do not make a distinction. When young children are asked to point to the writing on, say, a cornflakes packet or asked to point to the bit that says 'cornflakes', it becomes apparent that they have not yet learned the distinction between the writing and the picture as they may point to either.

As well as sorting out the differences between writing and drawing, children learn to make distinctions between writing and logographs (which are pictorial representations such as the ones found on the road sign for a school). It may be some time before children appreciate the differences between the two forms. This may not develop until the child learns more about the writing system and in particular about the correspondences between letters and sounds.

Children also learn to distinguish between letters and numbers as ways of representing things on paper. Although we write both, we are aware that only letters can be used in combinations to represent words. Initial attempts to write often involve children writing a mixture of both letters and numbers on the page while later they will begin to sort out this confusion. Again it is not easy to determine to what extent the initial mixing

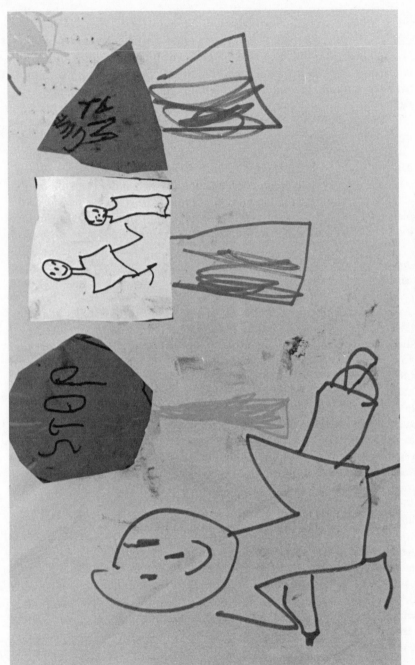

A child's picture involving drawing, writing and logographs

of these on the page indicates that children do not appreciate the differences between them as representations. It may well be that they are making use of what skills they have to make representations on the page. It is quite common though to find letters and numbers mixed through in children's early representations of writing. Certainly with increasing mastery over the representation of letters on the page, as described in the next section, the separation of letter forms from other forms develops.

For many children, of course, initial access to writing and letters does not involve having to write these. Plastic magnetic letters are very popular and may be found on fridges in many homes with young children. These letters can provide an excellent basis for discussion, helping children to separate out writing from other forms of representation such as drawings which may also be adorning the fridge door. In addition the concrete nature of the plastic letters and the ease with which they can be manipulated can help focus children's attention on the links between letters and speech sounds.

Bialystok (1991b), in a study exploring young children's understanding of written language, made use of these plastic letters. She worked with 3- to 5-year-old children most of whom could not read, but could recite the alphabet and correctly identify some printed letters. The children were given plastic letters and asked a series of questions including 'What can we make with these letters?', 'Can you make your name with the letters?', 'How many letters does it need to make a word?' and 'Can you make any other words with these letters?'. Children's responses to these questions were of interest. Of the children who could not read, many suggested that the letters could be used to spell words or names, or make the alphabet. A few children however, showed less understanding suggesting the letters could be used for such activities as counting, matching and making patterns, activities that indicate the letters were being regarded as objects with no special additional significance.

Slightly under half of the children who could not read were able to use the letters to spell their name, although several laid it out backwards. The children gave a range of responses about how many letters were required to make a word, ranging from one to three. Bialystok observed that the children who tended to say more than one letter were those who demonstrated higher levels of understanding about writing on other tasks. Finally, there was little success shown by these children in using the letters to make words. Two children who could not read produced some words but set these out backwards and a further two children produced words which could be read but did not follow conventional spellings. Many children strung together arbitrary letters and called them words. Bialystok comments, however, that generally the children enjoyed the opportunity to work with the letters and make their own words.

Consequently, the work of Bialystok which involved the systematic exploration of children's developing understandings, combined with much anecdotal evidence, reveals that many children prior to being given formal reading or writing instruction are showing signs of understanding key distinctions and familiarity with writing. They are also showing great interest in it.

## Letter Formation and Printing Skills

The mastery of printing skills by children is in many ways analogous to the mastery of articulation skills. In both cases the skills are required to produce the forms used in the language (sounds and letters), but the skills are not in themselves an integral part of the language. Just as children practise their articulation, they also practise writing letters on paper.

The actual form of young children's initial attempts to write will vary depending on which form of print in the environment seems to have influenced them most. For some children this appears to be the print that is found in books, newspapers, and magazines. This leads to the production of individual letter-like forms. Other children however seem more influenced by the cursive writing of adults and produce a linear scribble form where writing is represented as a continuous wavy line.

In both these cases it is evident that children put a great deal of effort into their writing. Neither case can necessarily be the direct product of copying because each is often produced in the absence of an available model. Further, each involves differences from the writing on which they are based that cannot be explained in terms of difficulties resulting from poorly developed motor skills. That is, children's attempts to write contain forms which are not found in printed text or in handwriting.

Perhaps the clearest example of this is the 'ball and stick' writing, $\sigma$, found so frequently during this period. The ball and stick letter is never found in any text (except ones about early writing) but shows that children have examined the printed form and extracted two of the main features of it – that many individual letters are made up of a straight line and a curved line. Children then use this information to produce their own writing.

Given the opportunity to practise, coupled perhaps with some input from an interested adult, children's approximations will become closer to those they are trying to represent. Children who initially base their representations on cursive writing will change to printing individual letters, be this a self-determined change or the result of adult intervention. Children who have been representing individual letters already will improve their

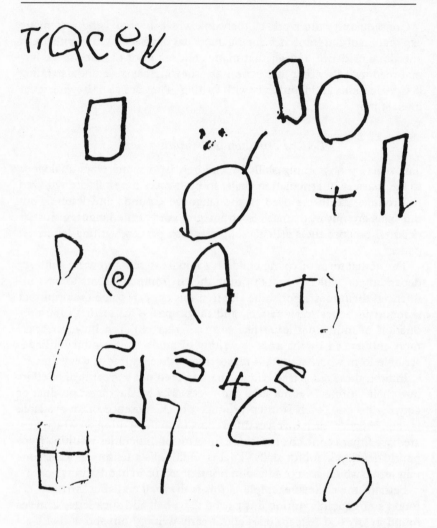

This child's writing includes her own representations (such as ball and stick), some conventional letters (such as A and T) and some numbers

letter forms either from their own striving to make better letters or from adult encouragement or both. Many children will introduce a few letters initially and will write these repeatedly on the page. These letters often come from their name as they have had many opportunities to see the written form of it and may also have watched it *being* written for them by an adult. They will then begin to try to write their name themselves and in time will make use of individual letters from it for other writing.

It must be stressed that at the time children are starting to write using their early forms of representation, many will have a very incomplete understanding of the purposes of writing or of the links between speaking and writing. Certainly many children produce letters and make use of these to represent words well before they know about the correspondence rules which govern the links between spoken and written language that are discussed below.

Once children start school there is usually considerable emphasis placed on letter formation. Understandably teachers see the need for children to learn a correct pencil grip and to write the letters in a clear form. Whereas we agree that children will benefit from assistance in these areas, it is essential that realistic expectations are held and that the training is not done in isolation from other activities. There is convincing evidence showing that about one-third of all children in the first year of formal school do not have sufficiently well developed perceptual-motor skills to produce letter shapes of the size and neatness so frequently expected of them (Laszlo, 1986).

Furthermore as these children have difficulty encoding the patterns of muscle movements involved in making each letter shape, they gain very little from spending many hours copying letters until they are at an age when they can memorize the muscle movements (Laszlo and Bairstow, 1985). It is very likely that these children will develop an extremely negative attitude to the entire writing process as they will perceive that it consists of spending substantial periods of time practising and perfecting letter shapes. It is surely much better to encourage the children to write for enjoyment and allow them to refine their printing skills gradually over, in some cases, a period of two to three years. Certainly such children should *not* be prevented from progressing into school or through the school grades because of poor printing skills. Children's natural interest in learning should be encouraged and teachers should avoid holding unreasonably high expectations of their printing abilities.

## The Functions of the Written Word

Like spoken language, written language serves many functions. Some of these were discussed in chapter 1 and include most of the functions found in spoken language plus some additional important ones, for example the use of writing as a memory aid (such as a shopping list) and as a more permanent record of transactions (such as in a bank when transferring money).

Children will eventually master, albeit gradually, the different functions of print and the conventions associated with each. Many children

Linear scribble

begin with a fairly vague initial understanding of one global function – that writing carries a message. In some cases there is an appreciation that the message must be placed in the writing, though this is not always so as the following anecdote indicates.

A teacher had set up her nursery to encourage children's interest in writing. In one corner she had placed a message pad next to an old telephone which the children used to pretend that they were talking to their friends. One day when a visitor was in the nursery, a small girl pretended to answer the telephone and made some marks on the message pad. She then took the visitor the sheet of paper and handed it to her saying, 'Here is a message for you.' The visitor held it out so that both she and the child could see the note and asked her what the message said. The child pushed the note back towards the visitor, making it clear whose responsibility it was to read it, and exclaimed 'I don't know but it is very important!'.

In this example the child believed that the writing carried a message – an *important* message. She further knew that adults can read messages and appeared to believe that she had represented writing on the page in a way that the adult could read it.

There are many such examples where children hold almost magical beliefs about the ability of print to carry a message without them necessarily having to put one there in the first place. Gradually though they seem to piece together their partial understandings and, as other skills develop, show an appreciation first of all that a message must be placed in the written word and then that the message must be written according to certain conventions so that another person can decode it. For most children, the written message at this point is another version of the spoken message. That is, they write down in some form the words as they are saying them. This provides the basis for determining the links between the spoken and the written word, an extremely important development for the mastery of both reading and writing.

The importance of being able to put a message in print and the potential benefits are clearly illustrated by Bissex (1980) in the opening paragraph of her book which described her son's developing mastery of both reading and writing. The situation that Bissex described is probably a familiar one to many parents although the child's solution is probably not. She was sitting reading while her son, Paul, had been trying to gain her attention. In her own words: 'After he tried unsatisfactorily to talk with me he decided to get my attention in a new way . . . Selecting the rubber letter stamps he needed from his set, Paul printed and delivered this message: RUDF (Are you deaf?!). Of course I put down my book' (Bissex, 1980, p. 3).

In this example Paul had a problem (getting his mother's attention)

Dear Nana we
are at Kendy
lit now and the
Snails are Dowg
lettuces, love From
michelle'

A letter to Nana

which he was highly motivated to solve. Consequently he made use of his fairly limited knowledge of writing to find the solution. The existence of a printing set saved him having to write each letter, though at the time he printed the message, he was also able to write messages using similar letter–sound strategies. As children learn more about the conventions of print (see next section), then they can make their messages much clearer until they will finally adopt, with varying degrees of accuracy, the spelling conventions of their language.

Many children gain initial access to writing through relatively vague notions that it represents some message, while others seem to develop much more specific access. For example, some children learn that written language acts as a label – their own name. These children are often taught to copy their name. This will lead them finally to learn the sequence of letters so that they can write it without the model being present. When they subsequently write their name on a painting or other creative piece of work, they understand that the name labels it as their property.

Other children are influenced by the conventions adopted when writing is used for particular functions. These children may get access to the general concept that print carries a message through one particular form. An example of this is the writing of shopping lists where children will follow the convention of writing items one under the other, often using a series of squiggles to do so. Another example found in the early period is writing letters to friends or relatives. In this case, children will start with a line that is equivalent to 'Dear . . .' and then represent lines of the message below this.

## Putting the Message in Writing

Once children become aware that writing carries a message and, more particularly, that when they are writing, *they* have to put the message there, they are then faced with the task of *how* to put it there. That is, they must find ways of encoding the message in their writing. In this section we argue that children do this through becoming aware that writing not only involves representing a message but involves representing a *spoken* message. This in turn leads children to work on the problem of how what one says is translated into marks on the page. By working on this task they will gradually discover the correspondence rules between speaking and writing.

Before examining the paths by which children finally master the rules, it is necessary to state our position in a little more detail. By claiming that children learn to represent messages in their writing by determining the links between speaking and writing, it is not our intention to suggest that writing is simply speech written down. As we discussed in chapter 1 and also elucidate below, there are many important differences between the written and spoken word. One of the main goals of early education should be to ensure children have the knowledge and experience required to develop complete fluency with both forms of the language without having to rely on one to work with the other. In particular they should become sufficiently fluent to be able to move directly between the meaning and the written text without always having to represent the written text first as speech in order to gain access to the meaning.

Nevertheless, although such fluency should be the outcome for children who are in the process of mastering the challenges of writing, the encoding of messages is learned by encoding speech. In making this claim, we support the position adopted by Vygotsky (1962, 1978) that writing is learned as a second-order representation. According to this position, spoken language is acquired as a first-order system because the child learns that words, or more correctly sound patterns, stand for objects, relationships, actions and so on. For example, they learn that the sound pattern which constitutes the word **table** represents the object 'table'. In contrast, children's access to writing is by learning that a combination of written symbols represents the spoken symbols. Thus the written word for children is a second-order representation as it does not represent the object directly but represents the spoken form of the word which in turn represents the object.

Children therefore must learn the correspondence rules so that when writing they can translate the spoken form into the written form. In English, as in many languages, the main rules that children must give early attention to are that:

- the temporal sequencing of speech is represented in writing by left to right, return left, and top to bottom spatial sequencing on the page;
- speech is represented in writing by combinations of letter strings;
- words in speech are represented in writing by grouping the letters on the page using spaces to separate the groups.

We will consider these in turn.

The description of the ways in which children develop an understanding of these rules is not easy. We still have a great deal to learn about the processes and at this stage can only give an indication of what may be involved. The situation is further complicated because, as discussed in the previous chapter, there will be aspects of the spoken language that many children have not had cause to reflect upon until they are learning to read or write. To take a specific example, children's understanding of *words* will vary tremendously. Some children may never have given any thought to what constitutes a word at the time they start to write (see Bowey, Tunmer and Pratt, 1984). Other children may have some understanding and have identified nouns as words while not accepting that other ones (such as pronouns and articles) are. This is quite understandable when one considers the nature of the speech signal. There are often no gaps between words in speech and even when there are, the gaps within words are frequently bigger than those between the words. It is therefore very difficult for children to identify words in speech. Thus even if children do learn that in writing they should leave gaps, they are still likely to encounter difficulties because they cannot determine with any degree of precision what the individual words are from the speech signal.

*Mapping the temporal sequencing of speech onto the spatial sequencing in writing* Many children who begin by writing individual letter shapes on the page do not initially follow any rules governing sequencing. They will frequently fill pages or sections of pages by starting at one point and moving to another part of the page at random. It seems that these children focus more on the representations on the page than the spatial sequence in which they should appear.

Children who first represent writing as linear scribble are much more likely to follow some spatial conventions, mainly because the form of the scribble dictates that it will be written across the page. This reduces the scope for making errors to possible left–right confusions or top–bottom ones, although once these children start to write individual letters rather than the linear scribble they too may make directional errors.

Children learn to impose spatial order on their early writing from various sources. For some it is likely to result from informal input from a parent or teacher who will point out that writing should follow certain rules. Others may extract the principle themselves as they watch an adult writing, particularly if that adult is writing something short that the child is dictating. And for other children it will be generalized from formal or informal reading instruction.

Once children learn the general principles, often there remain two difficulties both of which result in variations in the final form. One of these is the familiar left–right confusion that occurs. Here children are aware that writing should proceed in a sequence across the page and follow this principle. They start however at the right hand side of the page and proceed to produce mirror writing in a right to left direction. This writing is of an equivalent standard to the writing they produce when they start at the left side of the page suggesting that they find it equally easy, or difficult, to write in either direction. Although some adults show concern when children produce mirror writing, this is unfounded. The child has acquired the overall principle of spatial sequencing, a very important development, and the minor confusion about left and right does sort itself out. This can be said with full confidence as there is no evidence of this mistake occurring in older children or adults, many of whom now experience considerable difficulty producing mirror image writing. Further the mistake is very easily corrected by placing a small mark on the top left hand side of the page to act as a starting point for children who tend to make the error.

The other difficulty experienced by some children occurs when they run out of space on the page. Observing the behaviour of these children suggests that they have a general understanding of the conventions but do not fully appreciate that they must always be followed. These children will start somewhere near the top corner of the page and will write words from left to right and top to bottom. They will often leave large spaces around their writing and not use the page economically. The result is that they reach the bottom of the page before they have finished their message. Their solution is to use up the spaces on the page in the left or right hand margins which again violates the spatial sequencing conventions.

*Speech is represented in writing by combinations of letter strings*    In conjunction with the developing understanding that you write by starting at one point on the page and progress across the page, children also develop the understanding that combinations of letter strings represent chunks of speech. This is a very important breakthrough which in turn leads to the discovery of letter–sound correspondences or as they are referred to, grapheme–phoneme correspondences. The discovery of grapheme–phoneme correspondences and the subsequent learning of these correspondences is at the very heart of learning to write and to read.

As a way of illustrating the difficulties that children face when working out the rules of correspondence (either with or without formal assistance), let us first of all examine what grapheme–phoneme correspondences involve. Broadly speaking, graphemes may be equated with the letter forms of the language (Ellis, 1984). However, we can represent the same letter using different graphic forms. Each letter has an upper case form and a lower case form which usually differ (for example, **A** and **a**, **B** and **b**), and many letters also have different forms within one case (for example, the printed **a** and the written **ɑ**). All variations of the letter represent the same grapheme.

Individual children are likely to write an individual letter initially using the same graphic form, allowing, of course, for variations that result from problems with fine motor control. However, as these letters are produced as *their* individual representations of the print they see in the environment, they must still develop an understanding that the same letters may have different forms.

Phonemes are the individual sounds of the language. As discussed in chapter 7, the phonemes in speech are not produced as separate units one after the other. There is considerable overlap in their production. Liberman (1987) pointed out that this coarticulation has a distinct advantage for speech as it means that it proceeds at a satisfactory pace, making it easier to interpret than if the units were produced one after the other in a string. The coarticulation also results in a distinct disadvantage for the child who is in the process of trying to work out the correspondence rules. It makes the task of identifying the phonemic units to which the graphemes correspond more difficult.

Furthermore in many languages, including English, there is not a one-to-one correspondence between letters and sounds. Many of the individual letters in the alphabet can represent different phonemes (such as, the letter **c** in 'ice' and 'cream') and in many cases different letters can represent the same phoneme (such as **c** and **k** in 'call' and 'king'). In addition a small group of two or three letters is often required to represent a single phoneme (such as **igh** in 'thigh' or **ea** in 'meat'). At times, two letters separated by another letter may combine to produce one phoneme (such as the **a** and **e** in late).

The initial step involves establishing that there is some correspondence between the letters on the written page and the sounds of the language. How children develop this principle is difficult to determine, particularly as individual children will gain access to it in very different ways. This may be illustrated by comparing children who differ in the knowledge they bring to the task. Some children have some knowledge of the alphabet and can recognize a few letters and give them their letter names. Other children do not have this knowledge. Children who know some of the alphabet may not initially appreciate the significance of what they have learned, having acquired the skill through rote learning. But once these children start writing letters, they are in a position to name these. Then as they start to copy words in the environment or words provided specifically for them to copy, they will begin to realize that a sequence of letters not only conveys the overall sound pattern of a word or string of words but that individual letters convey segments of the overall sound pattern. Furthermore because the children are writing the words rather than reading them, they are creating the word one letter at a time and therefore are much more aware of the individual components of words.

Children who have not learned the alphabet will not have access to the names of letters and when copying a word are less likely to make the association this way. These children may develop an initial understanding that the correspondences are at the level of the word. They may then take considerable time to move from this to discovering the correspondences that exist within words, that is, the grapheme–phoneme correspondences.

The way in which children become aware of the individual correspondences will be a result of an interaction between the knowledge they bring to the writing task and the different types of encounters they have with the written word once they start to write. For children who have not been given the opportunities to interact with print by trying to write and who are receiving a formal approach to literacy, the understanding that there are correspondences is likely to develop from reading instruction. For many other children the understanding will develop in different ways, perhaps, as in the example of the first child above, as a result of beginning to make connections between a rote learned alphabet and one or two letters in words.

The social writing sessions that often occur at nursery school, where small groups of children stand or sit round a table writing provide individual children with the opportunity to begin to discover that there are correspondences. They may notice that their name has different letters in it to another child's and make some comment about it (for example, as one child said at nursery, 'Why has your name got two of these letters in it' – pointing to the **n**s in '**Ann**e' – 'while mine has only one?' – pointing to the **n** in 'Jane'). This can serve as a basis for further learning. They may even ask directly why names are spelled differently. Children who make use of writing centres (that is, centres set up by a teacher, usually in a nursery school or preschool, with pads of paper, pencils and pens), also have the opportunity to observe and interact with children who may be at a more advanced level of understanding and who may be sounding out the letter names or sounds as they produce their writing.

Once children realize that there are correspondences between letters and sounds, they must develop **strategies** to produce these correspondences. The main strategies they use have been described by Clay (1975) and include inventing strings of letters, copying from a variety of sources (books, another person's writing), asking another person how to spell a word, and reproducing whole words or parts of words from memory.

Initially many children invent the spellings of words so that they create a novel sequence of letters for each word. They often do this without any appreciation of the rules of correspondence. They are simply aware that different words consist of different letter strings and make use of this principle when writing. As appreciation of possible correspondences develops, children will use their knowledge of letter names and sounds to spell the words. This leads to the creation of many rules of correspondence that are not the recognized ones of the language. The area of **invented spelling** has been extensively researched by Read (1986) and we will consider the main points of his work below.

In a study of American children attending preschools and kindergartens, Read found that when children spelled words creatively, they frequently made systematic substitutions. Thus when he examined children's spellings of words that contained a vowel sound equivalent to the name of the vowel (such as the sound /i/ as in '**meat**' and 'lad**y**' which has the same sound as the letter name for **e**) over 70 per cent of spellings used the letter name (such as '**met**' and 'lad**e**').

Consistent substitutions and in some cases omissions also occur with consonants. Omissions are of particular interest as they draw attention to the fact that we tend to assume many sounds are represented in speech much more clearly than they are. The nasalized consonant /ŋ/ in words such as 'we**n**t' and 'can't' is a good example. Children frequently omit the **n** in such words spelling them as 'wet' and 'cat'. Although Read has shown experimentally that young children can detect the difference in the sounds of word pairs such as 'bet' and 'bent', and 'cat' and 'can't', children do not know how to encode the difference and often write the words in the same way.

The difficulty that children experience may seem puzzling at first, but this is because we have been influenced in our perception of the spoken word by our knowledge of the written word. Because we are so familiar with the written form of a word, a form that is very clear and consistent, we tend to assume that spoken words are also clear and consistent. This is not so. In the case of words such as 'went' and 'can't', we overgeneralize from the clarity of the written form and assume the **n** is sounded clearly in the spoken form as a nasalized consonant. Yet it is not evident as a nasalized consonant. In the spoken word, especially in American English, it is heard more as a nasalization of the vowel, that is, it has the effect of making the **e** sound more nasalized. As Read found, this leads to quite consistent errors in children's early spelling.

Since Read's work examining invented spelling, a number of other researchers have continued to study children's early spelling attempts in more detail. Treiman (1993) for example, in her book *Beginning to Spell* studied the early writing of 43 children in grade 1, again in America. These children, drawn from two successive years, were all in a classroom where the teacher expected them to write for half an hour each morning.

The teacher valued writing and saw it as an important part of children's developing mastery of the written language. Clearly it is not possible to adequately describe all of Treiman's work as reported in her book and in a series of other publications (such as Treiman, 1994; Treiman, Zukowski, and Richmond-Welty, 1995). In essence though, her works confirms much of Read's findings in so far as she found for example that children will make use of letter names they know to represent sounds, and will omit consonants from consonant clusters especially for nasalized consonants such as /n/ when it preceded /t/.

Treiman's (1993) work extends beyond that of Read, however, as she examined a range of other developing understandings. These included children's knowledge that certain graphemes are restricted in the positions in which they occur in words. For example, the grapheme **ck** which represents the sound /k/ can appear in the middle (for example in 'chi**ck**en') or end of words (for example in 'bla**ck**'). It does not appear at the beginning of words where other letters, **c** or **k**, are used. Treiman found 38 instances where children had used **ck** when it was not part of the correct spelling of a word. If children were unaware of the constraints on position then it would be assumed that these instances would be equally distributed across beginning, middle and end positions. However, Treiman only found two occasions when **ck** appeared at the beginning of words and in these cases there seemed to be confusion with **ch**. For example one child used CKES for 'cheese'. In contrast **ck** was used 11 times in the middle of words (such as MRCKUT for 'market') and 25 times at the end of words (such as BICK for bike). Similarly, Treiman found that children would use double consonants (such as **ss** or **ll**) at the ends of words but very rarely did these appear at the beginnings of words. Thus while children strive to establish the general correspondence rules for writing they are also extracting important information from their interactions with print about positional constraints on the use of certain graphemes.

As children develop their knowledge about correspondence rules and the positional constraints on these, they also extract rules based on grammatical considerations to determine the use of particular graphemes to represent phonemes, that are determined by the grammar. Nunes, Bryant and Bindman (1997) investigated the extent to which 6– to 8–year-old children's knowledge of spelling in English reflects an understanding of morphological and grammatical constraints on the use of graphemes. As these authors point out, the letter group **ed,** the morphological representation of past tense in English, corresponds with the phoneme /t/ when it is used at the end of *verbs* such as 'kiss', to produce 'kissed'. Similarly, the letter **s** when placed at the end of nouns such as 'car' to signal a plural, 'cars' represents /z/.

Their findings are of considerable interest and here we will focus on the developing use of **ed**. Nunes et al. found the basis of a developmental sequence in their work linked to measures of children's grammatical awareness. Essentially they found that there were many examples of children making errors and representing the past tense of verbs using the letter **t** such as spelling 'kissed' as 'kist'. However, they also noted that children who used **ed** would generalize this to verbs that do not follow regular rules for the past tense. Children would for example, spell the past tense of 'sleep' as 'sleped' to represent 'slept'. That is, they knew the past tense is pronounced 'slept' but spelled it incorrectly. Interestingly, these researchers also found that as children developed the use of **ed** for /t/ there were cases of overgeneralization beyond verbs such as 'sofed' for 'soft' and 'necsed' for next. Eventually, of course, for most children such errors disappear as they derive the grammatical and morphological constraints governing correspondence rules. In contrast therefore with position constraints within words, children take much longer to determine the grammatical and morphological constraints and make many more errors as they do so.

Consequently when children are striving to represent speech, they have to cope with words in which the sounds will not be heard as clearly as we think having been influenced by our knowledge of their spelling. It is hardly surprising they 'invent' spellings for words. It is also very likely that there will be individual and regional differences in children's invented spelling that result from the different pronunciations found in different dialects. As mentioned, Read and Treiman conducted their work with American children whose systematic substitutions in their invented spelling differ from children in other (English) speaking countries. Beyond that children need to determine the grapheme–phoneme correspondence rules as they encode speech and constraints within the language that influence what rules are used at different locations within the word and for morphological variations to particular parts of speech.

The second strategy that children use from very early stages before they have learned correspondences is really a group of strategies all of which involve copying words from various sources. Many children make use of this technique to extend their writing ability. They will often start by copying their name or some letters they see on a sign. Following this, they will then start to ask for words to use for copying. At first children may start to copy because they want to write and this provides a means to achieve the goal. They will, however, have little knowledge of the fact that the letters represent sounds and that each word has a different but consistent spelling. This is different to a later phase in development when children do appreciate these principles and copy words to ensure that they spell them consistently and, hopefully, correctly.

Children copy from a variety of sources and these vary depending on where the child is writing. Some common sources at nursery school, for example, are books, writing displayed on the wall by the teacher, and the child's own product from a previous occasion. Copying from their own product is of interest, as it reveals that children have developed an understanding that words should be spelled consistently but do not appreciate that their own spelling may not be accurate. The copying of one's own spelling may involve copying from the same piece of writing if the word has been used already, or copying from an earlier piece of writing as illustrated in the following example observed in a nursery school.

Mary, aged approximately 4 years 6 months, was standing at a table in the nursery school writing a description of her painting. She stopped and asked the teacher if she could go over and look at the writing she had done the day before to see how she had written the word 'her'. Mary went over and read her earlier writing until she found the word 'her' and returned to write it exactly as she had done on the previous occasion – 'hir'. She then completed her description which read as follows: 'This is as playing at Nicole's has weth Sarah is well and hir mum is geteg our lanch read' (This is us playing at Nicole's house with Sarah as well and her mum is getting our lunch ready). In this case the child went to a great deal of effort to check her previous writing. She demonstrated that she had remembered what she had written the day before and that her spelling was to be kept consistent.

A strategy that is closely related to copying occurs when children ask how to spell or how to write a word. This frequently results in copying if the other person responds by writing the word for the child to use as a model. On other occasions the spelling will be dictated letter by letter. For this to be effective the child who is receiving the dictation must be able to recognize the name given to each letter and produce the shape of the letter on the page. Observation of children engaged in this activity indicates that they will often rely on cues from the adult. That is, they engage in the activity before they are completely familiar with the shapes associated with each letter name. Consequently the adult will frequently cue them by drawing the letter in the air and trying to describe the main characteristics of the letter (for example, 'You know **d**, the one that goes straight down and then has a round bit at the bottom').

This method of gaining information about the grapheme–phoneme correspondence provides the basis for much learning as the interactions between the child and adult often involve explicit discussion about individual letters, their shapes, the names of the letters, and the sounds that they make. What is more, because it involves interaction between child and adult, and is initiated by the child, it is likely that the discussion will be pitched at an appropriate level which the child can understand.

Children will also generate sequences from memory when writing words. For many words, children seem to commit the entire sequence to memory and although they clearly write it letter by letter, they do not associate the letters with the sounds of the words. It is very likely that for many children their name is remembered this way as after they copy their name a few times they will then produce the letter sequence from memory without requiring a model to copy. Indeed as Bissex (1980) has observed, some children will continue to ask for assistance in spelling words that involve the same sound patterns as their names. For example, a child who could write his own name, Dwight, correctly and whose other writing indicated he was able to work at the level of letter–sound correspondences, required assistance with words such as 'light' and 'fight'. This indicates that he had memorized his name as a complete sequence and had not realized it could be broken down into constituent sounds which could be used for other words.

Evidence that children commit the letter sequences of many words to memory from an early stage of writing is seen when one watches them producing written words. If one observes children who are writing words by sounding out the individual phonemic components, and who then get to one they know, they will often be seen to write it more quickly and without sounding it out. At times the relief can be seen on a child's face particularly if he or she has been struggling with some more difficult words. A child may even comment on this knowledge – 'I know how to write *cat.*'

Further evidence that children learn many words as the entire sequence is found in their ability to write some words correctly and almost effortlessly without sounding them. For example, many children probably learn to spell words like 'you' and 'the' correctly from early on in their writing encounters.

At times of course children will use a combination of strategies in writing a sentence using different strategies for different words. They may also mix strategies within a word as shown for example when a child wrote 'refyous' for 'refuse'. Following some initial letter–sound correspondence, **r e f**, the child realized that he knew how to represent the sound u and so inserted his representation of it – **you** – in the word.

Gradually through frequent participation in the process of writing, if the opportunity is provided, children learn more about the written word and become increasingly adept at writing. Frequently children will not be writing by and for themselves but will be interacting with adults and other children about their writing. This process helps children become more efficient at producing written material directly and it results in them becoming more aware of the language and more fluent in communicating with others about both written and spoken language.

It must be recognized that as children learn to encode messages in writing, they will make many mistakes, and it is worth digressing briefly to consider the reactions that others may have to words which children spell incorrectly as a result of some of the strategies they adopt.

The reactions of many adults to children's early writing, especially invented spelling, is, to say the least, extremely mixed. Some adults may be greatly amused at incorrect spellings. This reaction is often only found when children have grasped the basics of the correspondences and are correctly representing words at 'their level of development'. That is, they are misspelling words that are deemed to be too hard for them. Essentially this is the reaction when children have received formal instruction and it is felt that their development is under 'control'.

Quite a different reaction often occurs when children are in the very early phases of writing and are misspelling all words or almost all words. Some adults become very concerned by this and will actually prevent or discourage a child from writing. This reaction is extremely puzzling for we do not react this way in other areas of development. When young children start to produce their first attempts at spoken language, parents do not gag their children and forbid them to talk until they can say the words properly. Such an action would be universally regarded as ludicrous for it is recognized that children need to practise speaking for some time before they develop full mastery of the sounds. Until then they will produce many approximations and will also substitute some sounds for others (see chapter 4). Instead parents respond with delight when they hear early approximations to speech and encourage the child to produce more sounds, recognizing that the approximations will be refined with practice and that the mispronunciations will be replaced with correct ones.

Similarly when young children produce drawings of a legless and armless person, their parents are likely to be pleased even when told it is a drawing of one of them. Again there is no expectation that children should produce an adequate drawing first time nor is there any great concern that children will develop bad habits and continue to draw limbless bodies for evermore. Instead parents will respond with words of encouragement and may also act in a way that leads to children developing their skills further. For example, they may ask the child where daddy's arms are or suggest these are added.

Why then should early writing be so different? We believe it is because the dominant view is that writing is a very complex skill that requires formal teaching and that any mistaken ideas the child develops will need to be unlearned before the correct learning can take place. Because writing has traditionally been regarded as a skill requiring formal instruction, it is not viewed from a developmental perspective. We argue however that it *should* be viewed from a developmental perspective and that the benefits of allowing the child to explore writing far outweigh the disadvantages, if indeed any exist.

*Words in speech are represented in writing by grouping the letters on the page using spaces to separate the groups*   One other important convention that children learn is that they must represent individual words by leaving spaces between them. As mentioned above, this presents difficulties for many children because they do not have a clear understanding of what constitutes a word. Thus even when children have learned the general principle that it is necessary to leave spaces between words when writing, they will often continue to run some words together simply because they do not regard them as separate words.

The ways in which children find out about the need to leave spaces varies greatly and illustrates the diversity found in early writing. Many children will extract and develop the principle themselves at a very early point in their attempts to write as they try to copy writing on a page. Others may become quite fluent writers and have mastered the basics of grapheme–phoneme correspondence but still run words together. They need to have the principle pointed out. Bissex (1980) reported the latter occurred in the case of her own child who had reached quite an advanced level but still presented all letters in a string. She then commented one day about the need to leave spaces and he immediately incorporated the principle into his own writing, correctly representing some divisions while still stringing some words together.

There are numerous other conventions in writing that children have to learn, many of these being grouped under the heading **punctuation**. For most the same principles will hold as for those covered above. Some children will notice a particular mark (such as a full stop) themselves and try to work out how to use it. They may even ask an adult to tell them about it. Other children will probably need to have their attention drawn to it at an appropriate time. For all children though the correct application of the principle will depend on their understanding of the concepts involved. Thus they may come to understand that full stops go at the end of sentences but remain hazy about what constitutes a sentence, with the result that they cannot apply the principle correctly at all times.

## Beyond Writing Speech

The previous sections of this chapter have focused on early writing in children and have traced some of the paths that children follow when learning to encode messages in the written language. The actual path that children follow and the enthusiasm with which they do so will vary. Nevertheless with varying degrees of assistance from parents and teachers, the majority of children will progress to the point where they can encode their spoken language in writing. Moving beyond this point presents many additional challenges for children and we briefly indicate what some of these challenges involve.

As discussed in chapter 1, there are many differences between spoken and written language. Children must become acquainted with these if they are to develop their writing skills. Many differences are stylistic and involve the development of **register** which Martin (1983) argued is the most interesting aspect of linguistic development in children once they reach primary school age.

Register is concerned with the appropriate use of language in different contexts. Children must develop an understanding that there are certain lexical items and syntactic forms that are used more appropriately in one language mode than the other. Thus as Green and Morgan (1981) claimed, it is more appropriate to use lexical items such as 'kids' and 'have to' when speaking and to replace these with 'children' and 'must' when writing, unless one deliberately selects the other form for effect.

Similarly there are many syntactic forms that occur in the written form of language which never appear in everyday conversation and would only be heard if someone was reading from a book. Children who have been read to a great deal and who also read themselves will be more familiar with forms that are not used in the spoken language and will find it easier to include them in their own writing.

There are many differences between the spoken and written language that operate at the discourse level (that is, beyond the lexical and syntactic level). These differences result from two fundamental contrasts between speaking and writing. When we speak, the recipient of the message is, with a few exceptions (such as a radio broadcast), there to receive the message and can, if need be, interrupt and seek clarification of the message. As discussed in chapter 6, the meaning can be negotiated during several rounds of a conversation. It may even be that the hearer thinks he or she has understood the message but the content of the reply indicates to the speaker that the message has been misunderstood, thus providing the speaker with another cue to restate the original message. With writing, again with a few exceptions (such as a bank teller), the receiver of the message is seldom there at the time it is written and therefore cannot signal problems of comprehension directly to the writer.

The other fundamental contrast between speaking and listening is that when we speak the message is soon lost. Spoken messages are fleeting with each word disappearing as soon as it is uttered. All that remains of it is a memory trace which may be incomplete and which will fade with time. The written message however is much more permanent and is available to the writer for review and editing.

As a result of these two contrasts, it is necessary to ensure that the written word is clearly expressed and in a way that avoids unnecessary repetition. The onus is on the writer to assess when a reader may have difficulty understanding part of the discourse. The writer must judge when to repeat a proposition in a different form in case it is not understood initially, and when to summarize an argument or story to ensure the reader will extract the main points without any misunderstandings. Equally because the writing is there to be reviewed by the writer, steps must be taken to avoid going on at length when this is not justified. The writer must try to avoid unnecessary repetitions when this does not add to the clarity and may distract from the fluency. Children have to learn to deal with all these aspects of the written word.

Writing is an exacting process. Children must learn to assess the knowledge of the readers of their creative stories and factual accounts. When reviewing their own work they must be able to break free from their own perspective. They must be prepared to see different interpretations in their writing if they are to minimize the possibility of misunderstandings and maximize the likelihood of the reader extracting the message as intended.

It is also necessary to develop an understanding of discourse rules that govern writing if a writer wishes to produce a fluent text, be it an expository or a narrative text, for the reader. As Scinto (1983) wrote, it is essential that the text has coherence.

In a narrative, the writer must set the scene for the reader and introduce the main actors. A theme must also develop that provides a link across the propositions of the story. This requires careful planning on the part of the writer. Although this skill appears to develop naturally in some children, there are many who need assistance and encouragement to develop their skills to this level of mastery and fluency.

## Individual Differences, the School and Writing

Given the complex network of understandings about writing that children must construct, it is hardly surprising that there are large individual differences between children. Even for those that have been fortunate enough to have their interest stimulated during the preschool years there will be major differences. Indeed as Dyson (1985b) commented in her paper, which provides an excellent description of the writing development of three children, 'the differences between the children were more striking than the similarities' (p. 118). Of the three children that she described, Tracy was interested in acquiring the labels for particular persons and objects in her writing, while Rachael was less concerned about individual words but spent a lot of time exploring the purposes of writing with a particular emphasis on the communication of messages. Perhaps as a result of this differing interest, Rachael knew less letter names than Tracy and could write less words correctly. The third child, Vivi, seemed more intent on determining how the system worked and spent more time figuring out the nature of the alphabetic code. In some senses Vivi was more involved at a metalinguistic level than Rachael who was more concerned with using her limited skills to communicate through writing.

Clearly, as these children enter the phase in their lives when they receive formal education, they will be bringing different types of understandings to the writing task. The challenge facing teachers is to provide writing opportunities in the classroom that enable them to develop an appreciation of each child's knowledge and enable all children to develop their skills at a level that is appropriate to their individual needs and interests. This approach should be followed by teachers instead of imposing a formal curriculum that involves spending long periods of time having all children practising writing in contexts that have little meaning for them and which do not take account of the knowledge they bring to the task. For there is another equally important challenge that these children pose for teachers. Although they differ greatly in their understandings and interest, all have one very important thing in common – they all have a natural enthusiasm and interest in writing. The challenge for teachers is to continue to provide writing experiences in ways that maintain interest and extend the children's skills.

There are many children of course for whom the educational challenges are totally different. These are children who have not developed an interest in writing either because they come from backgrounds where there is little interest shown in the written word or because they have been discouraged from writing as a result of the mistaken belief that it will negatively affect school learning. The main challenge facing teachers of these children is the one described by Vygotsky (1978). Environments must be created that lead children to learn to write through processes of discovery because they *want* to work out how to write rather than learning in a rote fashion because they are told they need to learn to write. Essentially children should be writing because they want to achieve some goal rather than learning to write being presented as the goal.

This fundamental principle of learning holds for all of us and we should not expect children to be any different. There are many adults who feel quite threatened if they are told they must learn to use a computer, particularly if they see no purpose in it, and will avoid doing so at all costs. They are in a sense scared of the unknown. Yet these adults will often use computers in other contexts without realizing it (such as an automatic teller machine for banking transactions). Further if they then find that for some reason they are motivated to learn more (for example, they want to reap the benefits of word processing), then they will overcome their negative feelings and frequently become very proficient in making use of the facilities provided by the computer.

Teachers should create opportunities for children to encounter writing in ways that result in them wanting to learn. This will stimulate development in these children so that within a very short period they too will be actively working out the early principles. Once these children get to this point, then the educational challenges are the same as the ones for children who come to school with their interest already stimulated. Writing activities must continue to be presented in ways that maintain interest and in ways that allow teachers to discover and react to the individual differences in children's understandings of and interests in writing that will always exist.

Moreover, while it is important to make sure that children also learn to follow spelling, layout and punctuation conventions when writing, care must be taken to ensure that this does not become the dominant goal for the teacher or in the eyes of the child. Wray (1993) has provided some cautionary evidence in this regard. With the assistance of teachers working in schools in England, he collected information about what children think teachers value in writing. Over 400 children ranging in age from 7 to 11 years were asked to write advice to a child who was either one or two years younger. The advice requested from the older children in the study was about how to write a composition that will be considered good by the teacher. The younger children were asked to say what writing would be like and what they would have to do to be good at writing. Almost all children provided sufficient advice in their responses to be included in the analysis. Wray classified all advice according to a set of categories which fell under two major headings, namely secretarial and composition. The 'secretarial' heading included spelling, neatness, layout and punctuation and the 'composition' heading included ideas, structure and characters.

In total over 2500 pieces of advice were given by children with 68 per cent of these falling within the secretarial classification. The most frequently mentioned within this category was spelling followed by neatness, with punctuation also rating quite highly. Ideas was the most frequently mentioned for composition and this rated at an equivalent level to punctuation. The results overall, however, raise considerable concerns. As Wray comments, 'The results seem rather an indictment of the approach to writing in the classrooms from which these children were drawn. In a situation in which the assessment procedures for the National Curriculum in English place a 70 per cent weighting on the compositional aspects of writing and only 30 per cent on the secretarial, it seems ironic that these children's views are almost an exact reversal of these weightings' (Wray, 1993, p. 73).

Wray also considered changes with age. One is tempted to seek some reassurance from noting that there is a trend towards giving more importance to composition features with increasing age such that by 10 to 11 years of age children are mentioning composition and secretarial aspects equally often, that is about 50 per cent for each. However the contrast to this is that the youngest children, aged 7 to 8 years, mention secretarial issues about 80 per cent of the time. This suggests that the emphasis teachers place on spelling, punctuation, layout and neatness soon dominate young children's writing with the result that children become more focused on the appearance of the product than the process of generating stories and the content of them. When this is compared with many children's enthusiasm for conveying messages in print when they enter school, it suggests that teachers need to place more emphasis on what children are trying to write and the process of conveying meaning. Clearly spelling and other secretarial considerations are important, but they should be shaped up in a way that does not convey to the child that this is what writing is all about. Children should continue to write because they are motivated to encode meaning in text and should be encouraged to master different forms of the written language without being stifled by too much emphasis on presentation and spelling.

# CHAPTER NINE

# *Learning to Read*

In the last chapter we examined the development of writing in children. In this chapter we are concerned with another aspect of children's interactions with the printed word, namely, the development of reading. As discussed in the previous chapter, written language is learned as a second order system of representation with the words on the page corresponding to spoken words that in turn convey meaning. In learning to read therefore, children must establish the correspondences between written words and spoken words, so that they can determine the meaning being conveyed. Consequently children must develop skills for decoding the written word in order to find its equivalence in the spoken form. They must also develop the skills required to reconstruct the meaning that was placed in the print when it was written, skills which are central to the comprehension of the text.

We begin by examining the conceptions and skills children bring to the reading task, including their views about what reading is and their developing concepts about print. These are examined first because it is essential to determine what knowledge children bring to the learning task (Pratt and Garton, 1988). All development progresses by building upon existing expectations, knowledge and skills. Therefore as children will bring different understandings to a particular task, they will gain access to new skills in different ways.

Following consideration of the knowledge and skills that children bring to the task of learning to read and their understanding of print, we examine the period when children are learning the skills required to change the written text into the more familiar spoken form so that they may gain access to the message contained in the text. We will document the general progression in the acquisition of reading while recognizing that there will be some individual variation in development across individuals. This is followed by a section on the processes involved in comprehension and in monitoring one's comprehension. In this section we are concerned mainly with children's comprehension of more complex sentences and of connected prose. The chapter concludes with a section on individual differences, the school and reading. In this section, the responsibility of schools to cater for the large differences in children's abilities when they come to school is discussed.

## Early Skills and Understandings

Children will vary tremendously in the knowledge and skills they bring to the reading task. In this context, one area that is central to learning to read is spoken language development. As discussed in earlier chapters, children will vary in the command they have of the spoken language at the time they begin formal education. There will be large individual differences in children's vocabulary development, both in terms of content and amount; in their familiarity with different conversational styles; in their listening comprehension skills; and in their ability to reflect on the language they are using. All of these will influence the course of reading development from the earliest stages. Some, such as vocabulary development, will have fairly direct influences and may limit the number of written words the child can gain access to during the early stages of reading. Others, such as familiarity with different conversational styles may influence the ease with which children will be able to follow the teacher as they are instructed about reading.

Learning to read does not occur in isolation from other development. At the same time as children are developing reading skills, their spoken language skills will continue to develop. Whereas this needs to be taken into account in teaching programmes, we would not advocate that children are deliberately held back because of language delays, unless these are extreme. Essentially, if there is an appreciation that children will vary in their spoken language skills and if these differences are taken into account, then all children can make progress. Furthermore, the process of learning to read and the eventual mastery of reading will provide benefits for the spoken language development of all children.

In addition to considering children's spoken language skills, it is important to examine what understandings children have about reading when they first start learning to read. One source of information about reading is environmental print. It is difficult for children to escape the abundance of environmental print that exists in our society. What they make of this print though will vary. Unlike writing where children at least have the chance to observe the writer producing marks on the page, reading can

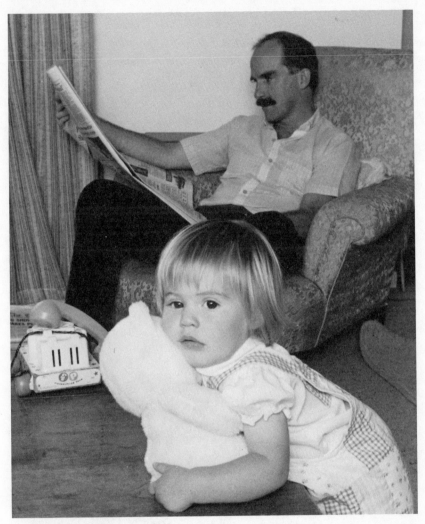

Reading is a mysterious skill

be a very private activity. If someone is reading silently, then a child observing this behaviour can deduce little of what reading involves. The child may conclude that when an adult is reading, he or she is sitting silently in a chair looking at some paper with funny markings on it and telling children to go away and play quietly! Similarly, many of the interactions that take place with environmental print can go unnoticed by the young child. Thus although parents might check whether it is the bus they want to get on, by reading the destination board or by checking the

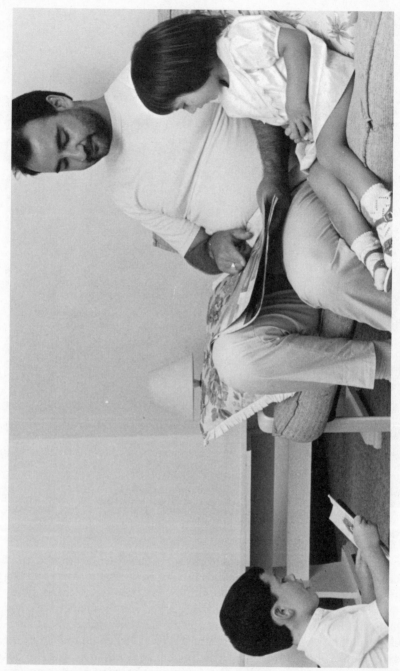

Children learn a lot from experience with books

number, young children may not even notice, unless their parents discuss what they are doing with them.

Some children of course have the opportunity to learn more about reading, as to them it is not simply interactions with environmental print. It is a shared activity with a parent or older sibling. They will sit on a parent's knee or lie in bed and listen to a story being read to them. Even with this opportunity to learn more about reading though, some children will pay little attention to the act of reading, being content to listen to the exciting tale. Although such children may gain much pleasure from being read to, they may still not show an interest in learning to read themselves. In this context we are reminded of a friend's child who when asked if he was looking forward to going to school seemed surprisingly lacking in enthusiasm. When it was pointed out that if he went to school he would learn how to read, he replied that he did not need to, as his big sister could read. This child enjoyed listening to books being read and having heard many, knew about the pleasure that can be gained from reading. But even with this background, he did not see the need to learn himself when others could do it for him. He was understandably unaware of all those times in his future life when there would be no one there to read something for him or of the pleasure that can be gained by reading a novel oneself. For this child reading was but one activity – listening to someone reading a story from a book.

Because it was not clear what understandings children may bring to the reading task, Jessie Reid (1958, 1966) asked children about reading at the time they started school. In her work, Reid interviewed a small number of 5-year-old children who had just begun school in Scotland. During the period when they were being given pre-reading exercises, she asked them if they could read yet, if their mother or father could read, if they had any books at home or at school and what was in these books. The children's answers indicated a range of understandings of the reading process. For example, although most children correctly stated they could not read, one child announced she was 'past reading', based on the fact that she had completed a 'reading readiness' book which involved a series of visual discrimination exercises.

In response to the other questions, Reid found that some children could not say whether their parents could read or not. They also demonstrated a limited knowledge about books with most children describing them by saying they contained pictures. Only one child stated that books contained words. Generally Reid (1966) concluded from these initial interviews that children 'had very little precise notion of what the activity (reading) consisted in' (p.60).

Reid's work made an important contribution to the teaching of reading by drawing attention to the need to consider the child's understanding and thus stimulating further research in the area. Downing (1970) replicated and extended Reid's research. Like Reid, he found that many children were confused about reading. However he discovered that when children were shown a set of pictures, some showing a person reading (for example, a teacher reading to a class) and some showing other activities (for example, a teacher talking to the class), children were able to identify correctly the ones depicting reading. This finding indicated that many children who remain confused about what reading involves, may have sufficient understanding to distinguish reading from other activities when given concrete examples. This early distinction could be used as the basis for discussion with children about what reading is and what people do when they read, discussion which would help develop clearer understandings.

It is evident then that educators cannot assume all children come to school knowing what reading is. Although many children come to school knowing that they will learn to read (because parents and others have told them), they may not know what this means. Some children will come from homes where there is little opportunity to see others reading. To these children, reading may simply be another one of those mysterious skills that you *have* to learn at school. For these children the mastery of this mysterious skill, reading, will itself be the goal rather than a means to achieve other goals, including gaining access to further knowledge and enjoyment by reading. Other children will have a greater understanding and in some cases will be much more enthusiastic about the opportunity to learn.

It is important to stimulate the natural curiosity of all children to learn. If children are presented with situations where they need to be able to read to achieve a goal, rather than reading being the goal, then they will show a much greater interest. Parents and teachers can create such situations. One example is to play a hiding game where an object is hidden and children are given simple written clues about where it is hidden. The clues can be kept short initially and help can be given with the reading of them. Gradually the help can be withdrawn as children become more competent. Children's attention should also be drawn to the many uses of reading in the classroom and the home so that they develop an understanding that reading is a very important means of achieving many goals.

## Concepts about Print

Clay (1979, 1985, 1991), in her work with young children, has recognized the importance of a range of understandings about many different

*Table 6*  Significant concepts about print (after Clay, 1972,1985)

| Concept | Knowledge or ability involved |
| --- | --- |
| Book orientation | Knowing which is the front of a book |
| Directional rules | Knowing that when reading you progress from left to right and at the end of the line you return to the left hand end of the next line |
| Print carries the message | Knowing that it is the print not the picture that carries the story |
| Letter concepts | Being able to point to a lower case letter and a capital letter |
| Word concepts | Being able to point to one word, two words |
| Punctuation | Knowing what a full stop, comma and quotation marks are for |

properties of the printed word. She refers to these as 'concepts about print' and a summary of the main concepts is given in Table 6. Some of these have already been discussed in the last chapter as they are concepts which the child must understand for both reading and writing.

Clay's concepts involve both knowledge of the conventions that exist in our written language, many of which are arbitrary (such as reading from left to right) and knowledge of the technical vocabulary of the language (such as 'word', 'sentence'). Although some children may have developed an understanding of some of the concepts, many will know very little about them until they are faced with reading instruction. As Clay pointed out, it is important for those involved in the teaching of reading to be aware of what children might know and also what they might have difficulty with. Conventions which are taken for granted by skilled readers can be very puzzling to the child who is learning to read.

A very clear instance of a child having difficulty with conventions was reported by Clay (1979). It involved an interaction between a child and his teacher. The child had written 'I am a dog' which the teacher copied onto another sheet of paper. She then cut up the sentence into words, and the word 'dog' into individual letters, and asked the child to make the sentence again. He produced 'dgo a am I', and when asked to read it, said 'I am a dog', while pointing from right to left. The dialogue which followed is given below (from Clay, 1979, pp. 101–2), as it illustrates very clearly the child's difficulty in understanding why we follow an arbitrary convention *and* the teacher's difficulty in explaining why.

*T*:  But you read it that way (*from right to left*).
*C*:  I know.

*T*:  But you can't do that.

*C*:  Why?

*T*:  Because we always read that way (*left to right*).

*C*:  Why?

*T*:  Because it's a rule.

*C*:  Why?

*T*:  Well if we didn't make a rule about reading and writing no one would know which way to start and which way to go and we'd get mixed up. Wouldn't we?

*C*:  How?

*T*:  (*picking up the book*). If I didn't know that the person who wrote this story kept to the rules and wrote this way I might read the top line like this 'Engine fire the at look.'

*C*:  (*long solemn look*): Ph.

*T*:  Haven't you always been shown to read that way?

*C*:  Ye–s. I didn't think it mattered.

*T*:  You are absolutely not allowed to go the other way in reading or writing

Although this child was able to read and write some basic sentences, he had not appreciated that at all times one reads from left to right. In contrast, other children will develop this understanding before they learn to read.

Ferreiro and Teberosky (1982), in a study conducted in Argentina, examined another aspect of children's concept about print, namely, their understanding of what print can and cannot be read. They presented 4- to 6-year-old children attending preschools and schools with a series of cards with different characters (letters and numbers) on them. All cards had one or more letters or numbers, with some cards having legitimate combinations of letters representing syllables or words while others had combinations that were not found in the language. The children were expected to sort the cards into two piles consisting of those that could be read and those that could not. Their findings indicated that some of the youngest children were not able to make any distinctions at all and divided the cards at random. Most children, however, did sort the cards systematically. The two criteria that were used most frequently were length and variation. Children rejected cards that had only a small number of characters on them or cards where the same character appeared several times without any other characters. Consequently according to these children, cards could only be read if they contained more than two characters or if the characters were not all the same. It did not matter to these children if the characters were letters or numbers or if they were in upper case or lower case.

Bialystok (1995) has examined in more detail children's early concepts of print in a study that follows on from the work of Ferreiro and Teberosky. Bialystok examined children's ability to judge whether an adult doll would be able to read material presented on cards. The cards contained printed and cursive style words, shapes, pictures, and squiggles. The squiggles were created so that some were scattered across the card, some were similar to printed words and some similar to cursive style words. The children in the study, whose ages ranged from 4 to 6 years, were carefully screened and selected on the basis that they could not read but could recite the alphabet, identify by letter name a series of letters presented on cards and write their own name. Bialystok found that the children were generally reliable in determining that print and cursive style writing could be read. However, the 4-year-old children in her study also stated that shapes, pictures and squiggles could be read about 50 per cent of the time. Except pictures, which remained around 50 per cent, these categories dropped to around 30 per cent of the time for 5- and 6-year-olds.

In a second task, the same children were asked to sort cards depicting print, cursive style writing and squiggles into three boxes, one for cards that adults could read, one for those children could read and one for cards no-one could read. Overall, children tended to put equal numbers of cards with print on them in the adult and child boxes, but favoured the adult box for cursive style writing and the no-one box for squiggles. The level of performance indicated that most children on this task, including the younger ones were demonstrating some understanding of the contrast between writing and squiggles.

Although the work by Ferreiro and Teberosky, and Bialystok is of considerable interest, one must be cautious in generalizing the findings. The criteria that these authors found being used were elicited from children in a situation where they were required to make judgements about cards or sort them into those that could be read and those that could not. These children may not have understood exactly the distinction between could and could not be read, but still completed the task by using some conspicuous properties of the stimuli. This would give the impression that they already possessed some understanding about what could be read. However they may never have thought about this distinction before.

Nevertheless, this research does demonstrate that children will strive to make sense of material presented to them. In so doing, they may form mistaken conclusions. It also demonstrates that children do not observe the same distinctions as adults, between, for example, letters and numbers.

An understanding of many of the other conventions discussed by Clay will develop as children continue to interact with the printed word. For example, children will learn to distinguish punctuation marks from letters, and develop an understanding that these serve different purposes. The letters provide information about the sounds that are being represented in words, whereas the punctuation marks provide information about such things as grammatical structure (for example, a full stop marking the end of a sentence) and the representation of direct speech (inverted commas).

In addition to learning about the conventions of print, children also have to learn the technical vocabulary used to refer to the different concepts encountered in print. Downing (1980) provided an impressive illustration of the need to take this into account when teaching children what may seem to be straightforward principles to adults. Consider the following passage provided by Downing:

> This is how you sove the zasp 'bite'. It is tebbed with the rellangs fly, ear, milk, wow. The last rellang is the holy wow. When you have a holy wow at the end of a zasp the ear says ear not ook like it does in the zasp 'bit'. (p. 17)

It makes little, if any, sense. Yet as the passage below illustrates, all Downing did was substitute terms that the reader does not know for the technical vocabulary (for example, letter, letter names, word) used in reading instruction. The effect for the reader is the same as for the child who is listening to the teacher and does not have this technical vocabulary. The child will not be able to follow the teacher's instructions.

> This is how you write the word 'bite'. It is spelt with the letters bee, eye, tea, ee. The last letter is the silent ee. When you have a silent ee at the end of a word the eye says eye not i like it does in the word 'bit'. (p. 36)

Even when children have developed quite a sophisticated understanding of the principles involved in decoding words, they may still find the technical vocabulary confusing, **as** illustrated by one child in Reid's (1966) study. Reid continued to ask children questions about reading during their first year at school as they were learning to read. Their answers to questions about the books they were reading, whether the books were hard or not, and what they did if they didn't know a word, revealed some remarkable insights into what is involved in learning to read and in the way it is taught. But the answers also revealed that throughout this first year some children were still unclear about some aspects of reading and confused the terminology.

An example of both insight and confusion is provided by Tommy half way through his first year. He was asked if there was anything funny about the word 'have' which appeared in his book. He replied: 'It's got an "e" on the end. It should only have three words instead of four words being there. You go to sound it and you hardly know what to say' (Reid, 1966, p. 58). Here Tommy was wrestling with the fact that the 'e' did not contribute to the overall sound pattern of the word and described the difficulty quite clearly, except the technical vocabulary still caused confusion. Tommy was confusing the terms 'word' and 'letter' in his explanation.

The importance of children developing an understanding of the concepts of print, including both conventions and technical vocabulary, was demonstrated in a study by Lomax and McGee (1987). Using selected items from Clay's test, along with a range of other items chosen to measure children's understanding of environmental print and recognition of written language units including letter, word and sentence, they investigated the relationship between concepts of print and decoding skills. Their results indicated that children's performance on the concepts of print task predicted performance on tasks measuring grapheme–phoneme correspondences which in turn influenced reading ability.

There can be no doubt that an understanding of some of the concepts of print is essential for the development of reading skills. For without the basic understandings, such as the left-to-right rule for English text, and an understanding of what words and letters are, it is impossible for reading to progress beyond a very basic level. There is a need therefore to take account of individual children's concepts of print as these will vary tremendously when children begin formal education. It must be recognized that many children will have poorly developed concepts of print when they come to school. These concepts should be developed in meaningful ways by reading to children and discussing the conventions adopted in books and other writing. Not only should children be read to, but the process of reading should be discussed with them For even when a book is read out loud to a child, there remain many mysteries about what the reader is doing. Some of these can be made less mysterious if the reader discusses with the child such principles as the need to turn the pages until one finds the writing, the starting point and the direction of movement along the line from left to right. The publication of very large books for use with small groups of children (for example, the 'Bookshelf' series published in the UK by Stanley Thornes, and the 'Storybox' series published in the UK by Macmillan) provides excellent opportunities for the teacher to discuss with children what is being done when reading and for the stimulation of discussion amongst the children (see Holdaway, 1979). These discussions lead to valuable learning for the children. They also lead to valuable learning for the teacher who can gain insights about the conceptions and misconceptions held by individual children.

As we discussed in chapter 7, the learning of technical terms may take some time as this learning requires the ability to focus attention on language, an ability many children will have had little opportunity to develop. Thus discussion about reading should also include many opportunities for children to develop an awareness of words (in both spoken and written forms) and of sounds and letters. An apparently simple statement that 'words are the bits that have spaces at each end' will do little to enhance the child's development of the *word* concept if children have never come across the term *word* before and if they have had little cause to focus attention on these linguistic units. Whereas many books should be read purely for the enjoyment of the story without interruptions to discuss concepts about print, at other times these concepts should certainly be discussed so that children's understanding will be enhanced.

Providing situations where children are motivated to try to write will also offer excellent opportunities for the development of concepts about print. The active involvement in the writing process often leads children to reflect on the units of language and ask questions about them.

Children should also be encouraged to 'read' books by themselves. Individual children who sit looking through a familiar book may discover some important information about the reading process. They may, for example, realize that the pictures do not tell the full story as they have heard it many times from a parent. They may start to examine features of the text and try to find some letters that they recognize. Alternatively, natural curiosity may lead them to ask questions about what is written in the book. These questions can then form the basis of informative discussions about reading, between adult and child.

The talk that stems from adults reading to children, from children trying to read and from their attempts to write, will all enhance the development of early concepts about print. This enhanced development will enable children to make progress in decoding the written word and gaining access to the meaning which will in turn lead to further understandings about concepts about print.

## Developing Access to the Message in the Printed Word

A few children begin school every year having learned to read, either as a result of explicit instruction from parents or from their frequent encounters with print, stimulating their natural curiosity to learn (D. Durkin, 1966). Most children however are not reading when they start school. Consequently the development of their reading skills will be influenced by the reading instruction they receive and in particular by the skills that are seen to be important by the educators who have devised the programmes. We start this section therefore by providing a very brief outline of some of the main characteristics of the different approaches that have been adopted in reading programmes.

In the past there has been an extensive debate about whether the decoding skills or the meaning should receive more emphasis in reading programmes and a comprehensive account of this debate is provided by Chall (1967; updated edition 1983) in her book *Learning to Read: The Great Debate*. The approaches that emphasize decoding involve some form of phonics teaching. Essentially the teaching of phonics aims to convey to the child the correspondences between the sounds of the language and the letters that represent these, known as letter–sound or grapheme–phoneme correspondences. In some phonics programmes the correspondence has been taught in complete isolation from other activities, with children spending entire lessons being shown a letter and rehearsing the sound it makes. Although most letters represent more than one sound, phonics approaches often teach only one letter–sound correspondence for each letter initially and then later introduce other sounds that correspond with the same letter as *exceptions* to the correspondence rule the children have already learned. For example, the letter **c** will be introduced as corresponding only to the /k/ sound, then later it is explained that **c** can also represent an /s/ sound.

In other cases the correspondences are taught in the context of learning words and the children may be required to sound out words. That is, they will be instructed to say '**c-a-t**' and then to 'blend' the individual sounds into 'cat'. (The problems with this blending were mentioned in chapter 7.)

In contrast, approaches that emphasize meaning provide children with sentences and encourage them to read these. These approaches are frequently based on the work of Goodman (for example, 1976) and Smith (for example, 1979). Goodman, in his 1976 paper, portrayed reading as a psycholinguistic guessing game suggesting that reading involves 'guessing' words based on surrounding context. Followers of this approach often emphasize reading 'real' books so that children can make use of the context to read unknown words. However, in some cases basal readers have also been used. Basal readers present children with short sentences involving very simple constructions that repeat words frequently. For example: 'This is John. This is Mary. This is Tip [the dog].' As one can see, the meaning is often very trivial and certainly not attention grabbing.

A related approach that has emphasized meaning is the language experience approach. The basis of this approach is that children are encouraged to talk about their experiences. Often the talk centres on a picture a child has drawn. The teacher writes down what the child has said about the picture and reads it back to the child. The child is then encouraged to read it to the teacher. Because the child has produced the language, it is argued that this approach has the advantage of using only language which is familiar to the child.

As Chall stressed, in most cases the debate revolves around the issue of which of the skills should be emphasized more, rather than which should be taught to the exclusion of the other. Granted there are some programmes that appear to teach either decoding or reading for meaning to the complete exclusion of the other. But in most cases children will be given some teaching in both, although one may be taught for a considerable amount of time before the other is introduced. As Chall pointed out, however, and has emphasized more recently, (Chall 1989), the inclusion of phonics or letter–sound correspondence training is critical to the development of efficient reading, a view strongly supported by many researchers, (for example, Snowling, 1996).

Clearly, decoding using knowledge of letter–sound correspondences and reading for meaning are both central to reading. Moreover, those who are strong advocates of developing effective word decoding skills based on knowledge of letter–sound correspondences, are all in agreement that the ultimate goal of reading is to extract the meaning, but recognize that doing so requires efficient and accurate decoding.

Consequently, all reading programmes should aim to ensure that children develop the skills involved in both efficient word decoding and extracting meaning from the text. Children should be given meaningful reading material so that they can make use of their developing decoding skills to extract the meaning. They should also be given a thorough grounding in decoding based on grapheme–phoneme correspondences. In practice, as we will see, some children will need more assistance with decoding skills while others may need to be encouraged to focus on meaning.

Thus in looking at how children learn to read and describing the path of development, it is important to remember that most children will be receiving formal reading instruction. The form that this instruction takes, along with the knowledge and skills the child brings to the task, will influence the path of development. A child who receives phonics training in isolation from reading words may learn about grapheme–phoneme correspondences before another child in a different school where phonics has not been emphasized. Consequently there will be large variations in children's learning and the descriptions that follow will not capture all of these. As mastery of the reading process is a large and complex area to cover, we have broken it down into subsections. These sections are visual discrimination, early word learning, grapheme–phoneme correspondences and combining strategies.

## *Visual Discrimination – or Learning Which Cues are Relevant*

When children start reading they sometimes make errors with letters that are the same shape but differ only in orientation, such as **b d p q**. In the past it was assumed this difficulty arose because children had trouble discriminating between the different letters visually, particularly ones that differ only in orientation. To help children surmount this *assumed* difficulty, they were given many exercises in visual discrimination. These exercises often involved presenting the child with a row of the same object (for example, cups) drawn on a sheet of paper. All the objects are identical except one, the odd one out, which is drawn as the mirror image of the others. The child's task is to circle the odd one out. The aim was to train children to detect different orientations of the same shape in preparation for finding these in the print. It is now clearly established that such training, though well intentioned, is misguided. As Tunmer (1988) has pointed out, children are able to make such visual discriminations well before they learn to read.

The mistaken approach resulted because the basis of the children's errors was misinterpreted. Children certainly do confuse letters, both in their reading and writing. But it is not a visual discrimination problem. It is a difficulty with determining what the salient features are that should be attended to. Before learning to read, children have spent four to five years learning, for example, that a chair is always a chair regardless of its orientation. That is, they have learned to ignore orientation when labelling objects. Although it may be important to have a chair the right way up when you sit down, it makes no difference to the labelling of it. Suddenly, though orientation is important for the labelling of one set of objects – letters (see figure 4).

Thus the child needs help, not in discriminating visually between letters, but in learning that when decoding them the orientation is important. Essentially, the difficulty with letter reversals illustrates a very important point for the learning of all letters. Children have to learn what features of print they should pay attention to in order to learn the rules which enable them to decode it. So, as they start to learn the associations between marks on the page and words or sounds, they are not only trying to find effective ways of memorizing this new and perhaps strange material, they are also working out which of the many features are important. Children must learn that some cues (such as orientation) will provide information that is relevant to their task while other cues will not.

Of course, even as they learn that orientation is important and become aware, for example, that **n** and **u** are different letters, they may still confuse them at times. But again this is not a failure of visual discrimination.

*Figure 4*   As chairs, each is labelled 'chair': as letters, they are labelled **b, d, p, q**.

When we learn new associations between two sets of stimuli, in the child's case between letters and sounds, confusions in learning arise more frequently amongst items in the stimuli that are similar (such as **n** and **u** or **n** and **m**) than between ones that are very different. This confusion is resolved in time through practising reading rather than practising discriminating the letters visually.

## Early Word Learning

Most children embark on the decoding process by starting to recognize some words which they encounter frequently on the basis of salient features. This has been described as recognizing words logographically (Ehri, 1987; Frith, 1985). The words that children recognize will vary from one child to another as will the cues they use for recognition. Many children first learn to recognize their own names and those of brothers, sisters and friends. Other commonly learned words for some children are those appearing on road signs (such as 'STOP') or on cars or emergency vehicles (such as 'FIRE'). At times the salient cues used may not even be part of the word. Thus although the word 'STOP' will be recognized immediately when it appears on a road sign, it may not be recognized in other contexts because the child is using the shape of the sign upon which 'STOP' is written as the cue rather than an intrinsic part of the word itself.

Even when children do make use of some properties of the words themselves, they may still adopt inappropriate strategies. They may, for example, remember a word because it has a distinctive outline (for example, 'bed' because the word looks like a bed) a distinctive feature (for example, 'dog', because it has a tail at the end) or it contains a certain shape (for example, the cross shape **x** in 'box'). Some children however may adopt strategies that are more appropriate. In particular, children who know their alphabet and can point to the correct letters as they say them, may make use of some of this knowledge to aid their memories. These children will begin to extract similarities between some of the letter names and words. For example, the word 'tea' may be remembered because the child recognizes that the first letter 'says t'. Alternatively children may recognize a word because it starts with the same letter as their name (for example, 'stupid' starts with the same letter as 'Sam' or 'Stephen'). The use of a range of strategies by different children reflects the fact that they are faced with a problem. They are confronted with the task of remembering many new words. They solve this problem using whatever means they have available to them.

Gough and Hillinger (1980) suggested that children may learn up to around 40 words using strategies involving visual cues before the system fails because there are insufficient visual features to distinguish new words. According to their view, the child begins by learning to associate a particular spoken word (such as 'dog') with a distinctive visual cue contained in the word (such as the 'tail' at the end of the word). Associative learning based on distinctive visual cues results in children recognizing the word on some occasions when they pay attention to the visual cue which triggers the association. However, on other occasions, children will fail to recognize the association when they fail to attend to the relevant visual cue in the word. With practice, children may become more adept at attending to the visual cues that are relevant to their learning. Sooner or later, another difficulty arises. As children are presented with more and more words to learn, they exhaust the number of distinctive visual cues that they can make use of effectively. Consequently, they must turn to other strategies based on the letter–sound correspondences.

Ehri and Wilce (1985) conducted a study to determine whether children who are just starting to learn to read use visual cues as Gough and Hillinger suggested or phonetic cues (cues that make use of the individual letter sounds). They created two lists of words for children to learn. In one list the spellings of the words were based on simplified phonetic spellings (for example, 'NE' for knee; 'BLUN' for balloon). In the other list the letters in the words did not correspond phonetically, but contained distinctive visual features (for example, 'Fo' for arm and 'WBC' for giraffe). Each list was designed so that only one of the strategies could be used. Thus the words in the visual features list could not be remembered using phonetic cues and the words in the phonetic list did not lend themselves to memory based on visual cues. Both lists were presented to three groups of children who varied in the number of words they were able to read on a standard word reading test.

The results indicated that children who could not read any words performed better when learning the list that provided visual cues than when learning the ones involving phonetic cues. In contrast children who could read a few words (up to 11) and children who could read more words (between 11 and 36) performed much better with the list that provided phonetic cues. Ehri and Wilce concluded from this that children make use of relevant phonetic cues earlier in the reading acquisition process than Gough and Hillinger claimed. Their results suggested that the children started to use correspondences between their knowledge of the names of letters and the sounds they represent as soon as they start reading.

Although Ehri and Wilce found that children could use letter names and sounds to help them remember the words, their performance could have been influenced in favour of using phonetic cues by several factors. The children may have been taught by a phonics based approach which would have emphasized the importance of letter–sound cues. In addition they were all given a pretest to assess their knowledge of letter names and sounds. This pretest would have drawn their attention to the relevance of names and sounds and could have increased the likelihood of using these when remembering the words. It should be noted, however, that the children in all groups did remember words in the list that required using visual strategies suggesting that they could make use of these cues. Finally, the lists were designed so that in each case the other strategy would not be used. That is, the phonetic strategy could not be used with the lists presenting visual cues and the visual strategy would not have been effective with the lists presenting phonetic cues.

The fact remains that if children have no knowledge of letter names or the sounds letters represent when they are first expected to remember the associations between written and spoken words, then they must resort to other means of remembering. It is also likely that children will use both visual and sound strategies in combination. For example, a child may learn to recognize both 'big' and 'box' because they both start with the letter **b** which represents the sound /b/, but distinguish them because 'box' has a cross-shaped letter in it. Such a combination of strategies may be used by children as they shift from relying on visual features to making use of their developing knowledge of grapheme–phoneme correspondences. Indeed, in a subsequent study, Ehri and Wilce (1987) recognized that children will use both visual and phonetic cues in the early stages of learning to read words.

## The Alphabetic Principle and Grapheme–Phoneme Correspondences

Within the range of the first 40 or so words, it is not of great importance exactly when children shift from learning words by remembering the visual features to decoding them using sound strategies, or whether some children make use of some letter–sound knowledge from the beginning. Of much greater importance is that all children **do** make the shift so that they become independent readers. For regardless of how many words are learned based on visual features, this strategy does not help the reader decode a word in print that has not been seen before. The decoding of a written word encountered for the first time requires a knowledge of the grapheme–phoneme rules of correspondence if the reader is to be certain that it has been decoded correctly. It may be the case that when a newly encountered word appears in a sentence context, the reader can make an inspired guess about it. However, there are few occasions where the context will completely determine what the word will be. For example, a child may read the words in a sentence 'He put the cake on the . . .', recognizing them by sight. However, if the last word is not known the child may then make an inspired guess that the word is 'table'. But it could have been 'plate' or 'rack'. Indeed calculations of the extent to which words can be correctly predicted from context is about 30 per cent according to Finn (1978). Moreover, as Gough (1983) points out, when one considers only content words, which usually have greater complexity than the more highly predictable function words, the predictability drops to about 10 per cent.

Learning the grapheme–phoneme correspondence rules is therefore of importance if children are to become independent and accurate readers. With regard to this, Share (1995) in a highly informative journal article refers to the self-teaching hypothesis. The self-teaching hypothesis describes the process by which individuals are able to decode words accurately using grapheme–phoneme correspondence rules, such that a small number of encounters with each new word will lead to that word being recognized in future on the basis of its orthography or spelling. That is, the self-teaching hypothesis accounts for the ability to decode words in text that have not been encountered previously, using grapheme–phoneme correspondences. On the basis of this process, following a relatively small number of encounters, they move to recognize the word from the entire sequence of letters, as discussed in more detail below. According to Share, this process is used by both skilled readers including adults, and by children learning to read. However, as children learning to read will clearly encounter many more words they do not recognize, they will rely more heavily on the process. It is essential therefore that as children are introduced to reading, they develop the knowledge and skills that underpin the self-teaching hypothesis.

We have already looked at the possible ways in which some children will begin to get access to correspondence rules through writing. Here we look at what may occur from the perspective of reading, recognizing that there should be considerable interchange between what is learned in both cases. It is important to appreciate that because the self-teaching hypothesis relies on a thorough knowledge of grapheme–phoneme correspondences, it also therefore relies on an understanding of the alphabetic principle. An understanding of the alphabetic principle involves knowing that the letters of the alphabet represent the sounds of the language. Clearly without understanding this principle, there is no basis to learn the individual correspondences between sounds and letters. Moreover, in turn, this principle relies on the awareness that the language is made up of individual sounds.

Traditionally, phonics approaches to reading have tackled the problem of teaching grapheme–phoneme correspondences solely from the perspective of learning the associations. This poses problems for many children as it is not possible for them to learn the associations between phonemes and graphemes if they are not able to focus attention on phonemes as units of language. Consequently they will have no basis to understand the alphabetic principle.

As we discussed in chapter 7, some children may gain initial access to the sounds in words through their experience with nursery rhymes. The study by Bryant, Bradley, MacLean and Crossland (1989), which established a relationship between knowledge of nursery rhymes and phonological skills, also examined the relationship between knowledge of nursery rhymes, phonological skills and early reading. Their results suggested that knowledge of nursery rhymes at age 3 was associated with the ability to detect rhyme in words. This in turn was related to performance on a phoneme oddity task, which required detection of individual phonemes, which correlated with reading scores at ages 5 and 6.

The early experience some children have in the home therefore leads them to become aware of the individual sounds of the language and provides them with practice in reflecting on these units. Consequently, when faced with learning to read they will find it less difficult to follow any phonics training they receive in school as they will be able to focus attention on the sounds in words and thus be more likely to make sense of such training. A few may even establish the alphabetic principle and the existence of grapheme–phoneme correspondences themselves without any formal phonics teaching.

Research by Byrne and colleagues (Byrne, 1996; Byrne and Fielding Barnsley, 1989; Byrne, Fielding-Barnsley and Ashley, 1996), however provides convincing evidence that most children are not able to extract the alphabetic principle and need explicit instruction to assist them. In a series of probing experiments, these researchers have managed to provide a considerable amount of information about how much young children are capable of understanding when first presented with print. For example, in one study they taught children who could not read previously to recognize word pairs printed on cards such as 'book' and 'books' and 'hat' and 'hats', thus providing them with the opportunity to work out that the letter **s** corresponds to the sound /s/. These children were able to generalize from learning the pairs presented to distinguishing between new pairs such as *cap* and *caps*. However, when presented with other contrast pairs which did not involve plurals, such as *bug* and *bus*, most children were unable to use their learning experience to identify the printed version of these words correctly. Thus children had focused on the presence of the **s** at the end of words as an aspect of meaning, in this case signalling the plural, rather than as representing a sound. Very similar results were found with word pairs such as *small* and *smaller*, which children could generalize to *mean* and *meaner*, but not to *corn* and *corner*, again suggesting that they are focusing on meaning and the relationship between word pairs, in this case signalled by **er**. As there is no meaningful relationship between 'corn' and 'corner' they are unable to generalize. In a final version of the task designed so that the key letters that changed were not morphological units associated with meaning as the plural **s** or the comparative **er** are, children were taught to identify the two written words *fat* and *bat*. However, once learned, they were unable to use this knowledge to determine whether a printed word presented to them such as *ball* was 'ball' or 'fall'. This research demonstrates that without drawing children's attention specifically to the alphabetic principle, namely that letters represent sounds, and providing training in grapheme–phoneme correspondences, children will face many problems with the mastery of written language. Thus explicit instruction should be given to assist children develop an understanding of the alphabetic principle and a knowledge of the grapheme–phoneme correspondence rules.

As mentioned above, the development of phonological awareness or phonological sensitivity is critical to understanding the alphabetic principle, the basis of mastering grapheme–phoneme correspondence rules. Amidst an initial debate about the relationship between phonological awareness and learning to read with some researchers and educators arguing it develops before learning and others arguing that phonological awareness is the outcome of learning to read, it is now widely, although

not universally, accepted that there is reciprocal causation with phonological awareness in part determining reading ability and the development of reading increasing levels of awareness (see for example Ehri, 1979;
Bentin and Leshem, 1993). However, it is important to note in the
context of the arguments for reciprocal causation that a key component
of phonological awareness, the ability to focus attention on the individual
sounds of language, is an essential requirement for the learning of
grapheme–phoneme correspondence rules. In addition, studies which
appear to show that phonological awareness at the level of attending to
individual phonemes, develops out of **learning** to read may in fact be
demonstrating that this awareness has developed from reading **instruction**. That is, because effective reading instruction, which must involve
teaching children grapheme–phoneme correspondences, relies on children being able to reflect on individual sounds of language, the process of
instruction may force the awareness to develop for the many children
who have not previously had cause to reflect on the individual sounds.
Consequently, if awareness is measured prior to learning to read, and
then following mastery of the printed word, or even at points in time
during the first year of learning, it may appear that the increase in awareness is linked solely to learning to read rather than being triggered by the
instruction process.

As an analogy, being familiar and at ease in water and being able to
float provide the individual with a considerable advantage when being
taught to swim. Attention can be focused on the details of the stroke
instruction in order to propel oneself forward. In contrast, if one is not at
ease in water and not able to float prior to instruction, especially given the
latter is an essential component of learning to swim, much energy and
attention will be devoted to this, reducing the effective learning that takes
place. Moreover, the individual who could not float before receiving swimming instruction will certainly have to learn to do so in order to achieve
the goal of learning to swim. Similarly, children who are familiar with
text and have developed an awareness of the sounds of language prior to
learning to read, will benefit much more from reading instruction than
those who are forced to extract the awareness from the process of being
instructed to read. Those children who have not developed an awareness
will need to do so as they are faced with instruction and work toward the
goal of learning to read.

The research by Bryant et al. (1989) showed that early experience with
rhyme was associated with greater of phonological awareness and also
predicted later reading performance. The importance of phonological
awareness in determining the course of reading development has also
been demonstrated by many other researchers including Cardoso-

Martins (1995) in Brazil, Lomax and McGee (1987) in the United States, Lundberg, Olofsson and Wall (1980), in Sweden, and Rohl and Pratt, (1995) in Australia. (For a more extensive discussion of the importance of phonological awareness and further details of studies in other countries the reader should consult Adams, 1990.) Essentially these studies show that phonological awareness measured before children learn to read, predicts reading (and spelling) performance in grade 1 and often in later grades, even when other possible influences such as intelligence, age, and vocabulary are taken into account statistically.

For example, Rohl and Pratt (1995) measured children's phonological awareness prior to reading instruction on a series of tasks including the ability to categorize words on the basis of similarities in the first or last sounds in the words, the ability to segment words into their individual sounds and to delete sounds from words. They also measured children's working memory capacity by asking them to repeat lists of letters and words forwards and backwards as well as repeating acceptable and anomalous sentences. The revised version of the Peabody Picture Vocabulary Test (Dunn and Dunn, 1981) was also administered. Using regression analyses, it was found that once the effects of age, vocabulary and working memory had been taken into account, all phonological tasks were significant predictors of reading and spelling at the end of grade 1 (the first year of reading instruction) and in the second half of grade 2.

With the interest in phonological awareness and reading now spanning several decades it has been possible to follow up the longer-term effects of differences in phonological awareness. For example, Stuart and Masterson (1992) examined the reading and spelling abilities of 10-year-old children whose phonological skills had been assessed at age 4, prior to reading instruction. Again they found significant relationships that point to the ongoing positive influence of prereading levels of phonological awareness.

It is evident from this research and a multitude of other studies that have shown clear associations between phonological awareness before children are introduced to reading and their subsequent reading performance that children with higher levels of awareness become better readers. Thus children who come from backgrounds where there is a focus on language will be better placed to benefit from reading instruction. However this is not very helpful for the many children who come from backgrounds where they have not had this early experience. What then can be done to assist these children? The answer to this question may be found in a number of studies that have provided children with training in aspects of phonological awareness. One early example of this is the study by Bradley and Bryant (1983). The children who participated in the study were aged 4 and 5 years when they were first assessed and had very low scores on a task in which they had to categorize words on the basis of sounds contained in them. These children are ones who would be expected to experience difficulty with learning the grapheme–phoneme correspondences in the course of reading instruction. Two groups of children were given training in sound categorization, while others acted as controls and received training not related to sounds. In one of the groups that received sound categorization training, the children were taught that the same word (for example, 'hen') shared with other words a common beginning (**hen h**at), common middle (h**en** p**e**t) and common end sound (he**n** ma**n**). Another group received the same training but plastic letters were used to demonstrate that the sounds were represented by letters of the alphabet. The training involved 40 10-minute sessions spread over a 2-year period. The results on reading and spelling tasks administered about three years after the initial training indicated that the reading and spelling levels of the two training groups were superior to control groups and that the group who was trained with plastic letters was superior to the other training group.

Other research by Byrne and Fielding-Barnsley (1993, 1995) confirms the benefits of explicit training in phonological awareness that provides the basis for learning the alphabetic principle and developing a knowledge of grapheme–phoneme correspondence rules. In their research they compared children who received explicit training in phonological awareness with a control group of children. The training programme was presented for about half an hour a week for 12 weeks and involved the children classifying items displayed in posters, worksheets and books on the basis of shared sounds, using a package developed by the researchers called *Sound Foundations* (Byrne and Fielding-Barnsley, 1991). For example, children had to search for all items that contained the sound /s/. Ample feedback was provided. Children in the control group were given an equal amount of training with the same materials but classified them on characteristics such as colour, shape and edibility. All training took place in the year prior to entering grade 1 and beginning formal reading instruction.

In follow-up studies at one year later (Byrne and Fielding-Barnsley, 1993) and two and three years later (Byrne and Fielding-Barnsley, 1995), children in the training group were still showing some reading advantages. However, the authors had noted that at the end of the preschool year, when the effects of training were being measured using a phoneme identity task requiring the ability to focus on initial and final phonemes, some children in the control group had spontaneously developed this ability. Consequently when Byrne and Fielding-Barnsley reanalysed their data in the follow up studies, examining the differences between children from both training and control groups who had developed an awareness of individual phonemes prior to reading instruction and those who had not, the differences in reading ability were very clear up to three years later. These findings are noteworthy. As the authors point out, their research confirms the importance of the development of phonological awareness prior to reading in determining the course of learning to read. However, as many more children in the training group developed this level of awareness as a result of the training than children in the control group who developed it spontaneously, the value of educational programmes which explicitly train awareness is evident.

Central to the issue of effective teaching of decoding skills therefore is an understanding that children will vary in their ability to reflect on phonemes when they start learning to read. The child who has not thought of language in terms of the sounds that are used to produce words will not be able to understand when, for example, the teacher says 'Look at this word – "box" – it starts with a /b/ sound.' Children should be given the opportunity to develop an awareness of the sounds in language before being given formal reading instruction. This can be done initially through rhyme and may involve children learning short poems containing clear rhymes and finding words that rhyme with one another. The latter task can be extended to include nonsense words that rhyme with real words (such as 'hen', 'sen') as this also has benefits for the development of other forms of awareness, particularly word awareness.

Later, children can be given tasks which involve finding words that begin with the same sound or end with the same sound. Bowey (1996) points out that teachers should work through these exercises with children, encouraging them to focus on the individual sounds. As children start to master the sounds and go on to make use of their skills to decode words using limited grapheme–phoneme cues (for example, recognizing the first and last letter in the word), then new challenges can be introduced to help them develop higher levels of control processing. One effective technique that can be used is to get children to search through words on a page to find any that have a particular letter in them. For example, in the following sentence children may be asked to circle all the words that contain a letter c: 'The clown picked an ice cream in a chocolate covered cone for the very excited child.'

This type of exercise caters for children of different levels as the ability to read is not necessary for finding the words with a c in them. Further, as long as the teacher takes care to demonstrate the task, children who do not have the technical vocabulary will still be able to follow what is required. Once the words have been found, the children can then try saying the words one at a time and listening to the different sounds the letter c can represent. Such activities provide children with the opportunity to develop skills required to reflect on the sounds of language. They also provide an opportunity for them to see the regularities that exist in the correspondence rules as well as the irregularities. That is, they can learn from examples with the letter **c** that it often corresponds to a /k/ sound or an /s/ sound, or combine with another letter, **h**, to produce a /č/ sound. Learning from an activity such as this one where the children are actively involved in finding letters is often more meaningful and more challenging than learning lists of associations between letters and sounds separate from the context in which they are used. Children are drawn into the activity as it presents them with problems they want to explore, leading to further learning of the associations between print and sounds.

## Combining Strategies

It is our view that all reading programmes should include teaching that ensures children develop an understanding of the alphabetic principle and learn the grapheme–phoneme correspondence rules. Furthermore good reading programmes will do this in a way that creates interesting challenges for the child. Our view should not be misinterpreted though as suggesting that children *must* use individual grapheme–phoneme rules at all times. Throughout the reading acquisition process, and even once the child is deemed to be a skilled reader, a range of strategies will be used.

Research by Goswami (1986, 1994), for example, has shown that children can make use of the sound patterns associated with letter strings when learning to read. She refers to this as reading by analogy. In one of her studies, 5- to 7-year-old children were given a written 'clue' word (for example, 'hark') and then asked to read seven test words. Some of the test words contained the same letter string as the clue word. This string either appeared at the beginning of the word (for example, 'harp') or at the end (for example, 'lark'). These test words could be read by children using the clue word to determine the sound pattern corresponding to the letter string. The other test words contained three of the letters from the clue word but these did not appear in the same sequence (for example, 'hair'). The results indicated that children who are in the early stages of reading were able to read more test words that contained the same letter strings than the test words that contained the same letters but in a different order. Moreover, through systematic investigation, Goswami has shown that children are more likely to make use of a clue word to read a test word if the rime is the same, (for example 'ark' in 'hark' and 'lark') than if other groups of letters which do not correspond to the rime are the same. Her research indicates that children can use the complete sound patterns corresponding to the string, especially, though not solely, if this string corresponds to the rime rather than the individual grapheme–phoneme correspondences contained within the string.

Kirtley, Bryant, MacLean and Bradley (1989) have suggested that children will continue to use the correspondences between letter strings and sound patterns and in some cases may never break these down into their constituent units. For example, Kirtley et al. pointed out that the string of letters 'ight' in words such as 'light' and 'fight' may be learned initially and subsequently recognized as a complete unit rather than as graphemes representing two phonemes. When children then encounter a new word involving this string, say 'sight', they may decode this by working out the initial sound from their knowledge of the correspondence rules and combining this with their existing knowledge that **ight** is sounded as 'ite'. Indeed in this case, trying to work out what sounds the individual letters **g**, **h** and **t** might represent will not be helpful.

Whereas this research demonstrates that children may make use of letter strings, it does not suggest that such strategies provide the basis for learning to read without children also knowing grapheme–phoneme correspondences. Clearly, to read the word 'sight' on the basis of knowing 'light' or 'fight', a child must still know that the onset, the letter **s**, corresponds with the sound /s/. The importance of grapheme–phoneme correspondence knowledge is illustrated in research by Ehri and Robbins (1992) and Walton (1995) on children's use of analogy. Walton's research, for example, showed that not only did children need to know the correspondence for the onset when reading words with the same rime (for example 'bat' and 'rat'), but that they were frequently also relying on the identification of the final consonant (in this case **t**) before reading it by analogy with the clue word. In addition, Bruck and Treiman (1992) in a study that examined predictors of children's ability to read by analogy, found that levels of phonological awareness were significantly correlated with reading using analogies. They concluded that in order for children to make use of the natural tendency to break words in onsets and rimes, and use rimes as a basis for decoding, they must **first** learn something about grapheme–phoneme correspondences.

Juel, Griffith and Gough (1986) have also pointed out that there are certain types of words where knowledge of the correspondence rules is not enough on its own to decode words. These include words where there is more than one option for the correspondence between letters and sounds. In these cases, children must develop specific knowledge about the words to assist them in their task of decoding. Thus, for example, for words that contain the pair of letters **ea**, the child must use his specific knowledge about the possible sounds it can represent together with the context in which it appears, in order to determine whether 'steak' sounds like 'stake', 'steek' or 'stek', or 'head' like 'hade', 'heed' or 'hed'. Frequently in order to establish what sound it represents, children will combine their knowledge of the possible sounds with clues about what word will fit from the context provided by the rest of the sentence. A sentence such as 'The boy had a cap on his head' is likely to provide a child with sufficient graphemic and contextual information to establish that the last word is 'head'.

Children should also be encouraged to use a combination of strategies to assist them when they encounter new words in print that they do not know at all. Earlier we gave the example of the sentence 'He put the cake on the . . .', and pointed out that the context did not provide enough information for the child to be sure of the correct word that completes the sentence. The context certainly suggests that 'table' is one possibility. The child may then look at the word for clues and see that the word starts with a /t/ sound and so deduce that it is 'table'. This approach may be especially useful to children when they encounter words with irregular spellings. Even words that we regard as having irregular spellings usually contain some clues to their phonemic representation. Tunmer (1988) gave the example of 'yacht'. Despite the irregular spelling, the first and last letters both give clues to the phonemic representation of the word. Thus even if children have difficulty reading the word in isolation, a context provided by other words in a sentence such as 'The man was sailing in his . . .', will probably enable them to decode it. They will be able to put together their knowledge about the world (people sail in boats that are often called yachts) with their knowledge of grapheme–phoneme correspondences (for example, knowing what sound the first letter in the word corresponds to). Tunmer claimed that children will use a range of cues to help them decode words that they have not encountered before. These include grapheme–phoneme correspondence rules, knowledge of the grammar of the language suggesting what grammatical category the word belongs to and semantic or pragmatic considerations based on one's knowledge of the world.

Certainly there is evidence from a number of studies that points to the relationship between grammatical awareness (and in some cases semantic or pragmatic awareness) and reading (see Blackmore and Pratt, 1997; Bowey, 1994; and Bryant, 1993, for further discussion of this relationship). Two studies are of particular interest here as they provide some account of the reason for children's awareness of the grammar and meaning of language assisting with their reading of words. The first is one reported by Rego and Bryant (1993) and also described in Bryant (1993). Towards the beginning of the first year at school, they gave children a series of tasks designed to provide measures of phonological awareness and semantic and syntactic awareness. The phonological awareness tasks were the phoneme oddity task and the phoneme tapping task. The semantic and syntactic tasks involved oral cloze tasks and sentence completion tasks, both of which involved children providing missing words in sentences, and a word order task in which children had to put strings of words into the correct grammatical order.

Five months later the children were given tasks including an invented spelling task, with children being asked to spell words they might not know, and a contextual facilitation task. This latter task was a measure of the number of words that children were able to read when the words were presented in context that they could not read when presented in isolation. Essentially the invented spelling task is taken as a measure of children's knowledge of grapheme–phoneme correspondence rules and the contextual facilitation task provides a measure of children's ability to use context to assist them in word decoding. As expected, Rego and Bryant found that children's phonological awareness scores were significantly related to their invented spelling scores but not to their contextual facilitation scores. In addition their syntactic and semantic awareness scores were significantly related to their contextual facilitation scores, but not to the invented spelling scores. This confirms the claim that syntactic and semantic awareness are of importance for assisting children make use of context when reading.

More recently, Tunmer and Chapman (1998) have explored in greater detail children's use of context to assist in the decoding of words. With a large sample of over 300 grade 2 and 3 children, they administered an oral cloze task similar to that administered by Rego and Bryant, a word reading task involving reading a list of words in isolation, a pseudoword naming task, and a context facilitation task. The pseudoword naming task involved asking children to read a list of single syllable nonwords that conformed to the standard rules of English but did not represent real words. The context facilitation task is of particular interest because, although similar to Rego and Bryant's task, the target words that were presented in isolation and in context were all irregular words. That is, they were all words which if not previously known could not be decoded by the application of grapheme–phoneme correspondence rules alone because the words do not follow the regular rules, (for example 'stomach', 'tongue').

The outcome of this study was of particular interest. Firstly, using regression analyses, Tunmer and Chapman showed that both decoding ability as measured by the pseudoword task and children's semantic and syntactic processing as measured by the oral cloze task were related to contextual facilitation. Secondly, in carrying out additional analyses, they found that children with very poor decoding skills were not able to make use of context for reading irregular words, and hence that a certain level of knowledge of grapheme–phoneme correspondence was required in combination with context to read words.

Consequently as the work of Tunmer and Chapman (1998) shows, reading for children can involve making use of both decoding skills and context. Children should be able to use their developing knowledge of grapheme–phoneme correspondence rules to extract from the text some sound cues, while also using their knowledge of language and the world to find words that match these cues. However this process cannot develop effectively if children encounter words in isolation. Reading material for children should be contextualized and meaningful.

We believe decoding and meaning are both essential for readers *at any stage* of the learning process, but this should not be taken to suggest that children should become too dependent on context for word recognition rather than developing a thorough knowledge of grapheme–phoneme correspondence rules. Accurate decoding at the level of the word provides access to the meaning. However, consideration of possible meanings can assist the process of decoding, especially when words do not follow regular correspondence rules. To illustrate this let us again consider the sentence 'The man was sailing in his yacht.' The process of deducing that the last word is 'yacht' may proceed in two directions. Some children who know the correspondence rule for the letter **y** and are able to establish the sound it makes can search through the words they know to find one that would fit the context. In so doing they will find the word 'yacht'. Other children who are having difficulty remembering the relevant rules of correspondence may start with the context provided by the rest of the sentence to search for a word that fits. They may then come up with 'boat' but realize from what knowledge they do have that the letter **y** does not sound like /b/. This may lead them to search for another word until they find 'yacht'. If this triggers any memory of the relevant rules of correspondence, they may be able to verify that it is the correct word.

Nevertheless, relying on a combination of decoding and context will not always yield correct answers and children will make mistakes. While many mistakes may result from an over-reliance on context, for example, using the context and not considering the graphemic structure of the word, at other times it may be that combinations of partial graphemic cues and contextual ones still lead to the incorrect word. In the sentence 'After school John went back to Peter's home', a child could understandably read the final word as 'house' using contextual cues and his knowledge of the sound corresponding to the letter **h** or the letters **ho**. Thus, the more children are aware of the grapheme–phoneme correspondence rules and the more they make use of these, even when encountering words that are not regular, the more likely they are to engage in accurate decoding.

The errors that children make provide valuable insights into the difficulties they may have (Goodman, 1967; Clay, 1991). These errors can be a valuable source of information for teachers. Consistent error patterns can indicate that children may be relying too heavily on one type of strategy. The child who frequently 'reads' words that fit the context but bear no relationship to their graphemic structure will be using context to the exclusion of other strategies. In contrast, the child who 'reads' words that contain a sound which relates to one of the graphemes, usually the first, but bears little relationship to the context may be using limited knowledge of correspondence rules and ignoring the context. By listening to errors, teachers can help provide children with assistance that is appropriate to their needs.

Children should be encouraged to make use of grapheme–phoneme correspondence rules and to become familiar with them. These rules can then be used to decode complete words or to constrain the range of possible words rather than providing only one or two cues to sounds that may be in the words. As children become more skilled in their reading, they will be able to use a combination of strategies, not simply to provide cues for decoding but to monitor the correctness of their reading performance. If the graphemic structure of the print suggests one word but the sentence (or paragraph) context suggests another, then it is likely that some error has been made. This can cue children to go back and check the sentence again to see if part of it has been misread. Here knowledge of the grapheme–phoneme rules of correspondence (leading to the word being read), pragmatic knowledge (for example, the meaning of the word as read leads to an anomalous sentence that does not describe the real world), and grammatical knowledge (for example, there is a lack of agreement between subject and verb) may all assist children with their reading.

With increasing experience of print children will, of course, develop a substantial vocabulary of words that they recognize by the entire sequence of letters, or orthographically. As discussed by Share (1995), relatively few exposures to each new word, if accurately decoded each time using correspondence rules, will lead to the word being recognized in future rapidly and with minimal effort and without the reader having to revert to the correspondence rules. While the processes underlying orthographic decoding of words, that is recognizing them directly from their spellings, are not fully understood, it is clear that we do move quickly from having to decode words phonologically to this level of recognition and a primary goal of reading instruction in school should be to provide children with sufficient opportunity and experience to build up a large vocabulary of words they recognize.

## Reading Comprehension

In the previous section we discussed how children use the meaning of one part of a sentence to assist in the decoding of a word they do not know in the sentence. These children are making use of the meaning they extract from the part of the sentence that they can read. One might expect therefore that as children become more efficient in decoding the text, the *comprehension* of it will follow without any difficulty. Efficient and accurate decoding is certainly of importance for comprehension. Fluent reading implies that much of the decoding of words proceeds automatically, requiring comparatively little cognitive effort. This fluency, coupled with the fact that children have been comprehending the language in its spoken form for some years, suggests they should be able to comprehend written language. However, the comprehension of what is read does not follow on automatically from being able to read the words. There are three reasons for this.

Firstly, reading comprehension depends heavily on listening comprehension skills and the latter may not be as well developed as may appear from observing children's day-to-day interactions with others. Secondly, the written language makes frequent use of syntactic constructions that are rarely if ever used in the spoken form of the language. Thirdly, comprehension of the written word often requires integrating complex information across extended discourse to a much greater extent than spoken language does. We will now look at each of these in turn, recognizing that in practice they will frequently combine to create comprehension difficulties for children.

### Listening Comprehension

It is well established that in addition to decoding skills, reading comprehension is largely dependent on listening comprehension (see, for example, Curtis, 1980; Gough and Tunmer, 1986). Hence it is important to consider what listening comprehension skills children bring to the reading task. As we discussed in chapter 6, by school age, many children may *appear* to have a good command of the basics of their language. But they will still have difficulty in comprehending the spoken language addressed to them in certain communicative settings. When language is used in conversations with young children they may well be able to follow much of what is said. The situation in which the language is spoken will provide many cues to help children interpret the meaning. Furthermore children will frequently be engaged in a conversation where the meaning of the language can be negotiated over several rounds of the conversation. Adults, often without realizing, will provide additional information to assist children in successive rounds of the conversation if they are having difficulty following what is being said. These factors contribute to creating the impression that children's language comprehension skills are better than they actually are. But as has been shown in the research on communication skills (see chapter 6), children frequently experience difficulty both with their listening comprehension and with their evaluation of the extent to which they have understood incoming information. They often act as if they are not aware that the messages they receive are inadequate and lack information. They also do not give any explicit signals when they hear something that is beyond their comprehension because it contains a word or words that they do not understand.

The difficulties that children have with listening comprehension become even clearer when the language presented to them is more similar to written language and lacks many of the cues usually found in daily interactions using spoken language. The study by Markman (1979), described in chapter 7, provides an illustration of this point. Markman read children short descriptive passages that contained deliberate contradictions. The fact that the passages were read to the children from a written form meant that Markman was examining children's listening comprehension. But the language was not embedded in any immediate context that provided cues to its meaning. Nor did it involve successive rounds of a conversation where the meaning could be negotiated. In this situation many children up to 11 years of age did not signal any difficulty with their comprehension of the material.

In another study, Tunmer, Nesdale and Pratt (1983) showed that children as young as 5 could evaluate the consistency of shorter passages. However, this relied on their attention being drawn to the fact that some passages contained inconsistencies. Performance, when attention was not drawn to the need to evaluate passages, was much poorer and dropped to chance level for children in the early school grades. Therefore, when considering reading comprehension, it cannot be assumed that children have fully developed comprehension skills for spoken language which will transfer to the printed form of the language. At the time they are learning to read, children still have much to learn about comprehension and in particular about the need to monitor their comprehension for cues that may signal misunderstandings.

## Unfamiliar Syntactic Constructions

The goal of teaching children to read is not simply to provide them with the skills required for reading basic material that in essence is only spoken language written down. The aim of teaching children to read should be to provide them with the skills they will need to engage in many activities that involve reading as a means of attaining other goals. These other goals will include following a set of instructions on how to play a new game or operate a new appliance, broadening one's knowledge from reading a variety of written material (such as, newspapers and magazines, textbooks, timetables, street maps, telephone directories) or reading purely for the enjoyment of the story in a book. All of these are likely to involve language constructions not used in speech.

Indeed one of the potential disadvantages of the language experience approach is that it may restrict the child's experience with written language because it takes the child's own language and writes it down. This means that there is an initial advantage for children as they are reading language with which they are familiar. But it is important that children are also given experience with the language forms in books and other written material, which, as we discussed in the last chapter, often involves a different language register.

It is likely to begin with, that unfamiliar syntactic forms will present children with some difficulties. Reid (1983) provided an excellent illustration of such a difficulty. It arose when a girl called Clare was reading 'The Sleeping Beauty'. Clare seemed somewhat upset and when asked what was wrong announced 'I can read the words but I don't know what they mean' (p. 152). Further discussion revealed Clare's difficulty. She was having trouble understanding the phrase 'seven in all' as it appeared in the sentence 'The princess's father and mother invited her fairy god-mothers, seven in all, to come to her christening.' In fact, Clare did know what the individual words meant in the phrase that presented trouble. Her difficulty was with the syntactic construction used to convey a meaning which could have been expressed as '. . . invited her seven fairy godmothers . . .'. It should be noted before leaving the example of Clare, that although she was having difficulty comprehending the text, Clare was developing another important skill – that of monitoring her comprehension. Through identification of her difficulty and subsequent discussion of it, Clare was learning to deal effectively with comprehension problems.

Clare's difficulty is certainly not an isolated one. She was reading a book specifically produced for the young reader. Indeed a survey of many of the early readers produced for children indicates that they contain constructions that are not found in spoken language (see Reid, 1983). Thus children must learn to process constructions that they have not previously encountered if they are to comprehend much of the reading material that is provided for them.

## Integrating Information

The studies of listening comprehension by Markman and Tunmer and colleagues revealed that although children can integrate information across sentences they frequently do not do so, particularly if the passages are more than a few sentences in length. Harris, Kruithof, Terwogt and Visser (1981) examined 8- and 11-year-old children's detection of anomalous information when reading short stories. They presented children with short stories, each of which contained an anomalous sentence. The sentence that was anomalous depended on the title that was given to the story. For example, in the following story, half of the children read the title 'At the hairdresser's', while the other half read 'At the dentist's'.

> John is waiting.
> There are two people before him.
> After a while, it's his turn.
> He sees his hair getting shorter. (A)
> Luckily there are no cavities. (B)
> After a while he can get up.
> John puts his coat on.
> He can go home.

Depending on which title a child read, either sentence (A) or sentence (B) was anomalous. Children read the story by moving a card that revealed one sentence at a time, so that a measure of the reading time for each sentence could be taken. The results showed that children took longer to read anomalous sentences than non-anomalous ones, suggesting that there was some awareness of comprehension difficulty at the time of reading the sentence. Further, many of the 8-year-olds and most of the 11-year-olds were able to identify the anomalous sentence after they had read the story if they had been told beforehand that the stories did contain anomalous information. In a second experiment where children were not told beforehand, the performance of the 8-year-olds was much poorer. Although they still took longer to read anomalous sentences, most were unable to identify such sentences when asked afterwards. Therefore, in both listening to stories and reading stories children will benefit from being encouraged to monitor their comprehension of the information that they extract from the passage.

Further valuable insights into the processes involved in compre-hension and in particular the difficulties that poor comprehenders experience in integrating information and making inferences have been provided by Yuill and Oakhill (Yuill and Oakhill, 1988, 1991; Oakhill, Cain and Yuill, 1998). While these authors recognize that accurate and efficient word recognition skills are necessary for good comprehension, their work has made it clear that these skills are not sufficient.

Indeed, in the introduction to their book, Yuill and Oakhill (1991) provide a compelling example of the dissociation that can exist between reading accuracy and comprehension. They used the Neale Analysis of Reading Ability Test (1966, updated 1989) which involves asking children to read short stories during which errors are noted by the person administering the test, and corrected for the child. In addition words the child does not recognize are provided. At the end of reading each story, a series of comprehension questions is asked. In the example, Yuill and Oakhill contrast two children, Lianne and Natalie, whose performances when reading a story differ greatly. Lianne hesitates frequently and makes many mistakes. Natalie reads the story with only one hesitation and two errors. However, Lianne's comprehension is almost perfect, giving correct answers to all but one question. In contrast, for Natalie, whose reading accuracy was close to perfect, many of her answers to the comprehension questions were, in the authors' words, 'either failures to re-member or confused confabulations mixed with repetitions of fragments of the wording' (p. 2). While Lianne's comprehension is impressive, the conclusion should not be drawn that good comprehension is possible without accurate decoding. As noted above, the administration of the test involves correcting all the child's mistakes and providing the words that the child cannot read. Clearly, had Lianne not had this input her comprehension score would have dropped considerably, given the number of errors and words she did not know.

The example of Natalie's reading accuracy and comprehension per-formance, however, provides convincing anecdotal evidence which clearly indicates that accurate decoding, while of importance for good com-prehension, does not guarantee it. Oakhill, Cain and Yuill (1998) refer to such children as having a specific comprehension problem and in their experimental research working mainly with groups of 7- to 8-year-old children, they have systematically investigated the differences between poor and good comprehenders, who have been carefully matched on decoding skills and accuracy, as well as vocabulary. All children in their work are reading at an accuracy level at least equivalent to their age but the poor comprehenders have comprehension scores well below that ex-pected for their age and reading ability. In contrast good comprehenders have scores at least equivalent to that expected for their age and reading ability.

The results from many of their studies indicate that as well as being matched initially for accuracy of decoding and vocabulary levels, good and poor comprehenders generally do not differ in their memory for texts they have read. Both groups remember similar amounts of information and are more likely to remember the main ideas, than peripheral ones. However, their work also shows that poor comprehenders have greater difficulty in drawing inferences from the text, even when this relies on an inference based on a single word, and in integrating information across sentences, especially if there is some distance between the pieces of information. With regard to inferences based on single words, Yuill and Oakhill (1991) observed that poor comprehenders frequently experienced difficulty with the following types of questions. At the end of a short story containing the sentence, 'A surprise parcel for Peter and Jane arrived on Saturday' the question 'How do you know that the children were not expecting the parcel?' is posed. The answer to this is based on a fairly straightforward inference from the single word 'surprise'.

With regard to integrating information across texts, Yuill and Oakhill (1988, 1991) have investigated linguistic devices referred to as anaphoric relations. These devices are used in stories to link information across sentences; for example, the linking of a pronoun in a sentence to the individual to whom it refers that has been mentioned in a previous sentence. Thus, for the two sentences 'The girl went into the shop. She bought some bread' the pronoun 'she' refers back to the noun phrase 'the girl'. Other anaphoric relations include substitution such as occurs in the two sentences 'Mary went home. John did too.' In this example 'did' is substituted for 'went home'. The findings from these experiments have shown that poor comprehenders have much more difficulty than good comprehenders with expressions which involve the integration of information across sentences.

In further work Oakhill, Hartt and Samols (1996) have shown in a task in which children were required to read through stories and state whether it was a story that made sense or one that did not and needed to be changed, that poor comprehenders were less likely to detect inconsistencies that had deliberately been placed in the stories. They were less likely to detect these inconsistencies than good readers even when they were contained in adjacent sentences. Moreover, when the inconsistencies were in sentences separated by three other sentences, good readers were not affected, whereas the performance of poor readers was even worse than in the adjacent sentence condition.

## Developing Children's Comprehension Skills

The work of Yuill and Oakhill and other researchers which has demonstrated that good comprehension does not always follow from accurate decoding of the text raises the important question of what can be done to assist poor comprehenders. Clearly given the goal of reading is to extract meaning from text, developing good comprehension skills is a very important educational issue.

The skills required for reading comprehension extend beyond those involved in the comprehension of spoken passages. Written material is often much longer and has a permanent existence which lends itself to methods of enhancing comprehension that are not available to the listener. Texts are organized into chapters which usually have titles. The chapters contain paragraphs which may be organized into sections with headings that give some indication of the content within them. The efficient reader often looks through the book before reading it to gain some overview of the material and to determine which sections may need more careful reading than others. The information in chapter and section headings can be used to inform readers in advance about what they may expect to learn from the text. They can also be used to assist readers evaluate their comprehension after having read the material.

One effective strategy used by some readers is to turn the section headings into questions and then evaluate whether they have understood what is in the section sufficiently to answer the questions. For example, the heading 'Reading Comprehension' can be used to generate such questions as 'What is reading comprehension?' and 'What processes are involved in reading comprehension?'. Readers can then evaluate whether they can answer these questions. If they cannot, they can then assess whether they have failed to comprehend or whether the information required is not given in the text. These strategies which involve organizing one's reading in advance and reviewing sections of the text after it has been read are of course not available to a person listening to spoken language.

Reading comprehension is therefore a complex process relying on the development of listening skills and of other skills tailored to deal specifically with written material. It is a dynamic process that involves the reader reconstructing the meaning that was placed in the text by the writer. Setting aside the existence of pictures in some books, reading comprehension relies entirely on the surrounding text to establish the context that assists the reader determine the writer's meaning in a particular sentence or set of sentences. To ensure efficient comprehension, readers must learn to interact with the text, evaluating what they read with respect to their existing knowledge of the language and of the world. They must be prepared for ambiguities that may occur in what they are reading and if found, readers should be able to look for cues in the surrounding linguistic context to enable these to be disambiguated.

Given the complexity of reading comprehension, how can children be helped to develop the skills that are involved? One important contribution comes from reading books to children. Those children who have come from home backgrounds where they have been read to frequently will be more familiar with the syntactic constructions used in written language. This will assist them in understanding these when they later come to read themselves. In addition to reading to children, the reader should also discuss the story and ask questions about it. These will help children appreciate the importance of listening carefully to what is read and of checking that they have understood it. Ideally the questions asked should not just be simple factual ones that can be answered by parroting part of the text that has just been heard. Questions should include many that require inferences which take the child beyond the immediate text or predictions about what may happen next. This will encourage the active reconstruction of the meaning in the text and the evaluation of the information gained. For example, from the story of Cinderella, we might find the following: 'Cinderella was dressed in rags. Her Ugly Sisters treated her very cruelly and made her do all the housework.' A poor question, requiring no inference on the child's part might be 'What was Cinderella dressed in?', while good questions would ask 'How do you think Cinderella felt when her sisters treated her cruelly?' or 'Why do you think the Ugly Sisters treat Cinderella cruelly?'. These latter questions require the child to go beyond the immediate meaning of the text, and therefore encourage skills other than simple decoding.

Thus at the same time as children are being helped to learn to read, parents, teachers and others should be reading to them and asking questions about what is being read. It is important to continue reading to children even when they become more fluent readers themselves. This encourages children to transfer the skills they develop while listening to stories and being asked questions about them to their own reading, particularly if they are given instruction about effective comprehension strategies.

Further development of children's comprehension skills should involve making children aware of a range of effective strategies for improving and monitoring their comprehension. The importance of this was shown in research conducted by Scott Paris and his colleagues (Paris and Oka, 1986; Paris, Saarnio and Cross, 1986; Paris, Wixson and Palinscar, 1986). They investigated children's understandings about reading comprehension, and the efficacy of a programme, the *Informed Strategies for Learning* (ISL) programme, designed to enhance the development of effective comprehension strategies.

One noteworthy finding from their research was the identification of the poor understanding many children in primary school grades had of comprehension strategies. They concluded that 'some children have very poor ideas about comprehension strategies [and that] . . . for example some 8- and 9-year-olds believe that skimming means to read only the "little" words' (Paris and Oka, 1986, p. 30). They also stated that 'the naïveté of even 10- and 12-year-olds often astonishes teachers when they teach students such simple tactics as thinking about the title and topic before reading, declaring reading goals, stopping periodically to paraphrase the text, checking to see if new information makes sense, and skimming or rereading as a review technique' (p. 31). Whereas we would agree that it is important to be aware that children do not have many comprehension strategies which we may take for granted, we would question whether it is appropriate to refer to these as simple tactics. We would also question the reference to the naïveté of children. It is probably more appropriate to refer to our own naïveté for assuming that children would develop an understanding of the principles described without some explicit instruction in this area – a point that Paris and his colleagues seem to recognize in their own work using the ISL programme.

The ISL programme was designed to teach children a wide range of strategies involved in comprehending written material. Children were encouraged to develop such skills as tracking down the main idea, integrating temporal and causal sequences, integrating ideas and using context, and error detection and self-correction. The programme aimed to instruct children about what these skills are, how to use them and when they should be used. The results of a study involving over 1600 children from 50 experimental classrooms where ISL was implemented and 25 control classrooms revealed that children benefited from instruction in the use of comprehension skills.

Yuill and Oakhill (1991) investigated a range of different training programmes in a follow-up to much of their work examining the differences between good and poor comprehenders matched for word decoding and accuracy. This work which was usually done with small groups of 7-year-old children demonstrated that significant gains could result from relatively brief training sessions designed to encourage the integration of information and the drawing of inferences. They also looked at training slightly older children, aged 9 to 10 years, to use imagery. Yuill and Oakhill chose this age group on the basis of previous work that had suggested imagery training was not successful with younger children. Their training involved three sessions, the first two of which made use of pictures to encourage children to create pictures of stories in their heads. The third session continued to give children practice in forming integrated mental images of the text, but without the use of pictures as aids. The training was successful and for the poor comprehenders there was a significant improvement in their comprehension when tested on different stories to those used in the training.

As Yuill and Oakhill acknowledge, all of their training studies have been implemented by researchers with small groups of children and so may not necessarily generalize directly to classroom settings. Nevertheless, the effectiveness of their short training programmes designed to assist children with the integration of information, to demonstrate that effective use of titles and pictures can assist comprehension and to encourage children to make use of mental imagery when reading, all provide useful information for the development of classroom-based programmes.

The research on comprehension provides evidence that many children will not spontaneously develop the range of skills required for reading comprehension, even when they have accurate decoding skills. They will however develop and make use of these skills when they are given the opportunity to do so and provided with strategies to assist them. Assistance with comprehension should be given from before reading begins, initially through the development of listening comprehension skills and later through assistance with skills related directly to reading comprehension. The benefits that arise are of course not restricted to reading comprehension *per se* but enhance the learning of all school work that requires the comprehension of school texts and other books.

## Individual Differences, the School and Reading

There will be large individual differences in children's interest and understanding of the reading process when they come to school. It is the responsibility of the school to cater for these differences and to ensure that all children become aware of the purposes and benefits of learning to read. Those children who come to school already reading should be provided with opportunities to develop their skills further and gain more enjoyment from reading. However, the majority of children are not reading when they begin formal education and programmes must be provided that enable them to develop their skills in meaningful contexts. It must be recognized that some children will have had little direct contact with reading and may also have had little cause to reflect on the components of spoken language. These children will require time to develop an aware-ness of the units of the language such as sounds and words. They will also benefit from being placed in situations where they become aware of the need to read to achieve a range of goals so that they develop a desire to read.

The importance of providing all children with adequate preparation for learning to read and then with reading instruction based on well-de-signed educational programmes cannot be overemphasized. As Stanovich (1986) clearly argues and as discussed in chapter 1, there are 'Matthew effects' in reading. Reading is a fundamental ability which underpins much of school-based learning in other subjects as well as providing the oppor-tunity for ongoing learning throughout one's life. However, it is clear that those who quickly become fluent readers, go on to read more and more, further developing their reading skills, and expanding their vocabulary and knowledge more generally. In contrast, those who struggle to learn to read and experience difficulty with text, read less and consequently have less practice and less opportunity to develop their vocabulary and knowl-edge. Thus, if there is no intervention, the gap between good and poor readers increases with time as the good readers become relatively better and the poor readers relatively worse. It is of great importance therefore that all children are given every opportunity to develop their reading, and that individual differences in children's knowledge and awareness of language prior to reading are recognized and addressed.

Educational programmes will interact with each child's own develop-ment, with children gaining different skills and knowledge from the in-struction. It is important to ensure that these programmes are balanced, providing each child with the opportunity to learn the alphabetic princi-ple and with the necessary decoding skills as well as emphasizing the importance of the meaning contained in the print. Strategies for both decoding and comprehension monitoring should be encouraged, as it should not be assumed that comprehension will follow from efficient and accurate decoding of individual words. When necessary, individual chil-dren who are relying too heavily on context to try to recognize works should be helped to focus on accurate word decoding and to use context for the monitoring of this accuracy.

Thus, encouraging children to develop sound strategies for decoding and comprehending text will provide the basis for them to make use of their reading ability in a variety of situations and for a diverse range of purposes. The process of learning to read will also raise children's awareness of language in general and increase their ability to exercise greater control over its use in both the spoken and written domains. The development of this control is central to the achievement of literacy.

# CHAPTER TEN

# The Accomplishment of Literacy

In the chapters of this book we have traced the development of spoken and written language up to the point where children are able to communicate in both modes reasonably fluently and effectively. We have shown how these developments are inter-related, and that accomplishments in one language domain have repercussions in the other domain. The active nature of the child learner has been emphasized throughout. The natural curiosity of all children to learn should be stimulated and encouraged through social interaction with other people. These people should support and assist children's entry into the worlds of spoken and written language. Together, a more experienced language user and the apprentice in literacy skills can make the process of language learning easier and more enjoyable.

## The Processes of Becoming Literate

At a theoretical level we have made two claims about the processes whereby spoken and written language are learned. We have claimed that social interaction, specifically facilitative, communicative interchange, between a more competent language user and the child, is necessary for language learning. We have further claimed that metalinguistic awareness has an important role to play in the development of literacy. Metalinguistic awareness while enabling reflection on language provides skills of choice and control. These skills are essential to the development of both spoken and written language.

Now we explore at a theoretical level the relationship between social interaction and metalinguistic awareness. How does social, communicative, interaction contribute to the growth of metalinguistic awareness? Or conversely, how does reflection on language facilitate communicative interaction? Both these questions deserve consideration. Although developmentally, as far as we can tell, children engage in social interaction before they are metalinguistically aware, the development of metalinguistic awareness further facilitates communicative interaction.

The proposed argument takes into account the active role of the child in the language learning process, the facilitatory role of the adult as external support and the growth of the child's awareness of the structure and functions of language. It also considers the relationship between such support, viewed as input to the literacy process, and literacy accomplishment, viewed as output, namely talking, reading and writing. We believe that via social interaction, children from infancy learn the cultural meanings and significance of actions. Thus we find adults interpreting children's cries and their actions such as head turning and reaching in an intentional way, even before they are produced intentionally by the child. As spoken language starts to be used, the interpretive system between parents and their children is well in place and language too becomes conventionalized for the child. Scaffolding, the facilitatory process described in chapter 3, provides for this interpretive mechanism. The parent, or scaffolder, interprets the child's actions and language in terms of culturally determined conventions. Thus, social processes ascribe meaning to the child's language, these meanings reflecting cultural conventions. The child acquires knowledge of the world that is determined by the meaning attributed to actions and words by a more experienced member of the particular culture. This view is broadly shared by a number of psychologists including Vygotsky, Bruner, Olson and Donaldson, and shares a common conception of the socio-cultural processes and determinants of literacy.

However, much of the relevant psychological research neglects the active role played by children in this process (for a notable exception, see Rogoff, 1990; see also Garton, 1992 for an alternative perspective). All the interpretation is conducted by the more experienced member of society. Children are however working on the language and the interpretations placed on early attempts at speaking, writing and reading. They are also developing systems of internal representation of the world around them. Language itself becomes a system of representation, a way of internally symbolizing the external world. Once language becomes a system of representation, then children can begin to reflect on these representations (Pratt and Garton, 1993). This is part of the process of becoming aware of language. Metalinguistic awareness thus depends on social interaction since children have to formulate their representations of language actively based on the support and interpretation provided by others. Parents who interact with their young children, interpret their gestures and words, comment on their early attempts at letter formation and encourage early attempts at book reading, are providing a socio-cultural interpretation of those activities for the children. They are also, perhaps unknowingly, indicating to their children the importance of these literacy-related activities for adequate functioning in the society in which the children are growing up. These interpretations form the basis of the mental representations created by the child. The representation of language is thus necessarily conventionalized.

While we acknowledge that children are innately predisposed to acquire language, the meanings and interpretations placed on that language are culturally determined. Children therefore reflect on the conventionalized representation of language. This comes to modulate the way in which metalinguistic awareness operates. Reflection can only take place on those rules and representations which are stored symbolically, hence are culturally determined. Therefore, we are claiming that social interaction and metalinguistic awareness are both essential components in the learning of literacy.

In describing the development of literacy, it is also important that a balance is maintained between considering what knowledge and abilities children bring to the learning process and recognizing their limitations. Only by doing this are we able to determine the continuities that exist in development and to provide learning experiences at home, at preschool and at school that result in further development.

A chapter by ter Laak (1994) makes an interesting contribution to the debate about the acquisition of literacy. While the chapter largely serves as a commentary on those preceding it in the edited volume, ter Laak distinguishes between literacy as information processing and literacy as a socio-cultural phenomenon. The former characterizes most of the research on literacy, both spoken and written language. Literacy is regarded as a complex set of skills that includes perceptual, representational and information processing ones. Despite acknowledging that literacy includes spoken language, reading and writing, ter Laak stipulates that the organizing principle (for reading) seems to be phonological processing. Research has examined both the effects of specific input (such as phonological training) for subsequent reading or the effects of social and non-social input on literacy acquisition more generally.

The latter characterization of literacy involves viewing reading as communication, as the construction of shared meaning, as participating in the world of the writer and in socio-cultural practices. It also rejects a notion of individual differences in literacy. While espousing the child as an active learner, there is more to this view than simple acquisition processes.

ter Laak believes that the social context is a common element to both approaches and what differs is the definition of (social) environment. A definition that permits the environment as something that affords opportunities for the purposive behaviours of child (as well as an adult) seems to allow both views to be adopted and to form the basis for research. ter Laak comments on the emphases and limitations to these approaches and concludes by noting that issues related to input for literacy acquisition, especially its duration, extent and timing and to the relationship between input and output are important since the causes of literacy acquisition vary with different ages. Inputs or causes are multiple and research needs to take account of the context in which literacy, however defined, is taking place.

There are several common assumptions sometimes made about the language development of young children, which, we believe, are now firmly dispelled. Firstly, it is often assumed that spoken language development is complete once children begin school, that is, children *can* talk like adults by this age. This then provides a basis from which reading and writing skills can be taught. We have shown, especially in chapters 5 and 6, that spoken language development is far from complete by the time children start formal schooling. While not wishing to add to the debate regarding the educational outcomes for children who have poor (noticeably delayed or deviant) spoken language skills on school entry, obviously children do come to school having experienced different types of interactions with spoken language. These differences should be acknowledged especially given the differences in input (such as quantity, quality and duration) which the child has experienced.

Secondly, it should not be assumed that children know nothing about reading and writing before they come to school. Again, children will vary in their knowledge of written language, with some holding apparently odd ideas about the nature and purposes of reading and writing. There is not the great division between spoken and written language, nor between home and school experience, that we might have formerly believed. Both the development of spoken language *and* the development of written language take place throughout children's early years. What varies between children is the nature of that experience and the extent to which they have had the opportunity to be actively involved. Further, it must be borne in mind that both spoken and written language can be fostered from very young ages through into the primary school classroom. The components of literacy as we see it, namely spoken language, writing and reading, are evolving continuously. They are not discrete developmental achievements, unconnected to one another. Teaching and learning in one domain can have benefits in the other.

The one constant factor that emerges is that social interaction is required for children to become literate. A supportive person, prepared to talk to the child, to read to the child, to encourage early attempts at literacy activities, is a prime ingredient in the development of spoken and written language. Such interaction need not always be one-to-one, but sensitivity to the child's needs, sensitivity to the child's accomplishments and a readiness to assist by providing literacy input and to encourage the child's efforts when talking, writing or reading are essential.

The nature of the support changes, sometimes of necessity, as children develop and particularly as they move from home to a broader world. The participants in the communicative interchanges vary and children interact with other children and with adults other than their mother. These people can offer differing kinds of support, such as those discussed in the preschool examples in chapter 8 and 9. Children's experiences are changing and expanding, but they bring to bear on each new situation their past knowledge and experience and their present language resources.

Those concerned with the literacy development of young children face the problem of agreeing on a definition of literacy. We believe that one fundamental issue of dissension concerns whether we regard literacy as a *goal* or a *process*. It has been suggested that in fact both these positions are tenable and each influences the teaching of literacy. For those who see literacy as a goal, the language teaching will concentrate on the child's recognition of words and how to spell correctly, that is, language or literacy output. Thus in the long run, the language learner will be able to function in society because of being able to read and write at a reasonable level. Others focus on the means by which literacy can be achieved and consequently teach ways to attain reading and writing, that is, concentrate on literacy input. They will therefore teach communication skills through discussion and interview, and other skills such as the reading of directions and the following of written instructions. It has been noted that there is often confusion between these two approaches, and many of those involved in the teaching of literacy espouse the latter but teach the former.

What we have described in this book are the normal ways by which children can learn spoken and written language. Ultimately, there is some goal, and this we have defined in relation to the accomplishment of the process. That is, it is assumed that the input and output are related. Literacy is not a socio-cultural or educational goal, but an outcome of the  learning process. By default, it will be educational because of the role of the school in the process, and cultural because parents and teachers are part of the prevailing society. However, by pointing out the continuities in literacy development, we are able to focus specifically on the processes, or inputs, involved in achieving the outcome, itself defined as literacy.

In this book we have been primarily concerned with children's early language experiences and how children learn to be literate. However, it is appropriate now to turn to consider the implications of this accomplishment. So we conclude with an examination of the consequences for children of becoming literate.

## The Consequences of Achieving Literacy

### *The Consequences for Further Language Development*

What are some of the implications for children of learning to use spoken and written language? Are there important consequences, and if so, what are they? We contend that early literacy experiences provide a solid basis for the development of subsequent language skills. Some of these skills will be deployed in communicative interaction with other people, whilst other skills will allow for the exercise of choice and control of language and knowledge (including remembering, thinking and problem solving).

As language development builds on existing skills, the accomplishment of literacy will lead to further language development. As a result of using spoken language in more and varied social interactions, there will be further spoken language development. The language skills learned in social interaction permit greater flexibility and scope in both the inter-personal and intrapersonal uses of spoken language right through life. Further language development also occurs through reading and writing. Unlike spoken language, mastery of reading and writing enables an individual to develop further without social interaction specifically (the so-called 'Matthew effects' whereby early literacy achievement fosters further educational benefits, Stanovich, 1986). Being able to read and write permits further language development to take place, through exposure to new vocabulary and the different language forms and functions found in the written mode.

A major contributor to subsequent spoken and written language development is the development of metalinguistic awareness. Metalinguistic awareness, itself an outcome of the development of both spoken and written language (see chapter 7) then permits greater choice and control over language. This enhances further language development. Olson (1988)  proposed the metalinguistic hypothesis to account for the relationship between early spoken and written language and thought (a later consequence of language). In this hypothesis, Olson suggested that making language into an object of thought, such as through learning to read and write, enables one to think about the world. He hypothesized that metalinguistic awareness is a product of learning to read and write. This contrasts with our proposal that metalinguistic awareness develops as a consequence of experiences with both the spoken and written word. However, Olson contended that spoken language is used to represent the world, and once language is learned, children can reflect upon the world. Subsequently, they learn written language, which then enables reflection on and awareness of the structure of the language. Thus, when learning to read and write, young children become aware of both the world and of the language. Therefore, it is a *sine qua non* that language and thought are related.

Finally, the accomplishment of literacy in the individual can contribute to the language development of others in two important ways. As experienced language users, literate people can assist in the language learning process of others, particularly children. Both spoken and written language development can benefit from the support of a literate assistant. Also, contributions can be made to the wealth of written language resources that exist in a society. Literate people can write, for example, novels, plays, poetry, advertising slogans, scientific articles and text books. These are permanent contributions to the language of a society.

## Cognitive Consequences of Literacy

Literacy enhances cognitive development through interactions involving spoken and written language. Not only do children learn language through social interaction but they also learn through interactions involving language. In the years before schooling commences, much learning results from interactions between children and others. As we discussed in previous chapters, communicative interchanges occur from very early on in a child's life, the contents and complexity of the language increasing as the child develops. Likewise, the dialogues that occur in the classroom introduce children to different ways of talking about the world and hence of thinking about the world. All of these increase children's cognitive skills and knowledge.

Children's natural curiosity and desire to learn often appear to be the motivation behind the use of language. Tizard and Hughes (1984) described the advantageous consequences of mother–child conversations for the child's subsequent learning and cognitive development. They described interactions where children asked their mothers questions in order to get answers. The children wanted information and to get it, they had to use language. Although the desire to learn motivates the use of language in such interactions, the language is **required** for the learning to occur.

With the shift to school, language is used by the teacher often to moti-vate the learning process. However, the learning is more disembedded for children, and requires greater cognitive control. Instead of children asking a question because they want to know something, the teacher uses language to tell children what they should know or to set them problems to solve. Whereas children may continue to satisfy their curiosity through asking questions, there are fewer opportunities to do so at school, al-though questions may still be asked at home. While, it is important to distinguish between situations where the desire for knowledge leads to the use of language by the child versus the use of language by another person leading to learning, both have cognitive benefits.

Written language too permits learning. The language of books and ex-tended written discourse is more disembedded than spoken language and, according to Donaldson (1978) and Olson (1988), it is written language that serves logical thought. So, learning to read and write also have important cognitive consequences.

The consequences of learning to read were explored by Francis (1987). She described four broad areas where children's learning to read could affect their thinking abilities. In considering reading, it is worth acknowl-edging that children may read because they are interested to get informa-tion and to learn, or children may read because the text is part of the curriculum and they have been told to read it. Francis firstly believed that learning to read extends children's mental representation abilities rather than causing any fundamental intellectual change. These changes were a function of the new knowledge rather than a function of new computa-tional skills. Secondly, she observed that in acquiring the written code, children were able to extend their knowledge of the world and were further able to reflect on this. She endorsed a close relationship between metalinguistic awareness and reading.

Thirdly, Francis looked at the relationship between learning and read-ing. She focused on how reading increases the opportunities for children to learn simply by making available a greater knowledge base from which to learn. She proposed that the home-based literacy activities that are related to later reading accomplishments achieve their success because children become aware that reading is an activity that provides them with new knowledge. Extending this argument into the classroom, Francis believed that by allowing children to find out about reading, its nature and its functions ('growing into literacy' as she termed it, Francis, 1987, p. 104), they then actually learn about learning.

Finally, Francis believed that learning to read takes away the authority for language from an individual speaker (such as the parent or preschool teacher) and places the authority firmly in the text itself. This uncoupling of the responsibility for the language is important for children's subsequent learning. By understanding that the truth of language is not always literal, children can decontextualize language and can begin to argue, to debate, to use language in a more abstract way.

We have continually highlighted the importance of a social framework for the development of the skills of literacy and for children to learn to become literate. Not all accomplishments require social guidance and monitoring. Children's early exploration of the world of objects and places can at times be a solitary activity, and can continue to be something that is done alone. Being literate increases the opportunities for learning for children, by expanding the range of materials available to them (such as text books, pamphlets and encyclopaedias). The scope for further learning is enhanced by being able to use the written mode. This learning does not necessarily involve social interaction. Such experiences are disembedded in so far as the learning from books does not result from direct experience. The learning and growth of knowledge that occur from encounters with the written language are a result of being able to detach thought from the immediate context. This in itself is a cognitive consequence of learning to be literate.

It is concluded therefore that learning to be literate increases the scope for further learning. The accomplishment of literacy further provides the opportunity for children (and adults) to contribute to the cognitive development of others through spoken language, including conversations, teaching and lecturing, and through written language, including the writing of books!

# References

Adams, M. J. (1990). *Beginning to Read: Thinking and Learning about Print*. Cambridge, MA: MIT Press.

Asch, S. E. and Nerlove, H. (1960). The development of double function terms in children: An exploratory analysis. In B. Kaplan and S. Wapner (eds) *Perspectives in Psychological Theory: Essays in Honor of Heinz Werner*. New York: International Universities Press.

Aslin, R. N., Pisoni, D. B. and Jusczyk, P. W. (1983). Auditory development and speech perception in infancy. In P. H. Mussen (ed.) *Handbook of Child Psychology* (4th edn) *Vol. I*, M. Haith and J. J. Campos (eds) *Infancy and Developmental Psychobiology*. New York: Wiley.

Assink, E. M. H. (ed.) (1994). *Literacy Acquisition and Social Context*. London: Harvester Wheatsheaf.

Astington, J., Harris, P. L. and Olson, D. R. (eds) (1988). *Developing Theories of Mind*. Cambridge: Cambridge University Press.

Atkinson, M. (1986). Learnability. In P. Fletcher and M. Garman (eds) *Language Acquisition* (2nd edn). Cambridge: Cambridge University Press.

Atkinson, M. (1987). Mechanisms for language acquisition: Learning, parameter setting and triggering. *First Language*, 7, 3–30.

Atkinson, M. (1992). *Children's Syntax: An Introduction to Principles and Parameters Theory*. Oxford: Blackwell.

Austin, J. (1962). *How to do Things with Words*. Oxford: Oxford University Press.

Axia, G. and Baroni, M. R. (1985). Linguistic politeness at different age levels. *Child Development*, 56, 918–27.

Baldwin, D. (1991). Infants' contribution to the achievement of joint reference. *Child Development*, 62, 875–90.

Baldwin, D. (1993). Infants' ability to consult the speaker for clues to word reference. *Journal of Child Language*, 20, 395–418.

Baldwin, D. and Moses, L. (1994). Early understanding of referential intent and attentional focus: Evidence from language and emotion. In C. Lewis and P. Mitchell (eds) *Children's Early Understanding of Mind*. Hove: Lawrence Erlbaum Associates.

Baroni, M. R. and Axia, G. (1989). Children's metapragmatic abilities and the identification of polite and impolite requests. *First Language*, 9, 285–97.

Barrett, M. (1995). Early lexical development. In P. Fletcher and B. McWhinney (eds) *The Handbook of Child Language*. Oxford: Blackwell.

Bates, E. (1976). *Language and Context: The Acquisition of Pragmatics*. New York: Academic Press.

Bates, E., Bretherton, I. and Snyder, L. (1988). *From First Words to Grammar: Individual Differences and Dissociable Mechanisms*. Cambridge: Cambridge University Press.

Bates, E., Dale, P. S. and Thal, D. (1995). Individual differences and their implications for theories of language development. In P. Fletcher and B. McWhinney (eds) *The Handbook of Child Language*. Oxford: Blackwell.

Bates, E. and MacWhinney, B. (1987). Competition, variation and language learning. In B. MacWhinney (ed.) *Mechanisms of Language Acquisition*. Hillsdale, NJ: Lawrence Erlbaum Associates.

Bentin, S. and Leshem, H. (1993). On the interaction between phonological awareness and reading acquisition: It's a two-way street. *Annals of Dyslexia*, 43, 125–48.

Berninger, V. (1994). Codes, connections, context and constructive processes: Integrating the Vygotskian and Lurian perspectives. In E. Assink (ed.) *Literacy Acquisition and Social Context*. London: Harvester Wheatsheaf.

Bernstein, B. (1960). Language and social class. *British Journal of Sociology*, 11, 261–76.

Berthoud-Papandropoulou, I. (1978). An experimental study of children's ideas about language. In A. Sinclair, R. J. Jarvella and W. J. M. Levelt (eds) *The Child's Conception of Language*. Berlin: Springer-Verlag.

Bialystok, E. (1986). Factors in the growth of metalinguistic awareness. *Child Development*, 57, 498–510.

Bialystok, E. (1991a). Metalinguistic dimensions of bilingual proficiency. In E. Bialystok (ed.) *Language Processing in Bilingual Children*. London: Cambridge University Press.

Bialystok, E. (1991b). Letters, sounds, and symbols: Changes in children's understanding of written language. *Applied Psycholinguistics*, 12, 75–89.

Bialystok, E. (1993). Metalinguistic awareness: The development of children's representations of language. In C. Pratt and A. F. Garton (eds) *Systems of Representation in Children: Development and Use*. Chichester: Wiley.

Bialystok, E. (1995). Making concepts of print symbolic: Understanding how writing represents language. *First Language*, 15, 317–38.

Bialystok, E. and Ryan, E. B. (1985a). Toward a definition of metalinguistic skill. *Merrill-Palmer Quarterly*, 31, 229–51.

Bialystok, E. and Ryan, E. B. (1985b). A metacognitive framework for the development of first and second language skills. In D. L. Forrest-Pressley, G. E. MacKinnon and T. G. Waller (eds) *Metacognition, Cognition and Human Performance*. New York: Academic Press.

Bissex, G. (1980). *GNYS AT WORK: A Child Learns to Read and Write*. Cambridge, MA: Harvard University Press.

Blackmore, A. M. and Pratt, C. (1997). Grammatical awareness and reading in grade 1 children. *Merrill-Palmer Quarterly*, 43, 568–90.

Blackmore, A. M., Pratt, C. and Dewsbury, A. (1995). The use of props in a syntactic awareness task. *Journal of Child Language*, 22, 405–21.

Bloom, L. (1970). *Language Development: Form and Function in Emerging Grammars*. Cambridge, MA: MIT Press.

Bloom, L. (1973). *One Word at a Time: The Use of Single Word Utterances before Syntax*. The Hague: Mouton.

Bloom, L., Lightbrown, P. and Hood, L. (1975). Structure and variation in child language. *Monographs of the Society for Research in Child Development*, 40.

Bonitatibus, G. (1988). Comprehension monitoring and the apprehension of literal meaning. *Child Development*, 59, 60–70.

Booth, J. R. and Hall, W. S. (1995). Development of the understanding of the polysemous meanings of the mental-state verb know. *Cognitive Development*, 10, 529–49.

Bornstein, M. and Bruner, J. S. (eds) (1989). *Interaction in Human Development*. Hillsdale, NJ: Erlbaum.

Bowerman, M. (1973). *Early Syntactic Development: A Cross-Linguistic Study with Special Reference to Finnish*. Cambridge: Cambridge University Press.

Bowerman, M. (1976). Semantic factors in the acquisition of rules for word use and sentence construction. In D. M. Morehead and A. E. Morehead (eds) *Normal and Deficient Child Language*. Baltimore: University Park Press.

Bowey, J. A. (1986). Syntactic awareness and verbal performance from preschool to fifth grade. *Journal of Psycholinguistic Research*, 15, 285–308.

Bowey, J. A. (1994). Grammatical awareness and learning to read: A critique. In E. M. H. Assink (ed.) *Literacy Acquisition and Social Context*. London: Harvester Wheatsheaf.

Bowey, J. A. (1996). Phonological sensitivity as a proximal contributor to phonological recoding skills in children's reading. *Australian Journal of Psychology*, 48, 113–18.

Bowey, J. A. and Tunmer, W. E. (1984). Word awareness in children. In W.E. Tunmer, C. Pratt and M.L. Herriman (eds) *Metalinguistic Awareness in Children: Theory, Research and Implications*. Berlin: Springer-Verlag.

Bowey, J. A., Tunmer, W. E. and Pratt, C. (1984). The development of children's understanding of the metalinguistic term *word*. *Journal of Educational Psychology*, 76, 500–12.

Bradley, L. and Bryant, P. E. (1983). Categorising sounds and learning to read – a causal connection. *Nature*, 301, 419–21.

Braine, M. D. S. (1963). The ontogeny of English phrase structure: The first phase. *Language*, 39, 1–14.

Braine, M. D. S. (1976). Children's first word combinations. *Monographs of the Society for Research in Child Development*, 41.

Brown, R. (1973). *A First Language: The Early Stages*. Cambridge, MA: Harvard University Press.

Brown, R. and Bellugi, U. (1964). Three processes in the acquisition of syntax. *Harvard Educational Review*, 34, 133–51.

Brown, R. and Hanlon, C. (1970). Derivational complexity and order of acquisition in child speech. In J. R. Hayes (ed.) *Cognition and the Development of*

*Language*. New York: Wiley.

Bruce, D. (1964). The analysis of word sounds by young children. *British Journal of Educational Psychology*, 34, 158–9.

Bruck, M. and Treiman, R. (1992). Learning to pronounce words: The limitations of analogies. *Reading Research Quarterly*, 27, 374–88.

Bruner, J. S. (1965). The growth of mind. *American Psychologist*, 20, 1007–1017.

Bruner, J. S. (1966). *Toward a Theory of Instruction*. Cambridge, MA: Harvard University Press.

Bruner, J. S. (1971). *The Relevance of Education*. New York: Norton.

Bruner, J. S. (1973). *Beyond the Information Given* (ed.) J. Anglin. London: George Allen and Unwin.

Bruner, J. S. (1975). From communication to language: A psychological perspective. *Cognition*, 3, 255–87.

Bruner, J. S. (1977). Early social interaction and language development. In H. R. Schaffer (ed.) *Studies in Mother–Child Interaction*. London: Academic Press.

Bruner, J. S. (1983). *Child's Talk: Learning to Use Language*. Oxford: Oxford University Press.

Bruner, J. S. (1984). Vygotsky's zone of proximal development: The hidden agenda. In B. Rogoff and J. V. Wertsch (eds) *Children's Learning in the 'Zone of Proximal Development'*. San Francisco: Jossey Bass.

Bruner, J. S. (1986). *Actual Minds, Possible Worlds*. Cambridge, MA: Harvard University Press.

Bruner, J. S. and Sherwood, V. (1976). Early rule structure: The case of 'peek-a-boo'. In R. Harré (ed.) *Life Sentences: Aspects of the Social Role of Language*. London: Wiley.

Bruner, J. S., Goodnow, J. J. and Austin, G. A. (1956). *A Study of Thinking*. New York: Wiley.

Bryant, P. E. (1993). Reading and development. In C. Pratt and A. F. Garton (eds) *Systems of Representation in Children: Development and Use*. Chichester: Wiley.

Bryant, P. E. and Bradley, L. (1985). *Children's Reading Problems*. Oxford: Basil Blackwell.

Bryant, P. E., Bradley, L., MacLean, M. and Crossland, J. (1989). Nursery rhymes, phonological skills and reading. *Journal of Child Language*, 16, 407–28.

Bryant, P. E., MacLean, M., Bradley, L. L. and Crossland, J. (1990). Rhyme and alliteration, phoneme detection, and learning to read. *Developmental Psychology*, 26, 429–38.

Bus, A. (1994). The role of social context in emergent literacy. In E. M. H. Assink (ed.) *Literacy Acquisition and Social Context*. London: Harvester Wheatsheaf.

Butterworth, G. and Grover, L. (1988). The origins of referential communication in human infancy. In L. Weiskrantz (ed.) *Thought without Language*. Oxford: Oxford University Press.

Butterworth, G. and Jarrett, N. (1991). What minds have in common is space: Spatial mechanisms serving joint attention in infancy. *British Journal of Developmental Psychology*, 9, 55–72.

Byrne, B. (1996). The learnability of the alphabetic principal: Children's initial hypotheses about how print represents spoken language. *Applied Psycholinguistics*, 17, 401–26.

Byrne, B. and Fielding-Barnsley, R. (1989). Phonemic awareness and letter knowledge in the child's acquisition of the alphabetic principal. *Journal of Educational Psychology*, 81, 313–21.

Byrne, B. and Fielding-Barnsley, R. (1991). *Sound Foundations.* Sydney, Australia: Peter Leyden.

Byrne, B. and Fielding-Barnsley, R. (1993). Evaluation of a program to teach phonemic awareness to young children: A 1-year follow-up. *Journal of Educational Psychology*, 85, 104–11.

Byrne, B. and Fielding-Barnsley, R. (1995). Evaluation of a program to teach phonemic awareness to young children: A 2- and 3-year follow-up and a new preschool trial. *Journal of Educational Psychology*, 87, 488–503.

Byrne, B., Fielding-Barnsley, R. and Ashley, L. (1996). What does the child bring to the task of learning to read. *Australian Journal of Psychology*, 48, 113–18.

Cardoso-Martins, C. (1995). Sensitivity to rhymes, syllables, and phonemes in literacy acquisition in Portuguese. *Reading Research Quarterly*, 30, 808–28.

Carraher, T. N. and Spinillo, A. G. (1984). Experimenter talk: Text or utterance? In J. den Haese and J. Nivette (eds) *Proceedings of Aila Brussels 84.* Brussels: Author.

Carter, A. (1974). The development of communication in the sensorimotor period: A case study. Unpublished doctoral dissertation, University of California, Berkeley.

Cazden, C. (1965). Environmental assistance to the child's acquisition of grammar. Unpublished doctoral dissertation, Harvard University.

Cazden, C. (1976). Play with language and metalinguistic awareness: One dimension of language experience. In J. S. Bruner, A. Jolly and K. Sylva (eds) *Play: Its Role in Development and Evolution.* Harmondsworth, Middlesex: Penguin.

Cazden, C. (1983). Adult assistance to language development: Scaffolds, models and direct instruction. In R. P. Parker and F. A. Davis (eds) *Developing Literacy.* Delaware: International Reading Association.

Chafe, W. L. (1985). Linguistic differences produced by differences between speaking and writing. In D. R. Olson, N. Torrance and A. Hildyard (eds) *Literacy, Language and Learning: The Nature and Consequences of Reading and Writing.* Cambridge: Cambridge University Press.

Chall, J. (1967). *Learning to Read: The Great Debate.* New York: McGraw Hill.

Chall, J. (1983). *Learning to Read: The Great Debate* (updated edn). New York: McGraw Hill.

Chall, J. S. (1989). Learning to read: The great debate 20 years later – A response to 'Debunking the great phonics myth'. *Phi Delta Kappan*, March, 521–38.

Chaney, C. (1992). Language development, metalinguistic skills, and print awareness in 3–year-old children. *Applied Psycholinguistics*, 13, 485–514.

Chapman, R. S. (1995). Language development in children and adolescents with

Down syndrome. In P. Fletcher and B. McWhinney (eds) *The Handbook of Child Language*. Oxford: Blackwell.

Chomsky, C. (1969). *The Acquisition of Syntax in Children from 5 to 10*. Cambridge, MA: MIT Press.

Chomsky, C. (1982). 'Ask' and 'tell' revisited: A reply to Warden. *Journal of Child Language*, 9, 667–78.

Chomsky, N. (1965). *Aspects of the Theory of Syntax*. Cambridge, MA: MIT Press.

Chomsky, N. (1968). *Language and Mind*. New York: Harcourt Brace Jovanovich.

Chomsky, N. (1981). *Lectures on Government and Binding*. Dordrecht: Foris.

Chomsky, N. (1986). *Knowledge of Language*. New York: Praeger.

Clark, E. V. (1973a). What's in a word? On the child's acquisition of semantics in his first language. In T. E. Moore (ed.) *Cognitive Development and the Acquisition of Language*. New York: Academic Press.

Clark, E. V. (1973b). Non-linguistic strategies and the acquisition of word meanings. *Cognition*, 2, 161–82.

Clark, E. V. (1978). Awareness of language: Some evidence from what children say and do. In A. Sinclair, R. J. Jarvella and W. J. M. Levelt (eds) *The Child's Conception of Language*. Berlin: Springer-Verlag.

Clark, E. V. (1979). Building a vocabulary: Words for actions, objects and relationships. In P. Fletcher and M. Garman (eds) *Language Acquisition* (1st edn). Cambridge: Cambridge University Press.

Clark, E. V. (1983). Meanings and concepts. In P.H. Mussen (ed.) *Handbook of Child Psychology* (4th edn), *Vol. III*, J.H. Flavell and E. Markman (eds) *Cognitive Development*. New York: Wiley.

Clark, E. V. (1988). On the logic of Contrast. *Journal of Child Language*, 15, 315–35.

Clark, E. V. (1990). On the pragmatics of Contrast. *Journal of Child Language*, 17, 417–31.

Clark, E. V. (1991). Acquisitional principles in lexical development. In S.A. Gelman and J.P. Byrnes (eds) *Perspectives on Language and Thought: Interrelations in Development*. Cambridge: Cambridge University Press.

Clark, E. V. (1995). Later lexical development and word formation. In P.Fletcher and B. McWhinney (eds) *The Handbook of Child Language*. Oxford: Blackwell.

Clark, H. H. and Clark, E. V. (1977). *Psychology and Language: An Introduction to Psycholinguistics*. New York: Harcourt Brace Jovanovich.

Clark, H. H. and Schunk, D. H. (1980). Polite responses to polite requests. *Cognition*, 8, 111–43.

Clay, M. M. (1972). *The Early Detection of Reading Difficulties: A Diagnostic Survey*. Auckland, New Zealand: Heinemann.

Clay, M. M. (1975). *What Did I Write?*. London: Heinemann Educational Books.

Clay, M. M. (1979). *Reading: The Patterning of Complex Behaviour*. Auckland, New Zealand: Heinemann.

Clay, M. M. (1985). *The Early Detection of Reading Difficulties: A Diagnostic Survey* (3rd edn). Auckland, New Zealand: Heinemann.

Clay. M. M. (1987). *Writing Begins at Home*. Auckland, New Zealand: Heinemann.

Clay, M. M. (1991). *Becoming Literate*. Auckland, New Zealand: Heinemann.

Cooper, C. R. (1980) Development of collaborative problem solving among pre-school children. *Developmental Psychology*, 16, 433–440.

Cooper, C. R., Ayers-Lopez, S. and Marquis, A. (1982). Children's discourse during peer learning in experimental and naturalistic situations. *Discourse Processes*, 5, 177–91.

Cross, T. (1975). Some relationships between 'motherese' and linguistic level in accelerated children. *Papers and Reports on Child Language Development*, no. 10, Stanford University.

Cross, T. (1977). Mothers' speech adjustments: The contribution of selected child listener variables. In C. Snow and C. Ferguson (eds) *Talking to Children: Language Input and Acquisition*. Cambridge: Cambridge University Press.

Cross, T. (1978). Mothers' speech and its association with rate of linguistic development in young children. In N. Waterson and C. Snow (eds) *The Development of Communication*. Chichester: Wiley.

Cross, T. (1979). Mothers' speech adjustments and child language learning: Some methodological considerations. *Language Sciences*, 1, 3–25.

Crystal, D. (1978). The analysis of intonation in young children. In D. Minifie and L. L. Lloyd (eds) *Communication and Cognitive Abilities: Early Behavioural Intervention*. Baltimore: University Park Press.

Crystal, D., Fletcher, P. and Garman, M. (1976). *The Grammatical Analysis of Language Disability: A Procedure for Assessment and Remediation*. London: Edward Arnold.

Cunningham, A. E. and Stanovich, K. E. (1990). Assessing print exposure and orthographic processing skill in children: A quick measure of reading experience. *Journal of Educational Psychology*, 82, 733–40.

Cunningham, A. E., Stanovich, K. E. and West, R. F. (1994). Literacy environment and the development of children's cognitive skills. In E. M. H. Assink (ed.) *Literacy Acquisition and Social Context*. London: Harvester Wheatsheaf.

Curtis, M. E. (1980). Development of the components of reading skill. *Journal of Educational Psychology*, 72, 656–69.

De Laguna, G. (1927). *Speech: Its Function and Development*. New Haven: Yale University Press.

DeLoache, J. and deMendoza, O. (1987). Joint picturebook interactions of mothers and 1-year-old children. *British Journal of Developmental Psychology*, 5, 111–23.

De Villiers, J. G. (1984). Form and force interactions: The development of negatives and questions. In R. L. Schiefelbusch and J. Pickar (eds) *The Acquisition of Communicative Competence*. Baltimore: University Park Press.

De Villiers, J. G. and de Villiers, P. A. (1973). A cross-sectional study of the acquisition of grammatical morphemes in child speech. *Journal of Psycholinguistic Research*, 2, 267–78.

Dias, M. and Harris, P. L. (1988). The effect of make-believe on deductive reasoning. *British Journal of Developmental Psychology*, 6, 207–22.

Dickinson, D. K. (1995a). Introduction: Directions in literacy theory and intervention programs. In D. K. Dickinson (ed.) *Bridges to Literacy: Children, Families and Schools*. Oxford: Blackwell.

Dickinson, D. K. (ed.) (1995b). *Bridges to Literacy: Children, Families and Schools.* Oxford: Blackwell.

Donaldson, M. (1978). *Children's Minds.* Glasgow: Fontana.

Downing, J. (1969). How children think about reading. *The Reading Teacher,* 23, 217–30.

Downing, J. (1970). Children's concepts of language in learning to read. *Educational Research,* 12, 106–12.

Downing, J. (1971). Children's developing concepts of spoken and written language. *Journal of Reading Behaviour,* 4, 1–19.

Downing, J. (1980). A reading puzzle. *Reading,* 14, 17 and 36.

Dunlea, A. (1989). *Vision and the Emergence of Meaning: Blind and Sighted Children's Early Language.* Cambridge: Cambridge University Press.

Dunn, L. M. and Dunn, L. (1981). *Peabody Picture Vocabulary Test – Revised.* Circle Pines, MN: American Guidance Service.

Durkin, D. (1966). *Children Who Read Early.* New York: Teachers College Press.

Durkin, K. (ed.) (1986). *Language Development in the School Years.* London and Sydney: Croom Helm.

Durkin, K. (1993). The representation of number in infancy and early childhood. In C. Pratt and A. F. Garton (eds) *Systems of Representation in Children: Development and Use.* Chichester: Wiley.

Durkin, K., Crowther, R. D. and Shire, B. (1986). Children's processing of polysemous vocabulary. In K. Durkin (ed.) *Language Development in the School Years.* London and Sydney: Croom Helm.

Durkin, K. and Shire, B. (1991). Lexical ambiguity in mathematical contexts. In K. Durkin and B. Shire (eds) *Language in Mathematical Education: Research and Practice.* Milton Keynes: Open University Press.

Durkin, K., Shire, B., Riem, R., Crowther, R. D. and Rutter, D. (1986). The social and linguistic context of early number word use. *British Journal of Developmental Psychology,* 4, 269–88.

Dyson, A. H. (1985a). Three emergent writers and the school curriculum. *The Elementary School Journal,* 85, 497–512.

Dyson, A. H. (1985b). Individual differences in emerging writing. In M. Farr (ed.) *Advances in Writing Research, Vol. II: Children's Early Writing Development.* Norwood, NJ: Ablex.

Ehri, L. C. (1979). Linguistic insight: Threshold of reading acquisition. In T. G. Waller and G. E. MacKinnon (eds) *Reading Research: Advances in Theory and Practice.* New York: Academic Press.

Ehri, L. C. (1987). Learning to read and spell words. *Journal of Reading Behavior,* 19, 5–31.

Ehri, L. C. and Robbins, C. (1992). Beginners need some decoding skill to read words by analogy. *Reading Research Quarterly,* 27, 12–26.

Ehri, L. C. and Wilce, L. S. (1980). The influence of orthography on readers' conceptualization of the phonemic structure of words. *Applied Psycholinguistics,* 1, 371–85.

Ehri, L. and Wilce, L. (1985). Movement into reading: Is the first stage of printed word learning visual or phonetic? *Reading Research Quarterly,* 20, 163–70.

Ehri, L. and Wilce, L. (1987). Cipher versus cue reading: An experiment in decoding acquisition. *Journal of Educational Psychology*, 79, 3–13.

Eisenberg, A. R. and Garvey, C. (1981). Children's use of verbal strategies in resolving conflicts. *Discourse Processes*, 4, 149–70.

Ellis, A. (1984). *Reading, Writing and Dyslexia*. London: Lawrence Erlbaum Associates.

Ely, R. and Gleason, J. B. (1995). Socialization across contexts. In P. Fletcher and B. McWhinney (eds) *The Handbook of Child Language*. Oxford: Blackwell.

Fernald, A. and Kuhl, P. (1987). Acoustic determinants of infants preference for motherese speech. *Infant Behaviour and Development*, 10, 279–93.

Ferreiro, E. and Teberosky, A. (1982). *Literacy Before Schooling*. London: Heinemann Educational.

Finn, P. J. (1978). Word frequency, information theory, and cloze performance: A transfer feature theory of processing in reading. *Reading Research Quarterly*, 78, 508–37.

Fodor, J. (1983). *The Modularity of Mind*. Cambridge, MA: MIT Press.

Forrester, M. (1992). *The Development of Young Children's Social–Cognitive Skills*. Hove: Lawrence Erlbaum Associates.

Francis, H. (1987). Cognitive implications of learning to read. *Interchange*, 18, 97–108.

French, L., Boynton, M. and Hodges, R. (1991). Beginning to talk with peers: The roles of setting and knowledge. In S. A. Gelman and J. P. Byrnes (eds) *Perspectives on Language and Thought: Interrelations in Development*. Cambridge: Cambridge University Press.

French, P. and Woll, B. (1981). Context, meaning and strategy in learning to read. In C. G. Wells (ed.) *Learning Through Interaction*. Cambridge: Cambridge University Press.

Frith, U. (1985). Beneath the surface of developmental dyslexia. In K. E. Patterson, J. C. Marshall and M. Coltheart (eds) *Surface Dyslexia*. London: Lawrence Erlbaum Associates.

Frith, U. (1989). *Autism: Explaining the Enigma*. Oxford: Blackwell.

Furrow, D., Nelson, K. and Benedict, H. (1979). Mothers' speech to children and syntactic development: Some simple relationships. *Journal of Child Language*, 6, 423–42.

Garton, A. F. (1982). The development of determiners in young children. Unpublished D.Phil. thesis, Oxford University.

Garton, A. F. (1983). An approach to the study of the determiners in early language development. *Journal of Psycholinguistic Research*, 12, 513–25.

Garton, A. F. (1984a). Social interaction and cognitive development: Possible causal mechanisms. *British Journal of Developmental Psychology*, 2, 269–74.

Garton, A. F. (1984b). Article acquisition: Theoretical and empirical issues. *Language Sciences*, 6, 81–91.

Garton, A. F. (1992). *Social Interaction and the Development of Language and Cognition*. Hove: Lawrence Erlbaum Associates.

Garton, A. F. (1993). Representation in problem solving. In C. Pratt and A.F. Garton (eds) *Systems of Representation in Children: Development and Use*. Chichester: Wiley.

Garton, A. F. and Pratt, C. (1990). Children's pragmatic judgements of direct and indirect requests. *First Language*, 10, 51–9.

Garton, A. F. and Pratt, C. (1996). Four-year-old children's understanding of others in collaborative problem solving. Paper presented at Ninth Australasian Human Development Conference, Perth.

Garton, A. F. and Renshaw, P. D. (1988). Linguistic processes in disagreements occurring in dyadic problem solving. *British Journal of Developmental Psychology*, 6, 275–84.

Gelman, S. A. and Byrnes, J. P. (eds) (1991). *Perspectives on Language and Thought: Interrelations in Development*. Cambridge: Cambridge University Press.

Gentner, D. (1988). Metaphor as structural mapping: The relational shift. *Child Development*, 59, 47–59.

Gentner, D. and Ratterman, M. J. (1991). Language and the career of similarity. In S. A. Gelman and J. P. Byrnes (eds) *Perspectives on Language and Thought: Interrelations in Development*. Cambridge: Cambridge University Press.

Gleitman, L. R. and Gillette, J. (1995). The role of syntax in verb learning. In P. Fletcher and B. McWhinney (eds) *The Handbook of Child Language*. Oxford: Blackwell.

Gleitman, L. R., Newport, E. and Gleitman, H. (1984). The current status of the motherese hypothesis. *Journal of Child Language*, 11, 43–79.

Gleitman, L. R. and Wanner, E. (1982). Language acquisition: The state of the state of the art. In E. Wanner and L. R. Gleitman (eds) *Language Acquisition: The State of the Art*. Cambridge: Cambridge University Press.

Goldfield, B. and Snow, C. (1986). Individual differences in language acquisition. In J. Berko Gleason (ed.) *The Development of Language* (1st edn). Columbus, Ohio: Charles E. Merrill Publishing Co.

Gombert, J. E. (1992). *Metalinguistic Development*. Hertfordshire: Harvester Wheatsheaf.

Goodman, K. S. (1967). A linguistic study of cues and miscues in English. *Elementary English*, 639–43.

Goodman, K. S. (1976). Reading: A psycholinguistic guessing game. In H. Singer and R. Ruddell (eds) *Theoretical Models and Processes of Reading*. Newark, DE: International Reading Association.

Gopnik, A. (1982). Words and plans: Early language and the development of intelligent action. *Journal of Child Language*, 9, 303–18.

Gopnik, A. and Meltzoff, A. (1986). Relations between semantic and cognitive development in the one-word stage: the specificity hypothesis. *Child Development*, 57, 1040–53.

Goswami, U. (1986). Children's use of analogy in learning to read: A developmental study. *Journal of Experimental Psychology*, 42, 73–83.

Goswami, U. (1991). Analogical reasoning: What develops?: A review of research and theory. *Child Development*, 62, 1–22.

Goswami, U. (1994). Onsets and rimes as functional units in reading. In E. M.

H. Assink (ed.) *Literacy Acquisition and Social Context*. London: Harvester Wheatsheaf.

Goswami, U. and Bryant, P. E. (1990). *Phonological Skills and Learning to Read*. Hove: Lawrence Erlbaum Associates.

Gough, P. B. (1983). Context, form and interaction. In K. Rayner (ed.) *Eye Movements in Reading: Perceptual and Language Processes*. San Diego, CA: Academic Press.

Gough, P. B. and Hillinger, M. L. (1980). Learning to read: An unnatural act. *Bulletin of the Orton Society*, 30, 179–96.

Gough, P. B. and Tunmer, W. E. (1986). Decoding, reading and reading disability. *Remedial and Special Education*, 7, 6–10.

Green, G. M. and Morgan, J. L. (1981). Writing ability as a function of the appreciation of differences between oral and written communication. In C. H. Frederiksen and J. F. Dominic (eds) *Writing: The Nature, Development and Teaching of Written Communication, Vol. 2, Writing: Process, Development and Communication*. Hillsdale, NJ: Erlbaum.

Greenfield, P. M. and Smith, J. H. (1976). *The Structure of Communication in Early Language Development*. New York: Academic Press.

Grice, H. P. (1957). Meaning. *Philosophical Review*, 66, 377–88.

Grieve, R. and Wales, R. J. (1973). Passives and topicalisation. *British Journal of Psychology*, 64, 173–82.

Grieve, R., Hoogenraad, R. and Murray, D. (1977). On the young child's use of lexis and syntax in understanding locative instructions. *Cognition*, 5, 235–50.

Grieve, R., Tunmer, W. E. and Pratt, C. (1983). Language awareness in children. In M. Donaldson, R. Grieve and C. Pratt (eds) *Early Childhood Development and Education*. Oxford: Basil Blackwell.

Hakes, D. T. (1980). *The Development of Metalinguistic Abilities in Children*. Berlin: Springer-Verlag.

Hall, N. (1987). *The Emergence of Literacy*. Sevenoaks, Kent: Hodder and Stoughton.

Halliday, M. A. K. (1975). *Learning How to Mean: Explorations in the Development of Language*. London: Edward Arnold.

Harris, M. (1992). *Language Experience and Early Language Development*. Hove: Lawrence Erlbaum Associates.

Harris, P. L., Kruithof, A., Terwogt, M. M. and Visser, T. (1981). Children's detection and awareness of textual anomaly. *Journal of Experimental Child Psychology*, 31, 211–30.

Heibeck, T. and Markman, E. M. (1987). Word learning in children: An examination of fast mapping. *Child Development*, 58, 1021–34.

Herriot, P. (1969). The comprehension of active and passive sentences as a function of pragmatic expectations. *Journal of Verbal Learning and Verbal Behaviour*, 8, 166–9.

Hewison, J. and Tizard, J. (1980). Parental involvement and reading attainment. *British Journal of Educational Psychology*, 50, 209–15.

Hickmann, M. and Schneider, P. (1993). Children's ability to restore the referential cohesion of stories. *First Language*, 13, 169–202.

Hirsh-Pasek, K., Kemler Nelson, D. G., Jusczyk, P. W., Wright Cassidy, K., Druss, B. and Kennedy, L. (1987). Clauses are perceptual units for young infants. *Cognition*, 26, 269–86.

Hirsh-Pasek, K., Treiman, R. and Schneiderman, M. (1984). Brown and Hanlon revisited: Mothers' sensitivity to ungrammatical forms. *Journal of Child Language*, 11, 81–8.

Høien, T., Lundberg, I., Stanovich, K. E. and Bjaalid, I. K. (1995). Components of phonological awareness. *Reading and Writing*, 7, 171–88.

Holdaway, D. (1979). *The Foundations of Literacy*. Gosford: Ashton Scholastic.

Hughes, M. (1986). *Children and Number*. Oxford: Basil Blackwell.

Hyams, N. (1986). *Language Acquisition and the Theory of Parameters*. Dordrecht: Reidel.

Hyams, N. (1987). The theory of parameters and syntactic development. In T. Roeper and E. Williams (eds) *Parameter Setting*. Dordrecht: Reidel.

Hyams, N. (1992). A reanalysis of null subjects in child language. In J. Weissenborn, H. Goodluck and T. Roeper (eds) *Theoretical Issues in Language Acquisition*. Hillsdale, NJ: Erlbaum.

Jespersen, O. (1922). *Language: Its Nature, Development and Origin*. London: Allen and Unwin.

Johnson, C. N. and Wellman, H. M. (1980). Children's developing understanding of mental verbs: Remember, know and guess. *Child Development*, 51, 1095–102.

Juel, C., Griffith, P. L. and Gough, P. B. (1986). Acquisition of literacy: A longitudinal study of children in first and second grade. *Journal of Educational Psychology*, 78, 243–55.

Karmiloff-Smith, A. (1979a). Language acquisition after five. In P. Fletcher and M. Garman (eds) *Language Acquisition* (1st edn). Cambridge: Cambridge University Press.

Karmiloff-Smith, A. (1979b). *A Functional Approach to Child Language*. Cambridge: Cambridge University Press.

Karmiloff-Smith, A. (1979c). Micro- and macro-developmental changes in language acquisition and other representational systems. *Cognitive Science*, 3, 91–118.

Karmiloff-Smith, A. (1984). Children's problem solving. In M. Lamb, A. Brown and B. Rogoff (eds) *Advances in Developmental Psychology, Vol. 3*. Hillsdale, NJ: Erlbaum.

Karmiloff-Smith, A. (1985). Language and cognitive processes from a developmental perspective. *Language and Cognitive Processes*, 1, 61–85.

Karmiloff-Smith, A. (1986a). Some fundamental aspects of language development after age five. In P. Fletcher and M. Garman (eds) *Language Acquisition* (2nd edn). Cambridge: Cambridge University Press.

Karmiloff-Smith, A. (1986b). From meta-processes to conscious access: Evidence from children's metalinguistic and repair data. *Cognition*, 23, 95–147.

Karmiloff-Smith, A. (1992). *Beyond Modularity: A Developmental Perspective on Cognitive Science*. Cambridge, MA: MIT Press/Bradford Books.

Karmiloff-Smith, A., Grant, J., Sims, K., Jones, M.-C. and Cuckle, P. (1996).

Rethinking metalinguistic awareness: Representing and accessing knowledge about what counts as a word. *Cognition*, 58, 197–219.

Karmiloff-Smith, A., Johnson, H., Grant, J., Jones, M.-C., Karmiloff, Y.-N., Bartrip, J. and Cuckle, P. (1993). From sentential to discourse functions: Detection and explanation of speech repairs by children and adults. *Discourse Processes*, 16, 565–89.

Kendler, T. (1969). Development of mediating responses in children. In J.P. de Cecco (ed.) *The Psychology of Language, Thought and Instruction*. London: Holt, Rinehart and Winston.

Kirtley, C., Bryant, P. E., MacLean, M. and Bradley, L. (1989). Rhyme, rime and the onset of reading. *Journal of Experimental Child Psychology*, 48, 224–45.

Klima, E. S. and Bellugi, U. (1966). Syntactic regularities in the speech of children. In J. Lyons and R. J. Wales (eds) *Psycholinguistic Papers*. Edinburgh: Edinburgh University Press.

Kogan, N. and Chadrow, M. (1986). Children's comprehension of metaphor in the pictorial and verbal modality. *International Journal of Behavioural Development*, 9, 285–95.

Laszlo, J. (1986). Development of perceptual motor abilities in children from 5 years to adults. In C. Pratt, A. F. Garton, W. E. Tunmer and A. R. Nesdale (eds) *Research Issues in Child Development*. Sydney: Allen and Unwin Australia.

Laszlo, J. and Bairstow, P. (1985). *Perceptual–Motor Behaviour: Developmental Assessment and Therapy*. London: Holt Saunders.

Liberman, A. M., Cooper, F. S., Shankweiler, D. P. and Studdert-Kennedy, M. (1967). Perception of the speech code. *Psychological Review*, 75, 431–61.

Liberman, I. Y. (1987). Language and literacy: The obligation of the Schools of Education. In *The Proceedings of the Orton Dyslexic Society Symposium: Dyslexia and Evolving Educational Patterns*. Virginia.

Liberman, I. Y., Shankweiler, D. P., Fischer, W. F. and Carter, B. (1974). Explicit syllable and phoneme segmentation in the young child. *Journal of Experimental Child Psychology*, 18, 201–12.

Lieberman, P. (1967). *Intonation, Perception and Language*. Cambridge, MA: MIT Press.

Lindow, J. A., Wilkinson, L. C. and Peterson, P. L. (1985). Antecedents and consequences of verbal disagreements during small group learning. *Journal of Educational Psychology*, 77, 658–67.

Lloyd, P. (1991). Strategies used to communicate route directions by telephone: A comparison of the performance of 7-year-olds, 10-year-olds and adults. *Journal of Child Language*, 18, 171–189.

Lloyd, P. (1993). Referential communication as teaching: Adults tutoring their own and other children. *First Language*, 13, 339–57.

Lloyd, P., Boada, H. and Forns, M. (1992). New directions in referential communication research. *British Journal of Developmental Psychology*, 10, 385–403.

Lomax, R. G. and McGee, L. M. (1987). Young children's concepts about print and reading: Toward a model of word reading acquisition. *Reading Research Quarterly*, 22, 237–56.

Lundberg, I., Olofsson, A. and Wall, S. (1980). Reading and spelling skills in the first school years, predicted from phonemic awareness skills in the kindergarten. *Scandinavian Journal of Psychology*, 21, 159–73.

Mackay, D. G. (1972). The structure of words and syllables: Evidence from errors in speech. *Cognitive Psychology*, 3, 210–27.

MacLean, M., Bryant, P. E., and Bradley, L. (1987). Rhymes, nursery rhymes and reading in early childhood. *Merrill-Palmer Quarterly*, 33, 255–81.

MacLure, M. and French, P. (1981). A comparison of talk at home and at school. In C. G. Wells (ed.) *Learning Through Interaction*. Cambridge: Cambridge University Press.

Macnamara, J. (1982). *Words for Things*. Cambridge, MA: MIT Press.

Maratsos, M. P. (1976). *The Use of Definite and Indefinite Reference in Young Children*. Cambridge: Cambridge University Press.

Markman, E. M. (1979). Realising you don't understand: Elementary children's awareness of inconsistencies. *Child Development*, 50, 643–55.

Markman, E. M. (1981). Comprehension monitoring. In W.P. Dickson (ed.) *Children's Oral Communication Skills*. New York: Academic Press.

Markman, E. M. (1991). The whole-object, taxonomic, and mutual exclusivity assumptions as initial constraints on word meanings. In S. A. Gelman and J. P. Byrnes (eds) *Perspectives on Language and Thought: Interrelations in Development*. Cambridge: Cambridge University Press.

Martin, F., Fraser, J. and Pratt, C. (1996). The use of orthographic and phonological strategies for the decoding of words in children with a specific reading disability and average readers. Paper presented at the ARC Special Research Initiatives Program On Reading and Developmental Dyslexia, Hobart.

Martin, J. R. (1983). The development of register. In J. Fine and R. O. Freedle (eds) *Developmental Issues in Discourse*. Norwood, NJ: Ablex.

McBride-Chang, C. (1995). What is phonological awareness? *Journal of Educational Psychology*, 87, 179–92.

McNeill, D. (1966). The creation of language by children. In J. Lyons and R. J. Wales (eds) *Psycholinguistic Papers*. Edinburgh: Edinburgh University Press.

McWilliams, B. J. (1984). Speech problems associated with craniofacial anomalies. In J. M. Costello (ed.) *Speech Disorders in Children: Recent Advances*. San Diego, CA: College-Hill Press.

Meisel, J. M. (1995). Parameters in acquisition. In P. Fletcher and B. McWhinney (eds) *The Handbook of Child Language*. Oxford: Blackwell.

Menyuk, P. (1977). *Language and Maturation*. Cambridge, MA: MIT Press.

Menyuk, P., Menn, L. and Silber, R. (1986). Early strategies for the perception and production of words and sounds. In P. Fletcher and M. Garman (eds) *Language Acquisition* (2nd edn) Cambridge: Cambridge University Press.

Merriman, W. and Bowman, L. (1989). The mutual exclusivity bias in children's word learning. *Monographs of the Society for Research in Child Development*, 54, nos 3–4 (serial no. 220).

Messer, D. (1994). *The Development of Communication: From Social Interaction to Language*. Chichester: John Wiley & Sons.

Mills, A. E. (ed.) (1983). *Language Acquisition in the Blind Child: Normal or Deficient?* London: Croom Helm.

Moore, C., Bryant, D. and Furrow, D. (1989). Mental terms and the development of certainty. *Child Development*, 60, 167–71.

Morse, P. A. (1979). The infancy of infant speech perception: The first decade of research. *Brain, Behaviour and Evolution*, 16, 351–73.

Murphy, C. and Messer, D. (1977). Mothers, infants and pointing: A study of gesture. In H.R. Schaffer (ed.) *Studies in Mother–Infant Interaction*. London: Academic Press.

Myers, J., Jusczyk, P. W., Kemler Nelson, D. G., Charles-Luce, J., Woodward, A and Hirsh-Pasek, K. (1996). Infants' sensitivity to word boundaries in fluent speech. *Journal of Child Language*, 23, 1–30.

Naigles, L. (1990). Children use syntax to learn verb meanings. *Journal of Child Language*, 17, 357–74.

Naigles, L. and Kako, E. (1993). First contact in verb acquisition: Defining a role for syntax. *Child Development*, 64, 1665–87.

Neale, M. D. (1966). *Neale Analysis of Reading Ability*, 2nd edn. London: Macmillan Education.

Neale, M. D. (1989). *Neale Analysis of Reading Ability*. Revised British Edition. Windsor: NFER-Nelson.

Nelson, K. (1973). Structure and strategy in learning to talk. *Monographs of the Society for Research in Child Development*, 38.

Nelson, K., Hampson, J. and Shaw, L. K. (1993). Nouns in early lexicon: Evidence, explanations and implications. *Journal of Child Language*, 20, 61–84.

Nelson, K. E. (1977). Facilitating children's syntax acquisition. *Developmental Psychology*, 13, 101–7.

Nelson, K. E., Carskaddon, G. and Bonvillian, J. (1973). Syntax acquisition: Impact of experimental variation in adult verbal interaction with the child. *Child Development*, 44, 497–504.

Newport, E. L., Gleitman, H. and Gleitman, L. R. (1977). "Mother, I'd rather do it myself": Some effects and non-effects of maternal speech style. In C. Snow and C. A. Ferguson (eds) *Talking to Children: Language Input and Acquisition*. Cambridge: Cambridge University Press.

Ninio, A. (1983). Joint book-reading as a multiple vocabulary acquisition device. *Developmental Psychology*, 19, 445–51.

Ninio, A. and Bruner, J. S. (1978). The achievement and antecedents of labelling. *Journal of Child Language*, 5, 1–16.

Nunes, T., Bryant, P. and Bindman, M. (1997). Morphological spelling strategies: Developmental stages and processes. *Developmental Psychology*, 33, 637–49.

Oakhill, J., Cain, K. and Yuill, N. (1998). Individual differences in children's comprehension skill: Towards an integrated model. In C. Hulme and R. M. Joshi (eds) *Reading and Spelling: Development and Disorder*. Mahwah, NJ: Erlbaum.

Oakhill, J., Hartt, J. and Samols, D. (1996). Comprehension monitoring and working memory in good and poor comprehenders. Paper presented at the 14th Biennial Meetings of ISSBD.

Ochs, E. and Scheiffelin, B. (1995). The impact of language socialization on grammatical development. In P. Fletcher and B. McWhinney (eds) *The Handbook of Child Language*. Oxford: Blackwell.

Olson, D. R. (1977). From utterance to text: The bias of language in speech and writing. *Harvard Educational Review*, 47, 257–81.

Olson, D. R. (1984). 'See! Jumping!' Some oral antecedents of literacy. In H. Goelman, A. Oberg and F. Smith (eds) *Awakening to Literacy*. Portsmouth, NH: Heinemann Educational Books.

Olson, D. R. (1985). Introduction. In D. R. Olson, N. Torrance and A. Hildyard (eds) *Literacy, Language and Learning: The Nature and Consequences of Reading and Writing*. Cambridge: Cambridge University Press.

Olson, D. R. (1988). Literacy as metalinguistics. Unpublished paper.

Olson, D. R. and Filby, N. (1972). On the comprehension of active and passive sentences. *Cognitive Psychology*, 3, 361–81.

Palermo, D. S. and Molfese, D. L. (1972). Language acquisition from age five onwards. *Psychological Bulletin*, 78, 409–28.

Paris, S. G. and Oka, E. R. (1986). Children's reading strategies, metacognition and motivation. *Developmental Review*, 6, 25–56.

Paris, S. G., Saarnio, D. A. and Cross, D. R. (1986). A metacognitive curriculum to promote children's reading and learning. *Australian Journal of Psychology*, 38, 107–23.

Paris, S. G., Wixson, K. K. and Palinscar, A. S. (1986). Instructional approaches to reading comprehension. In E. Rothkopf (ed.) *Review of Research in Education*. Washington, DC: American Educational Research Association.

Pea, R. D. (1979). The development of negation in early child language. In D. R. Olson (ed.) *The Social Foundations of Language and Thought: Essays in Honour of Jerome S. Bruner*. New York: Norton.

Perera, K. (1984). *Children's Reading and Writing: Analysing Classroom Language*. Oxford: Basil Blackwell.

Perner, J. (1988). Developing semantics for theories of mind: From propositional attitudes to mental representations. In J. Astington, P. L. Harris and D. R. Olson (eds) *Developing Theories of Mind*. Cambridge: Cambridge University Press.

Peters, A. (1995). Strategies in the acquisition of syntax. In P. Fletcher and B. McWhinney (eds) *The Handbook of Child Language*. Oxford: Blackwell.

Peterson, C. and McCabe, A. (1992). Parental styles of narrative elicitation: Effect on children's narrative structure and content. *First Language*, 12, 299–321.

Phelps, E. and Damon, W. (1987). Productive social interaction strategies for cognitive growth. Paper presented in the symposium 'Peer collaboration in problem solving', SRCD Conference, Baltimore.

Pinker, S. (1984). *Language Learnability and Language Development*. Cambridge, MA: Harvard University Press.

Pratt, C. (1978). A study of infant crying in the home environment during the first year of life. Unpublished D.Phil. thesis, Oxford University.

Pratt, C. (1981). Crying in normal infants. In W. I. Fraser and R. Grieve (eds) *Communicating with Normal and Retarded Children*. Bristol: Wrights.

Pratt, C. (1984). The referential communication game. *Australian Review of Applied Linguistics*, 7, 169–78.

Pratt, C. (1985). The transition to school: A shift from development to learning. *Australian Journal of Early Childhood*, 10, 11–16.

Pratt, C. and Garton, A. F. (1988). Early literacy development and school entry. *Australian Educational and Developmental Psychologist*, 5, 16–20.

Pratt, C. and Garton, A. F. (eds) (1993). *Systems of Representation in Children: Development and Use*. Chichester: Wiley.

Pratt, C. and Grieve, R. (1984). Metalinguistic awareness and cognitive development. In W. E. Tunmer, C. Pratt and M. L. Herriman (eds) *Metalinguistic Awareness in Children: Theory, Research and Implications*. Berlin: Springer-Verlag.

Pratt, C. and Nesdale, A. R. (1984). Pragmatic awareness in children. In W. E. Tunmer, C. Pratt, and M. L. Herriman (eds) *Metalinguistic Awareness in Children: Theory, Research and Implications*. Berlin: Springer-Verlag.

Pratt, C., Tunmer, W. E. and Bowey, J. A. (1984). Children's capacity to correct grammatical violations in sentences. *Journal of Child Language*, 11, 129–41.

Pratt, C., Tunmer, W. E. and Nesdale, A. R. (1989). Young children's evaluations of experience and non-experience based oral communications. *British Journal of Developmental Psychology*, 7, 83–92.

Prior, M. (1989). Reading disability: 'normative' or 'pathological'. *Australian Journal of Psychology*, 41, 135–58.

Rack, J. P., Snowling, M. and Olson, R. K. (1992). The nonsense word reading deficit in developmental dyslexia: A review. *Reading Research Quarterly*, 27, 28–53.

Ratner, N. and Bruner, J. S. (1978). Games, social exchange and the acquisition of language. *Journal of Child Language*, 5, 391–402.

Read, C. (1986). *Children's Creative Spelling*. London: Routledge and Kegan Paul.

Rego, L. and Bryant, P. (1993). The connection between phonological, syntactic and semantic skills and children's reading and spelling. *European Journal of Psychology of Education*, 8, 235–46.

Reid, J. (1958). A study of thirteen beginners in reading. *Acta Psychologia*, 14, 294–313.

Reid, J. (1966). Learning to think about reading. *Educational Research*, 9, 56–62.

Reid, J. (1983). Into print: Reading and language growth. In M. Donaldson, R. Grieve and C. Pratt (eds) *Early Childhood Development and Education*. Oxford: Basil Blackwell.

Robinson, E. J. and Robinson, W. P. (1977). Development in the understanding of causes of success and failure in communication. *Cognition*, 5, 363–78.

Robinson, E. J. and Robinson, W. P. (1978). Development of understanding about communication: Message inadequacy and its role in causing communication failure. *Genetic Psychology Monographs*, 98, 233–79.

Robinson, E. J. and Robinson, W. P. (1981). Ways of reacting to communication failure in relation to the development of the child's understanding about verbal communication. *European Journal of Social Psychology*, 11, 189–208.

Robinson, E. J. and Robinson, W. P. (1982). The advancement of children's verbal referential communication skills: The role of metacognitive guidance. *International Journal of Behavioural Development*, 5, 329–53.

Robinson, E. J., Goelman, H. and Olson, D. R. (1983). Children's understandings of the relation between expressions (what was said) and intentions (what was meant). *British Journal of Developmental Psychology*, 1, 75–86.

Roeper, T. and Williams, E. (eds) (1987). *Parameter Setting*. Dordrecht: Riedel.

Rogoff, B. (1990). *Apprenticeship in Thinking*. New York: Oxford University Press.

Rohl, M. and Pratt, C. (1995). Phonological awareness, verbal working memory and the acquisition of literacy. *Reading and Writing*, 7, 327–60.

Romaine, S. (1984). *The Language of Children and Adolescents*. Oxford: Basil Blackwell.

Rutter, M. (1985). Family and school influences on cognitive development. *Journal of Child Psychology and Psychiatry*, 26, 683–704.

Rutter, M. and Yule, W. (1975). The concept of specific reading retardation. *Journal of Child Psychology and Psychiatry*, 16, 181–97.

Savic, S. (1980). *How Twins Learn to Talk*. London: Academic Press.

Scaife, M. and Bruner, J. S. (1975). The capacity for joint visual attention. *Nature*, 253, 265–6.

Schiefelbusch, R. L. (1984). Assisting children to become communicatively competent. In R. L. Schiefelbusch and J. Pickar (eds) *The Acquisition of Communicative Competence*. Baltimore: University Park Press.

Scinto, L. F. M. (1983). The development of text production. In J. Fine and R. O. Freedle (eds) *Developmental Issues in Discourse*. Norwood, NJ: Ablex.

Scollon, R. (1976). *Conversations with a One Year Old*. Honolulu: University Press of Hawaii.

Searle, J. (1969). *Speech Acts*. Cambridge: Cambridge University Press.

Share, D. L. (1995). Phonological recoding and self-teaching: Sine qua non of reading acquisition. *Cognition*, 55, 151–218.

Share, D. L. and Silva, P. A. (1987). Language deficits and specific reading retardation: cause or effect? *British Journal of Disorders of Communication*, 22, 219–26.

Shatz, M., Wellman, H. and Silber, S. (1983). The acquisition of mental verbs: A systematic investigation of the first reference to mental state. *Cognition*, 14, 301–21.

Siegal, M. (1991). *Knowing Children: Experiments in Conversation and Cognition*. Hove: Lawrence Erlbaum Associates.

Silva, P. A., McGee, R. and Williams, S. (1985). Some characteristics of 9-year-old boys with general reading backwardness or specific reading retardation. *Journal of Child Psychology and Psychiatry*, 26, 407–21.

Skinner, B. F. (1957). *Verbal Behaviour*. New York: Appleton-Century-Crofts.

Slobin, D. (1966). Grammatical transformations and sentence comprehension in childhood and adulthood. *Journal of Verbal Learning and Verbal Behaviour*, 5, 219–27.

Smith, F. (1979). *Reading without Nonsense*. New York: Teachers College Press.

Snow, C. (1972). Mothers' speech to children learning language. *Child Development*, 43, 549–65.

Snow, C. (1986). Conversations with children. In P. Fletcher and M. Garman (eds) *Language Acquisition* (2nd edn). Cambridge: Cambridge University press.

Snow, C. (1989). Understanding social interaction and language acquisition: Sentences are not enough. In M. Bornstein and J. S. Bruner (eds) *Interaction in Human Development*. Hillsdale, NJ: Erlbaum.

Snow, C. E. (1995). Issues in the study of input: Finetuning, universality, individual and developmental differences, and necessary causes. In P. Fletcher and B. McWhinney (eds) *The Handbook of Child Language*. Oxford: Blackwell.

Snowling, M. J. (1991). Developmental reading disorders. *Journal of Child Psychiatry and Psychology*, 32, 49–77.

Snowling, M. J. (1996). Contemporary approaches to the teaching of reading. *Journal of Child Psychology and Psychiatry*, 37, 139–48.

Snyder, A. D. (1914). Notes on the talk of a two-and-a-half year old boy. *Pedagogical Seminary*, 21, 412–24.

Snyder, L. S. (1984). Communicative competence in children with delayed language development. In R. L. Schiefelbusch and J. Pickar (eds) *The Acquisition of Communicative Competence*. Baltimore: University Park Press.

Solan, L. (1983). *Pronominal Reference: Child Language and the Theory of Grammar*. Dordrecht: Reidel.

Spinillo, A. G. and Pinto, G. (1994). Children's narratives under different conditions: A comparative study. *British Journal of Developmental Psychology*, 12, 177–94.

Stanovich, K. E. (1986). Matthew effects in reading: Some consequences of individual differences in the acquisition of literacy. *Reading Research Quarterly*, 21, 360–407.

Stanovich, K. E. (1992). Speculations on the causes and consequences of individual differences in reading acquisition. In P. Gough, L. Ehri and R. Treiman (eds) *Reading Acquisition*. Hilldales, NJ: Erlbaum.

Stanovich, K. E. (1993). A model for studies of reading disabilities. *Developmental Review*, 13, 225–45.

Stark, R. (1979). Prespeech segmental feature development. In P. Fletcher and M. Garman (eds) *Language Acquisition* (1st edn). Cambridge: Cambridge University Press.

Stark, R. (1986). Prespeech segmental feature development. In P. Fletcher and M. Garman (eds) *Language Acquisition* (2nd edn). Cambridge: Cambridge University Press.

Stark, R. (1989). Temporal patterning of cry and non-cry sounds in the first eight months of life. *First Language*, 9, 107–36.

Stemmer, N. (1987). The learning of syntax: An empiricist approach. *First Language*, 7, 97–102.

Stevenson, R. (1992). Maturation and learning: linguistic knowledge and performance: A commentary of Clashen and Felix. In J. Weissenborn, H. Goodluck and T. Roeper (eds) *Theoretical Issues in Language Acquisition*. Hillsdale, NJ: Erlbaum.

Stuart, M. (1990). Processing strategies in a phoneme deletion task. *Quarterly Journal of Experimental Psychology Human Experimental Psychology*, 42, 305–27.

Stuart, M. and Masterson, J. (1992). Patterns of reading and spelling in 10–year-old children related to prereading phonological abilities. *Journal of Experimental Child Psychology*, 54, 168–87.

Sudhalter, V. and Braine, M. D. S. (1985). How does comprehension of passives develop? A comparison of actional and experiential verbs. *Journal of Child Language*, 12, 455–70.

ter Laak, J. J. F. (1994). Literacy acquisition and social context: Approaches, emphases and questions. In E. M. H. Assink (ed) *Literacy Acquisition and Social Context*. London: Harvester Wheatsheaf.

Tizard, B. and Hughes, M. (1984). *Young Children Learning: Talking and Thinking at Home and at School*. London: Fontana.

Tomasello, M. and Farrar, J. (1986). Joint attention and early language. *Child Development*, 57, 1454–63.

Tomasello, M. and Kruger, A. C. (1992). Joint attention on actions: Acquiring verbs in ostensive and non-ostensive contexts. *Journal of Child Language*, 19, 311–33.

Tomasello, M. and Merriman, W. E. (1995). *Beyond Names for Things: Young Children's Acquisition of Verbs*. Hillsdale NJ: Erlbaum.

Tomasello, M. and Todd, J. (1983). Joint attention and lexical acquisition style. *First Language*, 4, 197–212.

Torrance, N. and Olson, D. R. (1985). Oral and literate competencies in the early school years. In D. R. Olson, N. Torrance and A. Hildyard (eds) *Literacy, Language and Learning: The Nature and Consequences of Reading and Writing*. Cambridge: Cambridge University Press.

Torrance, N. and Olson, D. R. (1987). Development of the metalanguage and the acquisition of literacy: A progress report. *Interchange*, 18, 136–46.

Tough, J. (1977). *The Development of Meaning*. London: George Allen and Unwin Ltd.

Tough, J. (1983). Children's use of language and learning to read. In R. P. Parker and F. A. Davis (eds) *Developing Literacy*. Delaware: International Reading Association.

Trabasso, T., Stein, N. L., Rodkin, P. C., Park Munger, M. and Baughn, C. R. (1992). Knowledge of goals and plans in the on-line narration of events. *Cognitive Development*, 7, 133–70.

Treiman, R. (1993). *Beginning to Spell*. New York: Oxford University Press.

Treiman, R. (1994). Use of consonant letter names in beginning spelling. *Developmental Psychology*, 30, 567–80.

Treiman, R., Zukowski, A. and Richmond-Welty, E. D. (1995). What happened to the 'n' of sink? Children's spellings of final consonant clusters. *Cognition*, 55, 1–38.

Tudge, J. and Rogoff, B. (1989). Peer influences on cognitive development: Piagetian and Vygotskian perspectives. In M. Bornstein and J. S. Bruner (eds) *Interaction in Human Development*. Hillsdale, NJ: Erlbaum.

Tunmer, W. E. (1988). Cognitive and linguistic factors in learning to read. In P. Gough (ed.) *Reading Acquisition*. Hillsdale, NJ: Erlbaum.

Tunmer, W. E., and Bowey, J. A. (1984). Metalinguistic awareness and reading acquisition. In W. E. Tunmer, C. Pratt and M. L. Herriman (eds) *Metalinguistic Awareness in Children: Theory, Research and Implications*. Berlin: Springer-Verlag.

Tunmer, W. E. and Chapman, J. W. (1998). Language prediction skill, phonological recoding ability, and beginning reading. In C. Hulme and R. M. Joshi (eds) *Reading and Spelling: Development and Disorder*. Mahwah, NJ: Erlbaum.

Tunmer, W. E. and Grieve, R. (1984). Syntactic awareness in children. In W. E. Tunmer, C. Pratt and M. L. Herriman (eds) *Metalinguistic Awareness in Children: Theory, Research and Implications*. Berlin: Springer-Verlag.

Tunmer, W. E. and Herriman, M. L. (1984). The development of metalinguistic awareness: A conceptual overview. In W. E. Tunmer, C. Pratt and M. L. Herriman (eds) *Metalinguistic Awareness in Children: Theory, Research and Implications*. Berlin: Springer-Verlag.

Tunmer, W. E. and Nesdale, A.R. (1982). The effects of digraphs and pseudowords on phonemic segmentation in young children. *Journal of Applied Psycholinguistics*, 3, 299–311.

Tunmer, W. E., Nesdale, A. R. and Pratt, C. (1983). The development of young children's awareness of logical inconsistencies. *Journal of Experimental Child Psychology*, 36, 97–108.

Valian, V. (1993). Parser failure and grammatical change. *Cognition*, 46, 195–202.

Vosniadou, S. (1987). Children and metaphor. *Child Development*, 58, 870–85.

Vygotsky, L. S. (1962). *Thought and Language*. Cambridge, MA: MIT Press.

Vygotsky, L. S. (1978). *Mind in Society: The Development of Higher Psychological Processes*. Cambridge, MA: Harvard University Press.

Vygotsky, L. S. (1986). *Thought and Language* (new edn). Cambridge, MA: Harvard University Press.

Wales, R. J. (1993). The representation of spoken language. In C. Pratt and A. F. Garton (eds) *Systems of Representation in Children: Development and Use*. Chichester: Wiley.

Wales, R. J. and Coffey, G. (1986). On children's comprehension of metaphor. In C. Pratt, A. F. Garton, W. E. Tunmer and A. R. Nesdale (eds) *Research Issues in Child Development*. Sydney: Allen and Unwin Australia.

Walton, P. D. (1995). Rhyming ability, phoneme identity, letter-sound knowledge, and the use of orthographic analogy by prereaders. *Journal of Educational Psychology*, 87, 587–97.

Warden, D. (1976). The influence of context on children's use of identifying expressions and references. *British Journal of Psychology*, 67, 101–12.

Warden, D. (1981). Children's understanding of *ask* and *tell*. *Journal of Child Language*, 8, 139–49.

Warden, D. (1986). How to tell if children can ask. *Journal of Child Language*, 13, 421–28.

Weissenborn, J., Goodluck, H. and Roeper, T. (eds) (1992). *Theoretical Issues in Language Acquisition*. Hillsdale, NJ: Erlbaum.

Wellman, H. M. (1990). *The Child's Theory of Mind*. Cambridge, MA: MIT Press.

Wells, C. G. (ed.) (1981). *Learning Through Interaction: The Study of Language Development*. Cambridge: Cambridge University Press.

Wells, C. G. (1983). Talking with children: The complementary roles of parents and teachers. In M. Donaldson, R. Grieve and C. Pratt (eds) *Early Childhood Development and Education*. Oxford: Basil Blackwell.

Wells, C. G. (1985a). *Language Development in the Pre–School Years*. Cambridge: Cambridge University Press.

Wells, C. G. (1985b). *Language, Learning and Education*. Windsor: NFER-Nelson.

Wells, C. G. (1985c). Preschool literacy related activities and later success in school. In D. R. Olson, N. Torrance and A. Hildyard (eds) *Literacy, Language and Learning: The Nature and Consequences of Reading and Writing*. Cambridge: Cambridge University Press.

Wells, C. G. (1986). Variation in child language. In P. Fletcher and M. Garman (eds) *Language Acquisition* (2nd edn). Cambridge: Cambridge University Press.

Wells, C. G. (1987). *The Meaning Makers*. London: Hodder and Stoughton.

Wertsch, J. V. (1985a). *Vygotsky and the Social Formation of Mind*. Cambridge, MA: Harvard University Press.

Wertsch, J. V. (1985b). *Culture, Communication and Cognition: Vygotskian Perspectives*. Cambridge: Cambridge University Press.

Wertsch, J. V., McNamee, G. D., McLane, J. B. and Budwig, N. A. (1980). The adult–child dyad as a problem-solving system. *Child Development*, 51, 1215–21.

Wexler, K. (1982). A principle theory for language acquisition. In E. Wanner and L. R. Gleitman (eds) *Language Acquisition: The State of the Art*. Cambridge: Cambridge University Press.

Wexler, K. and Culicover, P. W. (1980). *Formal Principles of Language Acquisition*. Cambridge, MA: MIT Press.

Wexler, K. and Manzini, M. R. (1987). Parameters and learnability. In T. Roeper and E. Williams (eds) *Parameter Setting*. Dordrecht: Reidel.

Wilcox, S. and Palermo, D. S. (1974). *In, on* and *under* revisited. *Cognition*, 3, 245–54.

Wilkinson, L. C., Wilkinson, A. C., Spinelli, F. and Chiang, C. P. (1984). Metalinguistic knowledge of pragmatic rules in school-aged children. *Child Development*, 55, 2130–40.

Wolf, M. and Dickinson, D. (1986). From oral to written language: Transitions in the school years. In J. Berko Gleason (ed.) *The Development of Language* (1st edn). Columbus, Ohio: Charles E. Merrill Publishing Co.

Wood, D., Wood, H., Griffiths, A. and Howarth, I. (1986). *Teaching and Talking with Deaf Children*. Chichester: Wiley.

Wray, D. (1993). What do children think about writing? *Educational Review*, 45, 67–77.

Yopp, H. K. (1988). The validity and reliability of phonemic awareness tests. *Reading Research Quarterly*, 23, 159–77.

Yuill, N. and Oakhill, J. (1988). Understanding of anaphoric relations in skilled and less skilled comprehenders. *British Journal of Psychology*, 79, 173–86.

Yuill, N. and Oakhill, J. (1991). *Children's Problems in Text Comprehension*. Cambridge: Cambridge University Press.

Ziatas, K., Durkin, K. and Pratt, C. (1998). Belief term development in children with autism, Asperger syndrome, specific language impairment and normal development: Links to theory of mind development. *Journal of Child Psychology and Psychiatry and Allied Disciplines* (in press).

# Name Index

# Subject Index